Simon de Montfort

SIMON
DE MONTFORT

by

Margaret Wade Labarge

GREENWOOD PRESS, PUBLISHERS
WESTPORT, CONNECTICUT

Library of Congress Cataloging in Publication Data

Labarge, Margaret Wade.
    Simon de Montfort.

    Reprint of the 1963 ed. published by Norton,
New York.
    Bibliography: p.
    Includes index.
    1. Montfort, Simon of, Earl of Leicester, 1208?-
1265.
[DA228.M7L3 1975]   942.03'4'0924 [B]
ISBN 0-8371-8359-6   75-22643

This edition originally published in 1963 by W. W. Norton &
Company, Inc., New York

Reprinted with the permission of W. W. Norton & Company, Inc.

Reprinted in 1975 by Greenwood Press,
a division of Williamhouse-Regency Inc.

Library of Congress Catalog Card Number 75-22643

ISBN 0-8371-8359-6

Printed in the United States of America

PH 1-3-80

Contents

Preface	*page* x	
Prologue	xi	
Introduction: The Testimony of their Contemporaries	1	
1	Montfort-l'Amaury; the Family Background	15
2	The Earldom of Leicester	27
3	The King's Sister	39
4	Crusader and Warrior	53
5	The Peaceful Years	67
6	The Running of a Noble Household	85
7	The King's Lieutenant; Gascony	105
8	Simon de Montfort, Count of Bigorre?	128
9	The King's Envoy; France	141
10	The Common Enterprise	163
11	Arbitrations and Complaints	180
12	The King's Opponent	204
13	The Rise to Royal State	225
14	The Spin of Fortune's Wheel	244
15	Full Circle	259
16	Conclusion	274
	Appendix	278
	Notes	280
	Bibliography	297
	Index	304

Maps

England   *page* 13

Distribution by County of Simon and Eleanor's Lands   46

France   107

Counties of Manors settled on Simon and Eleanor,   159
    July 1259

Genealogical Tables

The Earldom of Leicester and the Montforts   xii

The Countess of Bigorre and her Descendants   132

TO MY MOTHER
AND THE MEMORY OF MY FATHER

Fortune speaks: "Is the insatiable discontent of man to bind me to a constancy which belongs not to my way? Herein lies my very strength; this is my unchanging sport. I turn my wheel that spins its circle fairly; I delight to make the lowest turn to the top, the highest to the bottom. Come you to the top if you will, but on this condition, that you think it no unfairness to sink when the rule of the game demands it."

Boethius, *Consolation of Philosophy*

Preface

This book originated in an enduring enthusiasm for medieval history kindled by the inspired teaching of Professors C. H. McIlwain and C. H. Taylor of Harvard, and by the illuminating scholarship of Sir Maurice Powicke of Oxford, who first interested me in the relations of Simon de Montfort and his wife with Henry III. The conviction of these men that the history of the Middle Ages can be both intelligible and fascinating has encouraged this attempt to picture one of the great men of thirteenth-century Europe in the setting of his time. My thanks are particularly due to Professor B. Wilkinson, of the University of Toronto, who read and criticized chapters 10 and 12; and to Rev. M. Sheehan, C.S.B., and Rev. J. A. Raftis, C.S.B., of the Pontifical Institute of Medieval Studies (Toronto), who most kindly read, criticized, and discussed the manuscript, and saved me from many errors.

I must also express my gratitude to the librarians who so cheerfully aided in the search for rare books; above all, to Miss Giffard and the staff of the Carleton University Library and to Miss Ewart and Mr Long of the Ottawa Public Library; also to the Parliamentary Library, the Public Archives of Canada, the University of Ottawa Library, the Toronto Public Library, the University of Toronto Library, the Medieval Institute Library, the New York Public Library, and the Harvard College Library.

For advice, suggestions, and assistance I am much indebted to Professor and Mrs Stephen Fuller, Dr W. Kaye Lamb, Miss Eleanor Milne, and especially to Mrs David Geggie, whose continued encouragement and capable criticism on matters of style were invaluable. Lastly, I must acknowledge my gratitude to my husband and children, who have regarded the increasing impingement of the thirteenth century on their life with cheerful tolerance, and who have given valuable aid.

Prologue

At Candlemas, 1239, Henry III presided in the great hall of Winchester among the prelates and barons who had gathered there to join him in the celebration of the feast. Henry loved Winchester, for he had been born in its castle, and the building was a vivid tribute to the king's interest in art and decoration. Opposite the lofty dais was the great Wheel of Fortune which he had ordered to be painted on the eastern gable. The brilliant symbol of the inscrutability of Fortune's change hung as a constant reminder to those present. But, for one noble among them, it was to have more significance than an artist's device. Henry had chosen this feast of Candlemas to invest his brother-in-law, Simon de Montfort, with the title of Earl of Leicester. Thus the king added the final touch to his series of gifts to the young Frenchman. Simon had been welcomed in England eight years before, given lands to which he had only a shaky claim, and had even received the king's sister in marriage. At this moment of triumph, when his position among the baronage of England seemed secure, the new earl no doubt overlooked the lesson of that looming wheel.

Fortune, good and bad, dominated the career of Simon de Montfort, and his story is well summarized by Winchester's great wheel. From relative obscurity, he spun to ever greater wealth and power. At the peak of his career, Simon was like the king whose image presided over the summit of Fortune's round, briefly controlling the whole kingdom. But the "rule of the game" was fulfilled as he toppled to the bottom. Through the terse language of the official records and the more voluble accounts of his contemporaries, the various stages of his journey, like the spokes of the wheel, can be traced one by one.

THE EARLDOM OF LEICESTER AND THE MONTFORTS

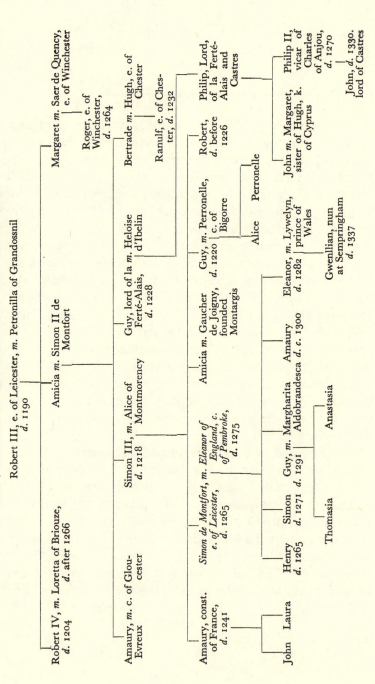

The Testimony of their Contemporaries

In his *Defence of Poetry*, Sir Philip Sidney puts his finger on the crucial problem of the historian when he remarks that it is "to pick truth out of partiality". Trying to reconstruct the life of such a couple as Simon de Montfort and his wife is something like doing a jigsaw puzzle. It requires the combination of innumerable bits of evidence, which unlike the pieces of the jigsaw, are not all equally useful. They mingle fact and fancy, prejudice and hero-worship, assertion and contradiction. Gradually, by sifting and sorting, by testing one piece of fact against another, the fragments may finally be arranged into a recognizable picture. But the historical puzzle is never quite complete. Always, one of the crucial pieces may be missing, and conjecture must substitute for fact. Often the available evidence is contradictory; all the accounts, even the contemporary ones, cannot be accepted at face value. Thus, it is illuminating to know the background of the records and, in those cases where personal authorship can be traced, to discover what the motives and prejudices of the authors were.

The royal records illustrate the will of the king, but in the prescribed forms of the chancery clerk. Only occasionally does some hint of the royal personality or the bare bones of some private tragedy peep through the official language. All the letters, charters, writs, etc., which were sent out in the king's name were copied by the chancery clerks on skins or parchment before dispatch. The completed membranes were then stitched together into a roll, and that roll was put away safely as a record of the king's business. By the reign of Henry III, these rolls had begun to be sorted into definite types. The two main classes were the

Patent and the Close Rolls. The Patent Rolls dealt usually with the more official business. They were quite formal in their address and in the list of witnesses who attested the grant or order. As their name would indicate, they were sent out open, with the king's seal hanging from them. In a partly illiterate age, the proper seal proved their authenticity to the ignorant as well as to the learned. The Charter Rolls, which were even more formal and permanent than the Patent Rolls, split off during this reign from the Patent Rolls and formed a separate set of records.

The Close Rolls covered an enormous number of subjects, usually more private in nature than the letters patent, but varying from the king's taste in fish to matters of national importance. The letters close were sent out folded very small, with the king's seal marked on a blob of wax holding the letter together. During Henry's reign, the Liberate Rolls, records of writs warranting or ordering expenditure, broke off from the Close Rolls and became a separate file. They are full of fascinating detail about the items on which the king considered it important to spend money. In them are to be found most of the royal orders for decoration and building, often in explicit detail, and frequently the exact description of his many gifts. They are a mine of information for the social historian, as are the records of cases heard before the king's judges, now being published as the Curia Regis Rolls. The Fine Rolls, which represent a record of a bargain made with the king which "finished" a matter and usually recorded a money payment, are the last important series of chancery records at this time. The Exchequer records, especially the Pipe Roll, which gave the settlement of accounts made at the Exchequer by the sheriffs and all others who owed money to the king, are, like most financial records, very useful, but not often full of human interest. Obviously, the letters and orders found on these rolls exemplify the king's will, except for the period between Lewes and Evesham, when Simon controlled the person of the king as well as the administration. They are never a connected history of events, but merely an unorganized record of the king's dealing with the affairs of the kingdom and his plans for meeting coming contingencies.

An attempt to build up a coherent picture of the period must utilize the monastic annals and chronicles, which give a running account of events. The monastic annals were almost as anonymous as the work of the chancery clerks. An annal was a record of the year's happenings, and many of the monasteries kept such an account. They included matters of importance to the monastery itself, and such general events as impinged on the monastic consciousness. Normally, they were compiled in a rather haphazard fashion. The monk who put together the Worcester annals, and who borrowed much of his text, including the preface, from the Winchester annals, says: "We have excerpted these things for you from old rolls and neglected parchments." Then he goes on to explain how the annal was compiled. A loose strip was hung from the manuscript, which was kept in the monastery library. On it, during the course of the year, any monk could note down in lead the death of illustrious men and anything particularly notable about the state of the realm. At the end of the year, the monk, whose charge it was, compiled what he found on the memorandum slip into more or less acceptable literary form for the benefit of posterity. The finished account was then added to the book of annals, the old slip was taken away, and a new one was added for the coming year.[1]

It is obvious that, under such conditions, a monastic annal is most likely to be of value for local matters, where they touch on national events. The annal of Tewkesbury, for example, one of the great abbeys of the rich Severn valley, has an enormous amount of information on matters that deal with the earls of Gloucester and their connections. The abbey was in the centre of the Gloucester lands and benefited from the liberality of the earls. But, as the earls of Gloucester played a leading role among the barons of thirteenth-century England, the Tewkesbury details are of general, not only local, interest. It is not surprising that the bias of a monastic annal is often determined by the simple fact of geography and the politics of the neighbouring lord. Naturally, the annal of the Cistercian abbey of Waverley, in Surrey, is extremely favourable to the Montfort family, all through the Barons' War. Waverley was only a few miles from Odiham Castle,

3

one of the main strongholds of Simon and Eleanor, and they had quite a record of liberality to the abbey and of friendship with its abbot.

Thus, there is often a traceable explanation for the bias of an annal. It is rather more difficult to be positive of their accuracy. These manuscripts were much passed around between houses, so that the identical information, written in the same language, will appear in several. The annals of Winchester, for example, were a favourite source for other monastic annalists, less close to the centre of news and less energetic. Much depended, too, on the judgment and intelligence of the particular monk whose duty it was to compile the annals. Their value often varies with a change of authorship. But despite all these defects, and the recognition of their often limited interest in matters outside their own lands and privileges, the monastic annals frequently are valuable sources. They give the local atmosphere, the local share in general events. Pieced together, they provide evidence from many corners of the realm that would be unavailable otherwise.

Most of the annals are not exciting reading, however, and it is often a relief to turn to the work of an individual chronicler, where a human personality, with all its faults and prejudices, enlivens and integrates the narrative. The thirteenth century is blessed with several chroniclers who add immeasurably to the pleasure of reading its history. In France, there is, of course, the lord of Joinville, whose chronicle of his friendship with St Louis and his share in affairs around the king is a classic in itself. Joinville not only told what he knew of the king he revered and loved, but also unwittingly held a mirror to the weaknesses and strengths of his own character.

In the simplicity of his old age, Joinville recalled for St Louis' great-grandson, and for the enjoyment of many generations, a picture of French noble society of his day. He had little to say about the earl of Leicester, but he gave the most vivid picture of the French court and some interesting sidelights on King Henry. The other French chroniclers, especially Guillaume de Nangis, have something to say about affairs in England and the place of

Simon de Montfort, but their information has none of the personal impact of the naïve narrative of Joinville.

Another truly personal chronicle of the period was that written by the Italian Franciscan, Salimbene. Born of a noble family of Parma, Brother Salimbene belonged to the second generation of Franciscans who still had much of the childlike simplicity and joy of life of St Francis himself, but his turn of mind was basically secular. Judged by his writings, he was a cheerful man who enjoyed the wandering Franciscan life and could vividly describe what he saw along the way. His chronicle was originally written for his niece, Agnes, who had entered the Poor Clares at the age of 15, and who, from her convent, thus shared in the far-flung wanderings of her irrepressible uncle. Only incidentally does Salimbene touch on English matters, and then only by hearsay. However, he spent some time in France and he has some sharp thumbnail sketches of leading French personalities which bring them to life across the centuries.[2]

But, naturally, it is to the English chroniclers that we must turn for an intimate picture of the events of English history in these troubled years. One name stands out, that of Matthew Paris, Benedictine monk of the abbey of St Albans.

St Albans had a great tradition of historical writing and it was ideally situated to learn the news quickly. The great abbey, probably the richest in England, lay just a day's journey north of London, astride the main route to the Midlands and the North. Its guest chambers and refectory echoed to the talk of many of the most important men of the realm. Even the king himself, with his large retinue, spent some time at St Albans. It was accounted as one of the good works of Abbot John of Hertford that he built a splendid new hall for guests with many adjoining bedchambers which were most up-to-date with closets and fireplaces.

The hall, too, showed the influence of the same passion for decoration and adornment which distinguished the royal castles and manors throughout the realm. Brother Richard, "an excellent craftsman", was detailed to see that it was "properly painted and delightfully decorated".[3] So, the chronicler at St Albans could count on getting much of his information first-hand, from the lips of important people who stayed at the monastery and who had participated in the events themselves. Being in this strategic location also meant that the basic obligation of the monastery to give food and shelter to all travellers often provided valuable stories for the chronicler. Royal and baronial messengers brought tales of the nation's business. Returned crusaders would have new accounts of the Holy Land. Then the abbot of St Albans, as one of the great magnates of the realm, would normally take his place in the councils of the king at the various feasts and ceremonies, and bring back an account of these affairs. The life of the monastery offered great possibilities for a monk who recorded history. Perhaps because of all these factors, St Albans was renowned throughout much of the Middle Ages for the high level of its chroniclers, as well as for real artistic competence.

Much of its reputation rests on Matthew Paris, but the facts about his life are sparse.[4] Matthew was born in about 1200 and took the habit at St Albans in 1217. Despite some controversy, it seems most probable that he died in June, 1259, unfortunately before the exciting events of the Barons' War. Most of our knowledge of him is negative. We are sure that he did not come from Paris, despite his name, but was English-born. He was not university trained. On one occasion only did Matthew emerge from the obscurity of his monastery to take part in directing affairs, instead of chronicling them. In 1248, he went on a mission to Norway, at the request of King Haakon, to serve as visitor for the abbey of St Benet Holm, on the island of Nidarholm. It was a compliment to the English monk and Matthew, with natural vanity, inflated the terms of his papal commission to make him visitor of all the Benedictine houses in Norway. But he tells us very little either about his stay or about the religious life of Norway at the time.* All he says is that he took letters from King Louis of France to King Haakon, and that a great fire was

* Norway, because of its remoteness from Rome, seems to have allowed some unusual practices. For example, Pope Gregory IX (*d.* 1241) had to send a papal brief to the archbishop of Drontheim warning him about the necessity of Norwegian babies, like other Christians, being baptized with water. It seems that, on account of a lack of water, they were accustomed to be baptized in beer! Paris, *Historia Anglorum*, III, p. xviii, n. 5.

burning in Bergen when he arrived in the harbour there. Apart from this one foreign expedition the life of Matthew Paris was that of an ordinary monk in which there were few events.

The thirteenth century put little emphasis on literary fame and had never heard of copyright. Thus, it is not surprising that much of Matthew Paris's work was borrowed with no acknowledgment or thanks by other less able chroniclers. His fame was, of course, upheld by his own monastery, from which came his best-known eulogy:

> At this time too, flourished and died Dom Matthew Paris; monk of St Albans, and an eloquent and famous man full of innumerable virtues; a magnificent historian and chronicler; an excellent author, who frequently revolved in his heart the saying: "Laziness is the enemy of the soul" and whom widespread fame commended in remote parts where he had never been.[5]

The eulogy went on to underline the fact that Paris was not only a chronicler, but also a worker in silver and gold, a painter of considerable skill, as well as a cartographer and heraldic expert. Matthew decorated his manuscripts with many different kinds of marginal pictures, including one of the first elephant that was ever brought to England. But, his art aside, it is interesting to find out what kind of person Matthew Paris was, and how it influenced his judgment in his chronicles.

Paris was a very copious writer, and the relationship of his chronicles and their continuations and abbreviations is best left to the careful judgment of the specialist. It is worth noticing, however, that he had a vivid realization of the difficulties of writing contemporary history. He writes, concerning his proposal to finish his chronicle:

> For if you speak or write truth about powerful men, they become your enemies, and if you are silent or substitute good for evil the work is mutilated, and through flattery and falsehood the whole work will be condemned.[6]

As far as he could, he tried to get his knowledge first-hand, and he had a remarkably long list of informants, including some of the most important men of the kingdom, as well as King Henry himself. The inquisitive monk was present at many of the most

7

ceremonial occasions, and thus could add his own personally observed touches to the scene. His greatest gifts were his vividness and his curiosity. Matthew was interested in almost everything. He seems to have incorporated into one or the other of his historical works an enormous number of irrelevant but interesting details. Matthew the man emerges very clearly from his work and, with all his many deficiencies, he was basically likeable.

A man of intense prejudices, they colour all his writing and often make him a very unreliable guide. As a black monk of an important and established house, he detested the upstart orders of friars, who seemed to be undermining the privileged position of the monasteries. Upholding the rights and privileges of his order, he thoroughly disapproved of bishops who exercised their proper right of visitation. As an Englishman, at a time when English national sentiment was just beginning to have real emotional force, he detested and despised all foreigners and was quite glad to attribute to their underhand schemings all the woes of England. He was exceedingly outspoken about these prejudices and had hard things to say about many of the important characters of his day, although occasionally he hid his own feelings under the convenient shield of "certain men say". His prejudices were those of a man of his time and position, a nationalist and member of a privileged caste.

For both these reasons, he comes out against any exercise of papal power in England, as well as its notorious abuses. He upholds the barons' constitutional efforts against the king, up to the time of his death, just as he upholds the monks against their abbot, or the canons against their bishop. Although due allowances must be made for the fact that Matthew was prejudiced, careless, and thus often unreliable, the history of the thirteenth century would be dull without him. He could tell an extremely good story. Unfortunately, when he was particularly successful, he had the bad habit of repeating the same story, but about a totally different character. He loved to repeat the scandalous rumours that circulated as gossip, and helped to embroider them himself. But he had a real flair for description and anecdote and for constructing a vivid conversation, which is usually true to character, though scarcely a trustworthy verbatim report. Although, through some of his informants and the resources of the abbey, he had access to a surprising number of important documents, it must be remembered that most of his writing was based on oral reports. Naturally, too, his informants tended to exalt their own share in the shaping of events. All these factors, as well as Matthew's own faults, tend to increase the inaccuracy of his account. But, if allowance is made for his omissions and prejudices, Matthew is a most enjoyable guide to the life of England, and indeed Europe, in the middle of the thirteenth century. Like Joinville and Salimbene, Matthew Paris emerges as a very real person, who, in writing the history of his time, has unwittingly drawn his own picture as well.

The other important individual whom we can discern behind his account of affairs is a very different person from gossipy, journalistic Matthew Paris. The chronicle of Thomas Wykes has always been recognized as one of the most valuable sources for the period of the Barons' War, but Wykes himself has only recently been rescued from his centuries of anonymity.[7] It has been hard to discover the relationship between the annals of Osney, an Augustinian monastery on Osney Island at Oxford, and the chronicle of Thomas Wykes, with their similarities and contradictions. Wykes entered the monastery at Osney in 1282, as a form of retirement in his old age, and took over the occupation of continuing the monastery annals from that year till about the time of his death in 1290-1. With what went before in the monastery's annals, he had no connection. But he had been writing his own chronicle before he came to Osney. His wider interests and different background explain the curious fact that the Osney annals, during the Barons' War, were very much in favour of the baronial party, while Wykes's personal chronicle for the same period is militantly royalist in tone.

The background of this enigmatic man is of special interest because he is the only chronicler who comes out strongly on the king's side. Thomas Wykes seems to have been born in Suffolk, probably in 1222, and was a student at Oxford between 1238-46. He was rector of Caister St Edmunds in Norfolk, and had as well, special knowledge and interest about affairs in London during and just after the civil war. His special knowledge and his friends combine to stamp him as a man from East Anglia. The family manor of Wykes was near both the great abbey of Bury St Edmunds and Richard of Cornwall's honour of Eye, and was held partly from each. Philip of Eye, Richard's treasurer for many years and later treasurer of England, was Thomas Wykes's friend and benefactor. It is almost certain that Wykes was closely associated with the household of Richard of Cornwall and by far the simplest and most sensible explanation is that this was due to his intimate connection with the Earl of Cornwall's treasurer.

Although Wykes's chronicle is royalist, it does not gloss over the defects of the king. Rather, it seems to look at events from the standpoint of the more moderate and much shrewder Richard. Quite possibly, Thomas received valuable material for his chronicle from Philip of Eye. He certainly had access to a much wider body of information than the average secular clerk, which made more valuable his unusual grasp of affairs and a strong vein of native shrewdness. Completely partisan, and unwavering in his disapproval of Simon de Montfort and the baronial party, he was not often inaccurate in matters of fact. His very sobriety is a surprising contrast to the more garrulous and discursive Matthew Paris. Historical detective work has provided him with "a local habitation and a name" but no personality kindles from his pages. However, without the revealing description which Wykes provides of the royalist version of events, our knowledge of these years would be much less complete.

There is, of course, other contemporary evidence besides these accounts. For example, the monk who continued Matthew Paris's chronicle at St Albans in the work known as the *Flores Historiarum* has much information about affairs in England during the crucial years of the Barons' War. Robert of Gloucester's metrical chronicle, which has been described as "doggerel verse in ballad metre",[8] is a hodge-podge compounded from many different sources. Nevertheless, it is contemporary for the period of the Barons' War and the author, close to the scenes he describes, had first-hand knowledge of the last tragic campaigns of the war.

Also, some of the chronicles written during the reign of Henry's son, Edward, deal with the troubled days of the civil war and occasionally have something to add. Such is the chronicle of the Dominican, Nicholas Trevet, the son of one of King Henry's itinerant justices. A well-educated man, he seems to have studied in London, Oxford and Paris. While in France, he collected the statements of French chroniclers which dealt with English affairs and thus brought the information of people like Guillaume de Nangis back into the stream of English knowledge. Although he wrote on Henry III's reign, he was too young to have known of matters personally, for he was probably born at the time of the Provisions of Oxford. Another later, but useful account, is the chronicle of Walter of Guisborough, a Yorkshire canon, who wrote at the beginning of the fourteenth century.[9] What he had to say of events at the time of the Barons' War was probably taken from the hearsay knowledge of various survivors and from people who had a special interest, political or territorial, in the troubles.

Both Nicholas Trevet and Walter of Guisborough were serious historians and relatively accurate. The chronicles of Lanercost and Melrose, which also come from the north and belong to the end of the century, are quite a different matter. They are not so much sober statements of fact as highly embroidered hagiography. They reflect the Franciscan tradition, which regarded Simon de Montfort as a saint and martyr, and considered him the saviour of the poor people of England. In much this same tradition were the political songs which become current around the middle of the thirteenth century. Many of them are rude, but effective, political satire.

The most important, the *Song of Lewes*, is a long and serious statement in Latin verse of the constitutional arguments of the barons. It, too, was probably written by a Franciscan. Most of the other songs, as well as Robert of Gloucester's doggerel, are in the vernacular and show the effects of the preaching in the popular tongue which had been one of the most important and successful parts of the mission of the friars. The friars served as the mouthpiece of the poor and lowly. In these songs, we see the secular application of ideas made current through their sermons. The sons of Lady Poverty were natural enemies of misrule and luxury, of injustice and vain display. Where the Latin chronicles and annals normally express the ideas and feelings of the more important and more educated sections of the "community of the realm", these scraps in the vernacular give us some idea of the popular feeling. Their enthusiasm helps to explain why Simon de Montfort was so strongly supported by the townspeople, especially by the Londoners, who were most influenced by the new orders of friars.

Unfortunately, the Middle Ages was not an era for autobiography. How much a medieval version of the ghostwriter could have added to our store of knowledge about the active, but uncommunicative, figures of those centuries! Nevertheless, about the earl and countess of Leicester, we have rather more personal information and family papers than are usual for this period. The most important and illuminating of these miscellaneous papers is the list of King Henry's complaints against Earl Simon, brought forward in the trials of 1260 and 1262, and the earl's replies to them, point by point.[10] The articles treat of many of the disputed facts of Simon's early career, though seen in the distorting glasses of conflicting memories. Then, too, in the French archives, there has been preserved a collection of manuscripts of the Montfort family, which were gathered together in the seventeenth century. In this there are some originals, and many copies, of letters and arrangements made by the earl and the countess dealing with their innumerable legal squabbles and incessant, but futile, arbitrations.[11] Another interesting fragment – brought back to England from France at the time of the French Revolution – gives a vivid glimpse of the domestic life of the couple. It is an incomplete roll of the countess's household accounts, covering six months of the year 1265, and it draws an unparalleled picture of the daily routine of a great noble household.[12]

The complete story of Simon de Montfort and Eleanor must be reconstructed from such small, and often confusing, pieces of evidence. With the many possibilities for error, and the varying judgments of his contemporaries, it is no wonder that the earl's portrait may be – and has been – painted in several ways. Perhaps this is part of the enduring fascination of this couple, who provoke such partisanship even across the centuries.

England

Montfort-l'Amaury; the Family Background

Simon de Montfort came from one of the important families of the Ile-de-France, that territory which was the essential domain of the French king and the source and centre of his royal strength. One of the early Montforts had settled and fortified the hilltop in the eleventh century, and named the stronghold after the Amaury who built it. About thirty miles south-west of Paris, Montfort-l'Amaury shelters among the hills and streams on the outskirts of the modern forest of Rambouillet. The fortress was the centre of a series of castles under family control, which were strong points on the road to southern Normandy. Up to the time of Simon's birth, there was continuous friction, and often open warfare, between France and the duchy of Normandy, which was ruled and administered by the king of England. Since the Montforts were settled in such a strategic border location, it is not surprising to find that they married into the great families of both Normandy and the Ile-de-France, and thus had interests on both sides of the line.

In Montfort-l'Amaury now there remain only ruins of the once great stronghold, although the town which grew up later around the castle still survives, old and charming. The "two black giants" of Victor Hugo, who lived in the town for a while, are the partial walls of the eleventh-century keep, or central tower. They are the sole remnants of the castle as it must have been in the time of Simon de Montfort. From the height of the "strong hill" it is easy to see what an excellent defensive situation Amaury de Montfort had picked out. The castle crowns the summit of a steeply rising slope, which, by itself, would have complicated the task of the attacker, even without the grim struggle to breach the walls.

Trying to trace the ramifications of the family tree of the early de Montforts is extremely difficult, and requires the work of a trained genealogist. It is made more complicated by the recurrent use of the same Christian names. Each generation had its Amaury, Guy, and Simon, and this only adds to the problem of disentangling them.* But, by the end of the twelfth century, it had become obvious that the Montforts had put into practice one of the cardinal principles of feudal society, the determination to marry well. Fortune favoured their efforts. In two generations alone, there were Montfort heirs to rich lands in England, in Normandy, and in Latin Syria, as well as to the growing family importance in France. Even two generations could spin a far-flung and useful series of connections and blood relationships.

But, despite the growing brilliance of their marriages and the inter-relation of the family with England, the Montforts would have been best known as argumentative figures in the law-courts, challenging the details of their inheritances, or as shadowy nobles at the king's court, if it had not been for the personal activities of Simon the Crusader. This Simon is most renowned for his leadership of the Albigensian Crusade. He combined strongly in his own person the dominant traits of the Montfort inheritance; deep religious faith, vigorous military ability, and enormous ambition. When he joined the misdirected Fourth Crusade, which substituted an attack on the Christian capital of the Byzantine Empire at Constantinople, for a frontal assault on the Holy Land, Simon would have nothing to do with it. He felt that it was an impious misuse to employ the crusaders against the Greek Christians, schismatics though they might be, and insisted on going directly to Palestine to fight the Saracens. In an age when many were devout, Simon the Crusader was notably so, and his contemporaries remarked on it.

Soon after Simon returned from this crusade, his ambition was whetted by a fortunate inheritance. Simon's father had married the sister of the earl of Leicester, a great landholder in both

* See Genealogical Table, p. xii.

England and Normandy. When the earl died without direct heirs in 1204, his large English inheritance was divided between his two sisters, Simon the Crusader's mother and Margaret, the wife of the earl of Winchester. The half share which thus came to the Montforts was glittering enough, for it included the earldom, the stewardship of England, and lordship over the borough of Leicester. Simon's father was already dead in 1204 and his older brother Amaury was busy with the French lands of the family, so the attempt to make good the claim to the earldom of Leicester was left to Simon.

In 1206, he obtained recognition as earl of Leicester and was granted certain of his lands by King John.[1] However, the growing tension between John Lackland and Philip Augustus of France meant that the old custom of holding lands in both England and France was more and more discouraged. Wherever possible, the kings forced their knights to choose between their lords, and then seized the lands and revenues within their own kingdom of those who chose for the other side. This is what seems to have happened to Simon the Crusader soon after his first acquisition of his English inheritance. In February, 1207, all his English lands were put in charge of the sheriff of Warwick and Leicestershire, a royal official, and the revenues went to the king.[2]

But Simon the Crusader had little time or energy to deplore the loss of his mother's inheritance, as he was soon to be actively engaged in the Albigensian Crusade. This Crusade was the final step in the efforts of Pope Innocent III to root out an extraordinary heresy which had spread widely in Languedoc and northern Spain during the preceding two centuries. These territories were quite different from the ruder districts of northern France, they were softer and more cultured. Christianity in the south was affected by its struggle with the still strong remnants of Moorish civilization, and with aggressive and prosperous colonies of Jews. In some obscure way Languedoc inherited from Asia Minor the dualistic doctrines originally known as Manichaeanism, which had been one of the earliest great heresies attacking Christianity. Now these heretics were called Catharists, or nicknamed Albigensians, from the town of Albi which was one of their strongholds. They believed in a body of doctrine which differed basically from that of the Catholic. According to the Catharists, there were two ruling principles in the world; one of good and one of evil, Spirit and Matter, God and the Devil. From this premise flowed the conviction that all the material part of man was essentially and inevitably evil, and must be shunned. Thus, they disapproved of marriage, of procreation – because it brought more material beings into existence – and justified suicide as a means of escaping from the evil weight of the body. This belief in the essential wickedness of matter also meant that they denied the Incarnation of Christ – God could not take on a real body, for the body itself was evil. Also they denied the doctrine of the Atonement, for they felt that man reached salvation through a series of progressive reincarnations.

The heretics were divided into two classes; the Perfect, who lived a most rigorous and ascetic life, more penitential than that of most religious orders; and the Believers, whose obligations were merely to reverence the Perfect, and to propose to become one of them before death. This division within the sect allowed the Believers, who were of course the great majority, to spend most of their lives unshackled by any of the normal rules of morality. It particularly encouraged a freedom in sexual behaviour which tended to undermine the foundations of the social structure. Yet much of the influence of the Perfect was due to the fact that they were convinced and ascetic men, whose moral standard reproached the luxurious lives of the great majority of the Catholic clergy, and even of many of the monks. Then, too, the Perfect were ardent preachers at a time when the parish clergy were neglecting their duty of instructing the people. But the movement was more than one of protest against the deficiencies of the contemporary church and clergy. It was essentially opposed to the basic dogmas of the church, and aimed to destroy its whole structure.

Despite the conditions which aided it, Albigensianism could never have spread so widely, or grown so powerful, if it had not been aided by the secular powers of the district. The men of Languedoc in the twelfth century were highly cultured and civilized. Their land was the centre of courtly poetry, the great literary movement of the day. It is not surprising that they looked down on the Frenchman from the north as a rude barbarian, and seized any possible pretext to proclaim their political independence and increase their power. The Catharist heresy appealed to the relaxed moral convictions of these lords, who were certainly not numbered among the Perfect, and it also provided them with a useful political weapon in their struggle for power.

During much of the eleventh and twelfth centuries, the church contented itself with frequent, but futile, condemnations of the heresy; even the preaching of the great St Bernard had no effect. By the end of the twelfth century, when the vigorous Innocent III became pope, stronger measures were required to fight its growth. Innocent first tried a campaign of persuasion. He sent preachers, and commissioned some of the best of the local Cistercians as his agents, but with little success. New and energetic legates were again appointed in 1202 who pressed the fight vigorously, especially against the bishops of the district, many of whom were secret sympathizers with the heretics. Several bishops were deposed or suspended, and in the next few years a busy campaign of preaching and education was carried on, most notably by St Dominic, who found in his work in Languedoc the inspiration for a new preaching order of friars. But the heretics were still supported by the great lords, especially Raymond count of Toulouse, in whose lands they were most strongly concentrated. The legate Peter de Castelnau tried vainly to deflect the count from Catharism. When all else failed he excommunicated Raymond, and laid an interdict on his territories.

This act roused such fury among the supporters of the count of Toulouse that one of them murdered the unfortunate legate. That act of violence opened a new chapter in the struggle against the Albigensians. The mission of preaching was put aside, and instead a crusade, a holy war, was declared against the heretics and the lords who supported them. Innocent decided that military methods must be used, and ultimately appointed Simon de Montfort as his lieutenant and the general of his armies.

It was this Albigensian Crusade which made the name of Montfort known and feared even in the mountain hamlets of the

Pyrenees. The expedition gave scope to Simon's undoubted military ability, and provided a marvellous opportunity for satisfying his ambition for power and riches, under the convenient cloak of enforcing religious orthodoxy. Simon's religious faith was deep and genuine, and he honestly believed in the necessity of putting down heresy, but his method was that of fire and sword, which left a long legacy of bitterness and hatred. There were other motives besides the religious one, for almost all the crusaders, and also for the great lords who fought on the side of the heretics. The enthusiasm of the king of France, who gave considerable financial support, and of most of the crusaders from the north, was due not to religious zeal, but to the very rich possibilities of conquest and confiscation in wealthy and cultured Languedoc. The great lords of the south fought as desperately to maintain their almost independent power against the spiritual sanctions of the pope and the lengthening shadow of control by the king of France.

For nearly ten years (1209–18), Simon led armies against heresy and the strongholds of the lords of Languedoc. In the process he won for himself the county of Toulouse and the duchy of Narbonne – valuable territories, which would have made him one of the greatest lords of the realm and, like his predecessors, almost an independent prince. Although the pope was rather wary of the Crusader's excessive ambitions in the south of France, he threw his weight on Simon's side in regard to his English claims. The pope's letters always address Simon de Montfort as earl of Leicester, and it was at the pope's request that the Leicester lands were committed to Ranulf, Earl of Chester, in 1215.[3] Ranulf was Simon's nephew, and was meant to hold the lands for his uncle's use. Thus Simon had another line of defence to fall back on if his dreams of power and glory in southern France proved a mirage. But all these dreams were brought suddenly to an end in 1218. While he was besieging the city of Toulouse, he died ingloriously, struck on the head by a stone pitched from a mangonel used to defend the city.

His death was a matter of European importance, commented on by chroniclers far away from Languedoc. An Englishman composed the floweriest of epitaphs, which compared the crusader to Mars, Paris and Cato:

> He was another Mars, because warlike, another Paris, because beautiful, another Cato, because adorned by good morals.[4]

Everywhere the judgment of his contemporaries was the same – Simon de Montfort was a strenuous and handsome knight. So widely had his reputation travelled that there is a curious story in one of the English annals. Simon de Montfort seems to have disturbed the dreams not only of the men of southern France, but even of King John. The story goes that, in 1210, when the king had gone to Nottingham, on his way to put down one of the frequent raids of the Welsh into the Marches, he heard a rumour of a conspiracy against him by his barons. This was not an unusual state of affairs. John and his barons wrangled continuously, to Magna Carta and beyond. This time, however, the rumour claimed that the barons had deposed John and elected Simon de Montfort as king of England.[5] It was only idle gossip, but it is revealing, because it shows Simon's importance in the eyes of his contemporaries.

When Simon died, the task of carrying on the Crusade devolved upon his eldest son Amaury, a young man in his early twenties. Unfortunately, Amaury had neither the military talents, the enthusiasm, nor the prestige of his distinguished father. He soon abandoned the struggle. After considerable negotiation as to the compensation that should be paid, he ceded all his rights in the south to the French king, giving up his rather shadowy title to Toulouse and Narbonne. It was a valuable political acquisition, for the king thus had another legal claim to back up his consistent efforts to expand his practical power. Amaury retired to a relatively peaceful life on the family domain.

Guy, the second son of Simon the Crusader, also shared his father's crusading activities in the south of France. Before his father's death – and by his father's arrangement – he was married to Perronelle, countess of Bigorre. This little southern county was valuable to the orthodox because its strategic position helped to discourage any invasion from Aragon, whose king favoured the heretics. Again, Simon had succeeded in combining ambition and religion, at once providing handsomely for his son and protecting the crusading army from outside attack. Guy had two daughters by Perronelle before his death at Castelnaudary in 1220. The interests and claims arising from this marriage were to preoccupy the young Simon when he was acting as the English king's lieutenant in Gascony, but he must have had very little personal contact with his older brother.

Amaury and Guy were considerably the elders of the family and were in an assured position before their father's death at Toulouse. Simon had another brother, Robert, who seems to have died before 1226. It is difficult to determine whether Simon or Robert was the elder and, so far, impossible to know the exact year of Simon's birth. The general weight of evidence, mostly negative, would suggest that it was around 1208.

Just as it is impossible to pinpoint the date of Simon's birth, so it is equally difficult to find exact information on his early years. The chronicles were not interested in such family affairs. But his upbringing must have followed the general pattern of any noble child. When he had graduated from the nursery, he would be free to run and play until about seven years of age. Then for the next few years his education would be supervised by the lady of the household. She would see that he learned the requirements of polite behaviour, the usages of the social code. Among his duties would be to serve in hall and to run messages for the ladies.

At this age, many boys of noble families were sent to serve as pages in other more important households. If their parents were distinguished enough they might even be sent to the royal court, where sometimes they had to serve not only as pages, but as hostages for the continued good behaviour of their parents. The one thing that we do know about this period of Simon's youth is that the Montforts were rather more insistent on book learning than was usual in their day for people of their rank. Simon seems to have had a thorough education, and was probably fluent in Latin, as well as the usual Norman French. Certainly he approved of education for the young, for he sent two of his own sons, Henry and Amaury, to be educated in the household of Bishop Robert

Grosseteste, the most learned man in England. Amaury was taught by Master Nicholas, one of the best mathematicians of his time, who was mentioned approvingly even by Roger Bacon, the censorious Franciscan. If Simon ever learned English – and it is specifically mentioned that he did not know it when he went to England[6] – it must have been much later. Quite possibly, he never really used it, for the general language of polite society in England in the thirteenth century was still Norman French, just as Latin was the language of the officials and the clerks.

Whatever specific education the young Simon did or did not receive, much of his knowledge and interests must have been determined by his family contacts. During the years of Simon's childhood his father was away, for the most part, in the south of France. Simon's mother, an energetic woman, frequently accompanied her husband. News trickled back to Montfort-l'Amaury through messengers, returning knights, travelling clerks on errands for pope or bishop, and visiting relatives. They would stop at Montfort-l'Amaury for a meal or a night or even a more extended stay, depending on the urgency of their business. These visitors brought the household the latest news, as well as the current rumours. In those days the upper levels of society were peripatetic. Everyone, including the king and his whole court, moved constantly from place to place, utilizing the different castles and manors in their possession. The laws of hospitality – probably the most strictly observed of all medieval laws – required both castles and monasteries to entertain, feed, and lodge the travellers who knocked at their gates. Just as the chroniclers at St Albans gained much of their information from the word-of-mouth accounts of their visitors, so the inmates of the castles learned of events from those travellers who had had some part in them, or from the reports of distant relations. The ramifications of family knowledge and interest were amazingly extensive. There is, for example, a surprisingly well-informed summary of Simon's character and of the English civil war in the chronicle of the Templar of Tyre. Although the author was primarily concerned with affairs in the Holy Land, he explained that his knowledge of English affairs came from his position. In his youth he had been page to the wife of John de Montfort, lord of Tyre, whose father, Philip, was Simon's first cousin, the son of his uncle Guy. Thus, the chronicler in the Holy Land had heard discussed in considerable detail the important events in England in which his lord had a family interest.

The closeness of family ties and the kaleidoscopic nature of feudal society suggests that one of the visitors at Montfort-l'Amaury during Simon's youth may well have been his great-aunt Loretta, the countess of Leicester,[7] who probably spent some time in France sheltering from King John's wrath. She was a remarkable woman in her own right, as well as in her far-flung connections. Loretta was a daughter of William de Briouze, one of the greatest lords of the southern Marches, and married Robert Beaumont, the fourth earl of Leicester and a member of the great Midland family. Childless and widowed very young, she saw the Leicester earldom divided between her husband's two sisters. If the harried countess went to France during the period of King John's attack upon her parents, she would undoubtedly have gone to Montfort-l'Amaury to see her sister-in-law's family. Perhaps she even saw Simon as an infant. But Loretta spent the greater part of her life – some forty-five years – as a recluse at Hackington, just outside Canterbury. There she lived in religious seclusion, but she was not completely cut off from the world she had renounced. Canterbury was a centre of pilgrimage, and many petitioners at the martyr's shrine also asked the noble recluse to aid them with their temporal business. She helped the first group of Franciscan friars to get established in England. But almost at the end of her long life, she touched again the life of her great-nephew, whom she may have held as a baby in France. For an instant she was part of the turbulent stream of political action from which she had turned away so long before. In the spring of 1265, when Simon was in fact ruling England, he had the king write to her about the rights and liberties which pertained to the stewardship of England. More than any one in the realm, she was supposed to have the best knowledge of it, since her husband, as earl of Leicester, had held the office, more than sixty years before. Unfortunately there is no record of her reply, but it is obvious that, even in her eighties, the old countess must have been regarded as a woman of intelligence and ability. All these things can be deduced from the bare bones of the records. If only the Middle Ages had thought highly of memoirs and autobiographies for others than the saintly, we would know so much more. If the gaps in Loretta's life could be filled, they might well help to illuminate the childhood days of young Simon too.

A rapid series of deaths deprived Simon of the elders of his family and of his glowing prospects. His father was killed in 1218, his second brother in 1220. His mother's death took place in 1221, when he was about thirteen. Soon the glittering conquests of Simon the Crusader slipped into the hands of the king of France, and the family treasure evaporated in the vain effort to pay their troops. Amaury, as the eldest son, was the lord of Montfort, at least. Guy's death meant that any rights he had had in Bigorre through his wife would pass to his two young daughters. The younger son was orphaned and unprovided for. He was still a youth who had to learn his trade as a fighting man, and he had no immediate prospects. These thoughts must have troubled Simon's mind as he struggled to acquire, by constant practice, the skill with horse and weapons which was the basic equipment of the knight. Perhaps he remembered the tales which circulated of the rise to fame and fortune of William Marshal. That aged baron had died only a few years before, regent of England and full of honour. Starting as a penniless knight, with extraordinary fighting ability, William had built up a reputation and a fortune. His early wealth came from victories in tournaments, where the vanquished had to surrender his horse and armour to his conqueror, and often pay a ransom as well. Then William Marshal married the rich heiress of Pembroke and became the greatest knight in England, whose strength and feudal loyalty were equally unquestioned. But such successful fortune-hunting was none too frequent, despite the encouraging songs of the minstrels. Nevertheless, something had to be done. By the time that Simon had reached his majority, his decision had been made. His older brother Amaury was comfortably secure in his French position and was willing enough to resign to young Simon the questionable claims to the English lands of the Montfort inheritance. Armed with his brother's agreement, Simon would go to England and try to claim the Leicester lands which had once been his father's. At the same time, he would begin to explore the possibilities of a rich marriage. Either, or both, would establish him in the feudal world and start the Wheel of Fortune turning.

2

The Earldom of Leicester

In 1230 Simon de Montfort emerges from the mists of conjecture to begin his career in the clearer light of historical records. Unfortunately we do not know what he looked like. There is a clerestory window in Chartres cathedral which has been generally accepted as a representation of him. But, like the effigy on his seal, it tells us nothing definite of his appearance, for it is merely a knight on horseback, with his helm closed. For all the distinguishing physical characteristics, it could be any knight of the period. He was probably handsome, for this is mentioned as a family characteristic by several chroniclers. For the rest, imagination must fill the gap. We know considerably more about what kind of person he was, both by his actions and by the judgments of his contemporaries. Their comments, of course, have to be evaluated in the light of their bias for or against him. The young man gave certain definite hints of the person he was to become. His admirers described him as pleasant and witty in speech, "commendably endowed with knowledge of letters", already giving promise of his notable reputation in warfare and the use of arms, and always marked by an unusual piety and reverence for the clergy.[1] All in all, he must have been an attractive and ambitious young man, ready to seek his fortune where the best opportunity lay.

It is hard for the modern mind, moulded, half-consciously by generations of nationalistic passion, to understand how little this feeling affected a medieval man. In the thirteenth century patriotism certainly existed, but it was still a regional patriotism.

27

The emphasis was on the province from which one came rather than on the larger national unit which was still in process of formation and had, as yet, none of the emotional force of the older grouping. For example, a chronicler of St Louis's time would normally differentiate between the different "nations" of French, Norman, or Poitevin. In such a situation, the real bond of loyalty was not abstract devotion to a distant king, but the actual feudal tie, the oath of fidelity taken personally to one's overlord. Homage rendered to the lord of the lands was a necessary condition for taking possession of an inheritance or answering for the lands acquired in a fortunate marriage.

When Simon de Montfort came to manhood he found himself in the position of many younger brothers. The family lands in France were held by the eldest, and were not adequate to support another as well. Since Simon held, as yet, no lands from the king of France, he was free, according to feudal law, to go and look elsewhere. But the young Montfort was much more fortunate than most younger sons, for one glittering possibility lay ready to his hand. This was the Montfort claim to the earldom of Leicester, to which his father had been too busy during the Albigensian Crusade to pay more than token attention. The first project, the one that promised the easiest success and the most brilliant future, was to pursue this English inheritance at the court of the young King Henry III.

The struggle to get possession, or "seisin" as they would call it in the feudal documents, of this lordship was not likely to be easy. After the Montfort half of the earldom had again been seized by King John in 1207, it was guarded for some years by royal custodians. In 1215, at the pope's request, the Leicester lands were commuted to Ranulf, the earl of Chester, to hold for the use of Simon the Crusader. Ranulf was Simon the Crusader's nephew, as well as one of the greatest men of his day. He was not a baron with whom King John could afford to quarrel. As earl of Chester, which was almost an independent buffer state between England and Wales, Ranulf ruled almost as an independent sovereign in the turbulent district of the northern Marches. His lands and castles were dotted all over England, and his revenues and knights' fees made him the most powerful lord in the realm after John himself.

Besides his English power, he still retained much from the vast grants in Normandy which Henry II had made his grandfather. Ranulf was viscount of the Avranchin, the district on the borders of Normandy and Brittany, and here, too, had valuable castles and a good supply of knightly vassals. Undoubtedly Ranulf was ambitious and greedy, but he seems to have had the same effect on the imagination of his age which Robin Hood has retained for ours. He was the hero of many popular ballads. Sloth, the lazy priest in *Piers Plowman*, admitted that he could not say his *pater noster* and knew nothing of Our Lord and Our Lady, but he remembered all the rhymes of Robin Hood and Ranulf, earl of Chester.[2] Until Simon the Crusader's death in 1218, Ranulf held the lands for his use. On the death of his uncle at Toulouse, the Leicester lands, following feudal law, fell back into the king's hands. When the earl of Chester returned from a crusading expedition in 1220, the advisers of young King Henry restored the Leicester lands to him. In 1230 this formidable cousin was still in undisputed possession of the earldom. Certainly his power and established position would seem a massive stumbling-block to the hopes of his youthful and landless French cousin. But, at this crucial beginning of his career, Fortune smiled on Simon de Montfort.

Simon himself described how he achieved the earldom some thirty years later when he was defending his rights in the court of a king no longer friendly. It was such an important matter that Simon's memory was likely to be accurate, and his reminiscences generally agree with what can be proved by the documents. But Simon's own account states only baldly, and the documents not at all, how important Earl Ranulf's generosity was. Impelled by an unknown mixture of motives – perhaps a tardy sense of justice to the rightful heir, perhaps the realization that his vast complex of lands and honours must inevitably be divided, since he had no male heirs – the elderly earl graciously acceded to the request of his young kinsman. Thus was put in motion the legal process by which Simon de Montfort, younger son of a French family, took up the hereditary claim to the earldom of Leicester and became one of the magnates of England.

Simon himself gave the most coherent account of the various steps of the affair:

> First, our lord the king says that he has done me great goodness in that he took me for his man, because I was not the oldest. And so that one may know what the goodness was, my brother Amaury released to me all the right that he had in our father's inheritance in England, if I could secure it, in the same manner that I released to him the heritage which I had in France. And I went to England, and prayed my lord the king that he would restore to me my father's inheritance. And he answered that he could not do it because he had given it to the earl of Chester and his heirs by his charter. Upon this I returned without finding grace. The following year my lord the king crossed to Brittany and with him the earl of Chester who held my inheritance. And I went to the earl at the castle of St James-de-Beuvron which he held. There I prayed him that I could find his grace to have my inheritance and he, graciously, agreed and in the following August took me with him to England, and asked the king to receive my homage for the inheritance of my father, to which, as he said, I had greater right than he, and all the gift which the king had given him in this he renounced, and so he received my homage.[3]

This story is borne out by Amaury's series of renunciations of his rights in Simon's favour, and the relevant entries on the close and patent rolls.[4] Simon had come to England in the early months of 1230[5] armed with his elder brother's charter. In it Amaury de Montfort had surrendered to his younger brother any rights he might have had in the Leicester inheritance. Diplomatically, the older man emphasized that his brother held nothing from the French king, and thus should be a much more acceptable English vassal than Amaury himself could be. Since Amaury was soon to become the Constable of France, as well as count of Montfort, he was certainly too powerful a figure in France to be allowed to take up a claim to an English earldom. Henry III did nothing concrete at first. In the presence of some of the great lords at Westminster, including Earl Ranulf, he promised that Simon should have the earldom and the honour of Leicester as soon as the lands ceased to be held by the earl of Chester. After Easter, when Simon sent over one of his knights to re-emphasize his desire to enter the English king's service, Henry promised him an annual payment of 400 marks* until he received the earldom.

During the spring and summer of 1230, Henry was engaged in the first of his personal attempts to reconquer his Poitevin lands. This most unwarlike expedition did little more than march south from Brittany to Bordeaux and back, providing a show of force, but none of the actuality of power. Earl Ranulf who had accompanied the king and actually done some fighting, stayed on, after the king had returned to England, at his Norman castle of St James-de-Beuvron, on the borders of Brittany, not far from the renowned abbey at Mont-St Michel. There Ranulf received his kinsman and agreed to an early handing over of the Leicester honour. The official letters of August, 1231, corroborate Simon's statement that Earl Ranulf took him to England then and begged the king to accept him as the rightful heir. On August 13th, the king ordered the sheriffs of Leicestershire, Hampshire, Dorset, and Wiltshire to give full seisin to Simon, as the king had received his homage for the honour of Leicester which belonged to him by hereditary right. From this time on, the Leicester lands and revenues belonged to Simon, although he was not invested formally with the title for another eight years.

The half of the Leicester inheritance which Simon thus acquired included the title of earl of Leicester, the office of Steward of England, the suzerainty of the borough of Leicester, and a miscellaneous collection of lands and rents with their privileges and obligations. To sort out the various elements, which together formed this great inheritance, may help to explain the kind of power and wealth that a great English noble had in the thirteenth century, and on what it was based.

The title of earl no longer bestowed the actual authority which the Anglo-Saxon earls had had before the Norman conquest, but it was still coveted for its prestige and the position of pre-eminence which it implied among the barons of the realm. Financially, too, it still paid the "third penny", i.e., one third of the profits of justice with the earldom. Like that of other barons, the earl of

* A mark was worth two thirds of a £.

Leicester's income would be derived from three main sources: profits from essentially public jurisdiction which he exercised by a royal grant; feudal payments in his position as feudal lord; and, most profitable of all, the revenues and rents from his own manors and those which he had rented out to others for cultivation. The earl of Leicester was not really wealthy like Richard of Cornwall, the king's brother, and the richest baron in the realm, who had a yearly income of between four and five thousand pounds, or even like the earl of Gloucester who had £1,800, without his Irish or Welsh estates.[6] The Leicester earldom had suffered financially by its division in half and its administration by custodians for the benefit of the king. Where others were rising, its value fell during the course of the century. In 1210, the Montfort's half of the honour of Leicester was worth £256, considerably less than the general average, and more than half of this came from the ownership of the borough of Leicester.[7]

Leicester was one of the old boroughs of England, for it figured as a borough in Domesday Book. The earl of Leicester held it from the king, but, within the borough, he had the right to exclude any of the royal officials from dealing with its inhabitants. The borough included not only the town, but a reasonably large extent of land around it. The forest and fields, together with the river Soar, which formed one of the boundaries of the town and a natural defence, provided all the necessities of life. There was wood for building and fires, pasturage, fields for cultivation, and the river to turn the mills. The lord's castle was in the south-west quarter of the town, moated by the river, and quite near the parish church of St Mary of the Castle. This castle served as the centre of the Leicester barony, although Simon de Montfort was to have more impressive castles than this relatively small one.

The rest of the lands, manors, and knights' fees which belonged to the earldom of Leicester cannot be exactly determined for the period when Simon claimed the inheritance. There are the accounts rendered to King John by his custodians, which give some idea of the number of fragments that made up the holding then,[8] but these are nearly twenty years earlier. The task is further complicated by the fact that Simon held other lands by the king's gift, and more by right of his wife. One thing is certain. The Leicester lands were scattered in several different counties, including Hampshire, Dorset, and Wiltshire, as well as Leicestershire. In 1251, Simon answered for at least 60 knights' fees, that is, he was responsible for the service of at least 60 knights to the king's army, or for a substitute money payment. Undoubtedly, the earl held more fees than that. The barons had succeeded by the middle of the thirteenth century in cutting down the knight service owed by them to the king. It was then about one sixth of what they had to give his grandfather, Henry II. This again was a possible source of profit for the lord, as he could levy a money payment, in place of military service, on all his holders of knights' fees, and his returns normally exceeded his debt to the king.

With this shifting complex of lands and rents and revenues it is not surprising that "a fair proportion of the English baronage was always in debt to the crown".[9] In 1230, in fact, some sixty per cent were thus indebted. It was always difficult for the barons to find the necessary cash for major expenses or investments in a society where land was the most valuable commodity and many rents were paid in kind. Merely to take possession of his barony would cost a baron a relief, or succession duty of £100 paid to the royal exchequer. Besides the ordinary feudal obligations of aids for the king as his overlord, and the costs of military service and crusading expeditions, a baron might also be tempted into more speculative expenditures. To buy the wardship of a young lord left orphaned before his majority or the marriage of a wealthy young heiress, promised rich financial gains. During the years of wardship the revenues of the ward's lands went to the controlling baron and a rich noblewoman could be auctioned off to the highest bidder of equal social rank. But the king only sold such prizes at stiff terms. Often the optimistic barons found they had paid too heavily for their privileges, and then they fell behind in their payments. The baronial incomes varied wildly. The most stable element, the manorial rents and revenues, will be discussed more fully later. Even these were severely affected by bad crop years or civil disturbances. The feudal aids and reliefs which their sub-tenants owed the barons were highly variable. Their franchise resources (i.e. the profits they took from the exercise of justice and public administration) were more constant. Naturally, the lords were always striving to extend the scope of their jurisdiction over their own lands, and over the lands of their tenants, for the purposes of revenue as well as for prestige and power.

The Leicester earldom was in particularly bad shape in 1230, or so Simon claimed. Of course, it had been administered for some years, during his father's lifetime, by royal custodians, who sought only to take an immediate profit for the crown, and cared little for its future value.[10] Thus the earl of Leicester would have a rather smaller income than many other barons of his political importance. Since it also fluctuated considerably from year to year, it is not surprising that he had trouble making ends meet. Normally, he would find himself indebted to the king, and perhaps also to the Jews or the Cahorsins or the Italians, the recognized money-lenders of the time. In this habitually money short society the king's gifts, in pensions, extra rents, or commutation of debts, assumed important political value. One of the constantly recurring grievances of the English nobility and the English churchmen was that King Henry squandered the wealth of England on foreigners. The underlying suggestion was, of course, that it would have been better spent on his own subjects.

The earl of Leicester also held the title of Steward of England. This office is rather a confusing one to define. Originally, it designated the person who served the king at ceremonial feasts, handing him dishes and food and drink. Although the duties were menial ones, the position itself became important because it provided a means of access to the king. As the official stewardship became hereditary in the family of one or the other of the great nobles, a new steward of the household developed. He was a royal official of much lesser importance, who actually supervised the king's domestic establishment. The Steward of England still carried out his ceremonial functions on important occasions, but during the thirteenth century a new theory of his office was developing. In a memorandum on the office and duties of the Steward of England, written in the time of Edward II, the Steward had become an official second only to the king. He had the right and duty to see that justice was administered properly and to supervise the king's counsellors, even to get rid of the bad ones by force, if necessary.[11] We do not know how much of this theory had been developed by the time that Simon de Montfort became earl of Leicester and Steward of England, but, at the very least, his acquisition of this office, with its wide and vague claims, was a considerable step towards greater power and influence in England.

It is characteristic of the ambitious young man that he wasted no time in claiming this miscellaneous inheritance. In fact, he asserted his new rights so strenuously that within six months the king had to intervene to curb his impetuosity. The king reminded the sheriff of Leicester that seisin given to Simon de Montfort did not mean that Margaret, the countess of Winchester and Simon's great-aunt, should be dispossessed from the lands given her in the partition under King John. Obviously, the enthusiasm of the new broom was trying to sweep away some of the old rights.

Simon's fortune was soon increased by royal gifts, for during these early years he rose quickly in King Henry's favour. In June, 1232, the king granted him any escheats from the "lands of the Normans" which fell within his fief.[12] Escheats were lands that fell back into the royal hands because of crime, treason or lack of heirs. Naturally, they were one of the most convenient sources of extra revenue for the king. However, they also provided a useful source of gifts, either as a reward for faithful service or merely as a mark of royal favour. The "lands of the Normans" were those fiefs in England which had originally belonged to Norman lords who had thrown in their lot with the French king and retained their French lands after Philip Augustus's seizure of Normandy in 1204.

Gradually, on both sides of the Channel, the nobles had been forced for the first time to take sides permanently. They had had to decide on one overlord, the English king or the French king, and, in most cases, to abandon their territories in the other kingdom. But, for a long time, the legal fiction was maintained that this was only a temporary expedient. During most of the thirteenth century the formula, "Until the land of England and

Normandy be united", was used to mark these grants as a conditional gift. This was little more than legal quibbling. In actual fact, the Norman lands were disposed of like any others in the king's free gift and only rarely did a Norman ever gain back his lands. The king had given Simon a valuable right, which he exercised fully.

Here was, at least, the first half of a feudal success story, which was to be repeated many times in England because of King Henry's liberality to his Poitevin and Savoyard kinsmen. The popular contemporary romance, *Jehan and Blonde*, put the example of reality into story form. Jehan had to leave home, because there was no money or land left for him, and went to England to seek his fortune. A leading English nobleman accepted him as a squire. In the true tradition of romance, the young squire fell madly in love with the noble's beautiful daughter. At first nothing but gallantry came of the affair. Then Jehan had to go back to France on his father's death, which made him the owner of the family property and established him as a rising young seigneur. Once settled, he went back to England to seek his love and propose marriage. She was about to be married off to a great earl, but Jehan, in a notable fight against heavy odds, swept her away from under the Englishman's nose and took her back to France. The medieval version of the happy ending ensued. The French king came to knight the young Jehan and gave him a substantial revenue in rents. His mollified English father-in-law arrived with a retinue of thirty knights, and everybody enjoyed the subsequent great feast and days of hunting.[13]

The story itself is typical of what any young and landless nobleman dreamed of doing. It shows too what means were necessary to ensure success – the serving of good and indulgent masters, and the conclusion of a prosperous marriage. But, surprisingly enough, this romance has a more intimate acquaintance with the career of Simon de Montfort than just its general illustration of the hopes and dreams of all impecunious nobles. There seems to be a personal link between its author, Philippe de Rémi, and Simon de Montfort himself. Philippe was a younger son, who had had to leave home when his father remarried. He certainly went to England, and there is a very strong possibility that he served as a page with Simon de Montfort. At the very beginning of 1265, when Philippe was about eighteen, he was called back to France and never returned to England. In the household of the earl of Leicester, the young French squire would have seen a living prototype of his story, a landless knight who had achieved fortune and enormous power, from the small beginnings of royal favour and a wealthy marriage. Philippe probably wrote his exceedingly popular romance while he was in his twenties. But his career as a romancer was put aside, as he inherited the family lands and the family title, so that he was known from then on as Philippe de Beaumanoir. The fortune-hunting squire became one of the French king's most trusted officials, and the author of the best-known treatise on French law in the thirteenth century.[14] If he served as Simon de Montfort's page during the eventful days of the Barons' War, he must have heard some of the continuous discussion about the technical difficulties of administration. His lord, too, would have had something to say about the basis for the power of the king and the rights of the nobles. It is tempting to see some residue of his experience with the earl, not only in the lighthearted gaiety of his romance, but in his considered judgment on the law.

Like that of Jehan, Simon's future was improved by the death of people who might have blocked his path. In October, 1232, Earl Ranulf of Chester died, depriving England of one of her great feudal personalities. But Simon de Montfort could now breathe more easily. The £200 he owed Earl Ranulf, too, would not have to be paid immediately, as the settling of his estate would take some time.

In the autumn of 1235, Amaury de Montfort came to England with nine of his knights. They were bound on pilgrimage to the shrine of St Thomas at Canterbury.[15] Probably Amaury journeyed out to Hackington to see his great-aunt Loretta in her cell, and perhaps he went on to London to discuss with the king the last details of the formal transfer of his claims to the Leicester inheritance to Simon. Whatever the details, they were at last satisfactorily settled. Amaury came to England once more, in 1239. In

Westminster Hall, during the Easter meeting of the magnates, Amaury made formal and final renunciation of all his claims in favour of his young brother, and his charter was witnessed by many of the great prelates and barons of the realm.[16] Simon had already ceremoniously received the title at the Candlemas celebrations at Winchester.[17]

Amaury was probably glad to settle this long-drawn-out affair before he left for the crusade. The following autumn he led the French contingent with disastrous personal results. No sooner had Amaury arrived in the Holy Land than he was made prisoner in the course of a raid on Gaza. The raid seems to have been inspired by no higher level of military strategy than pure jealousy of a successful, though unauthorized, coup by his companion, the count of Brittany. General opinion is tempted to echo the tart judgment of the French chronicler who felt that the count of Montfort's imprisonment was the just consequence of seeking "vain knightly honours instead of the true deliverance of the Holy Land", and disregarding the first rules of wisdom and prudence.[18] Despite papal efforts to get the ransom paid earlier, Amaury was forced to remain in prison until Earl Richard of Cornwall, Henry III's brother, freed the whole group of French prisoners as part of his crusading effort in 1240. Released from the Saracens, Amaury started home to France by way of Rome, hoping to visit the tombs of Sts Peter and Paul. The eternal city was to be the end of his earthly pilgrimage, for he fell ill and died there, and was buried honourably in the church of the Apostles.[19] His death, in 1241, as Earl Ranulf's nine years before, served the rising star of the young earl of Leicester. They made his possession impervious to quibbles of primogeniture or previous possession.

Having achieved the Leicester lands, with little danger of dispute, Simon now had to carry out the other part of the romance's suggestion for wealth and happiness. He should marry a rich wife. Here Fortune was to favour him even more encouragingly, for his wife was not only rich and beautiful but the sister of the king.

3

The King's Sister

One of the most valuable assets of a thirteenth-century king was a supply of marriageable daughters. They could be used to cement alliances, to steady the allegiances of powerful but wavering lords, and to extend family connections to all corners of Europe. Henry III not only had daughters, he was blessed with three sisters for whom he had the right to arrange the marriages, as their father, King John, had died when the eldest was barely six. Even at that early age, Joanna had already been promised to Hugh X le Brun, son of the count of La Marche, and had been sent off to Poitou to be brought up in the household of her future husband. By a startling reversal, Isabella, King John's widow and Joanna's mother, actually married Hugh herself, claiming that she only desired to safeguard her son's interest in Poitou.[1]

This sudden marriage was all the more surprising, because Queen Isabella had once been betrothed to her new husband's father. Ten-year-old Joanna was sent back to England and was soon married to Alexander II, king of Scotland. The alliance marked another attempt to keep good relations between England and her turbulent northern neighbour. Henry's second sister, Isabella, made the most glamorous marriage. In 1235, she married Frederick II, the remarkable Hohenstaufen emperor who flashed like a strange comet across the thirteenth-century sky. Her wedding in England to the emperor's proxy was a gorgeous affair, and Matthew Paris revelled in the account of it. He provided a detailed and enthusiastic account of her lavish trousseau, though he did think the cooking-pots of silver were excessive.[2] They were not used for long, for Isabella died in childbirth in 1241, having served as a shadowy link between two of the most dissimilar of medieval monarchs.

The two eldest sisters made royal marriages, which took them out of English life. Eleanor, the youngest, married twice and both times within the realm. In 1224, when she was only nine, she was married to William Marshal the younger, the eldest son and heir of the great noble who had been regent for Henry III. This marriage was planned as a kind of insurance. William was one of the most powerful nobles of the land, for he had his title as earl of Pembroke and an impressive extent of lands in England, Ireland, and Wales. Besides, by a special concession, the Marshals had been allowed to keep their lands in Normandy which they held from the king of France. When the council of magnates discussed the marriage, as they did almost interminably, they hoped that the union with the king's sister might safeguard his loyalty, which a foreign marriage might endanger. William's support was essential for the peace of the realm and the safety of the young king. The council's discussions were so long and so inconclusive that William Marshal finally petitioned the king either to allow the marriage to take place, or set him free to marry another lady.[3] The marriage took place, but Eleanor was only sixteen and childless, when he died in 1231.

His death left Eleanor a very wealthy young woman. She had two sources of wealth, her marriage-portion and her dower. A marriage-portion was land given by a father to his daughter on the occasion of her marriage. Since English law provided that all the inheritance at death should go to the male heir, the marriage-portion provided a share in the family wealth for the daughter and her children. Eleanor's brother, King Henry, had assigned her marriage-portion, since her father was dead. He granted her ten manors, with the unusual proviso that they were to pass to her husband's heirs, after her life-interest. These scattered manors were worth just over £200 a year.[4] Soon after William Marshal's death, the king confirmed her lifetime possession of these lands.[5] However, the major part of her wealth was to come from the dower. The prevailing law of dower, as it had been clarified in the reissue of Magna Carta in 1217, gave the widow one third of all the lands possessed by her husband during his life. This held true unless some other special arrangement had been made "at the church door", as the Charter phrased it, before the wedding.[6]

During the course of the thirteenth century the law of dower was growing steadily more favourable to the widow. Bracton, the great lawyer and judge, writing in the middle of the century, also insisted that the wife's dower was supposed to be free of the husband's debts – of which there were likely to be many – and that a widow did not lose her dower by remarriage.[7] Bracton was not stating any new principles, but merely codifying the accepted usages of his day, which were very favourable to the widow's rights. This explains why a frequently married widow was such a welcome prize on the marriage market!

Immediately after William Marshal's death, Henry ordered Eleanor to remain at the great Marshal manor of Inkberrow, about twenty-six miles east of Worcester, while the machinery was set in motion for the assignment of her dower.[8] Normally, this was done within forty days, but, in this case, it was not easy to arrive at an equitable settlement. Richard Marshal was not at all fond of his sister-in-law. The records are full of his efforts to take over manors that were part of her marriage-portion, or to charge her with his brother's debts, which were really his own responsibility. The problem of Eleanor's dower was further complicated by the vast extent of the Marshal lands. They were, in fact, so widely scattered that separate settlements were made about her dower rights in Ireland and Wales, and her dower rights in England. Since the vexed question of Eleanor's dower was to be mixed up in affairs of state until her death some forty years later, it is necessary to describe briefly the beginnings of the trouble. A purely personal quarrel between the king and his sister became a magnet which attracted a series of complaints and exasperated later relations.

The Marshal lands were worth £3,350 a year, including the lands in Ireland as well as those in England and Wales. A settlement was finally arrived at in 1233 between Richard Marshal and his sister-in-law about her dower rights in Ireland. She agreed to accept a payment of £400 a year, paid semi-annually, in place ᴏᴏ the actual lands and rents at first assigned to her.[9] But this settlement unfortunately settled nothing. First, the Marshals were very lax in their payments. Richard Marshal seems to have defaulted almost immediately. Gilbert Marshal succeeded his brother after Richard's death in Ireland in 1234, and he had to arrange to give Eleanor the revenues of certain important Marshal manors in England for £400 of his own arrears and £350 of Richard's.[10] The king himself became first the surety for payment and ultimately the payor of the sums, forcing the Marshal heirs to repay him. The Exchequer rolls are filled with the records of payments and debts, but, as so often in medieval finance, the debts were a great deal more prominent than the payments. This non-payment of dower was one of Eleanor's greatest grievances, and she pursued it legally all her life. Her second grievance about her dower was that it was not sufficient, that her brother had let Richard Marshal escape with paying less than the proper amount. Much later the negotiations for the treaty of Paris in 1259 were interrupted by this claim. Eleanor argued vehemently that the settlement with Richard Marshal had been made when she was in King Henry's power, and had been sealed with her seal without her consent. Henry had been willing to accept for her one third of what her dower was really worth.[11] She overstated the case, but there seems to have been fair ground for her grievance. She should have received almost half as much again for her dower rights in the Irish lands as she actually did.

The same problem seems to have arisen over her dower rights in England. Her English lands brought her about £400, but this included the lands nominally given her for her marriage-portion. The last of the sons of the old Marshal died in 1252 and none of them had any direct heirs, some said owing to a bishop's curse on their father. All the Marshal lands thus had to be divided among the five sisters and their heirs. At that time, the family lands in England and Wales were worth over £2,075; Eleanor's £500 was far short of a third. These technical matters about the inequity of Eleanor's dower are touched on because they were the backlog of her later complaints against her brother the king, the subject of much litigation and attempted arbitration. Always they sounded a nagging undertone of personal exasperation in the shrill chorus of political controversy.

In the early period after William Marshal's death, while these legal problems were only at the beginning of their complexities, Eleanor was placed in the care of a gentlewoman called Cecily de Sanford. Cecily was also a widow and served as governess and teacher of morals – and probably chaperone – for her young charge. Matthew Paris described her most enthusiastically as noble in blood, but more noble in manners, very learned, eloquent, and courteous.[12] This paragon was an extremely pious woman and, it would seem, a forceful one as well. Cecily decided to take a vow of chastity before the saintly archbishop of Canterbury, Edmund Rich, and encouraged, or influenced, her charge to do likewise. Both the governess and the young girl took a vow of celibacy, and accepted the ring that marked an espousal to Christ. They did not take the veil which usually marked the solemn sealing of the pact. As another token of celibacy and the putting away of the things of this world, they began to dress in russet, the coarse homespun material which was worn by peasants and given as alms to the poor.

This vow, even though it was not altogether complete, caused a good deal of trouble for Eleanor some years later. When she had recovered from the shock of her husband's death and had begun to outgrow the dominating influence of Cecily de Sanford, perpetual widowhood seemed much less attractive and fine dress more so. The determined governess, however, remained faithful to her vow till death. The gossip Matthew Paris picked up all the details of the story from Cecily's confessor, the Dominican Walter of St Martin, when he brought her body to St Albans for burial in 1251. As she lay dying, the friar had tried to take the ring off her finger. The semi-conscious woman revived sufficiently to warn him that "living or dead, no one could take away her ring, which she would carry to the tribunal of God in testimony of her inviolable chastity". So saying, she curved her fingers around it, so that her servants could not slip it off, and then died.[13]

Despite the vow and her semi-religious state, Eleanor seems to have spent her time like that of any noble lady. She travelled

43

from place to place with her retinue, and where she had no manors of her own on which to call, her brother the king would order his officials to provide lodging for her. At Tewkesbury in 1235, for example, she was to have sufficient houses for all her household for as long as she wished to stay, as well as hay for the horses and wood for the fireplaces.[14] Then she was naturally concerned about the upkeep of the buildings on her manors. Again the king's generosity provided her with oaks from the royal forests for building a hall at Wexcumb, or rebuilding her burned-out houses at Kemsing.[15] Through the rolls, too, are sprinkled the report of gifts of deer, caught in the royal forests and sent to the king's sister. But, in the normal pattern of events, Eleanor probably spent much of her time at court. Certainly she would have been present when Henry celebrated the main feasts of the year. At these times, the king was accustomed "to wear his crown" and call the great magnates of the realm together for discussion of the most important affairs of state. In other words, he held a council, or, as it was gradually coming to be known, a parliament.

The great social event of these years of Eleanor's widowhood was the king's marriage. Henry was married in January, 1236, to Eleanor of Provence, the younger sister of St Louis's queen. The solemn coronation at Westminster and the banquet which followed it were magnificent affairs. The city was scrubbed and decorated with wreaths and flowers, candles and lamps, and all kinds of flags and hangings to do honour to the young queen. London looked magnificent, with all the citizens dressed in their richest attire, showing off the paces of their horses before the royal procession. At the banquet many of the nobles and some of the towns had certain ceremonial functions. Londoners had the right to pass the wine – in gold cups – and the citizens of Winchester cooked the feast.[16]

For the first time, Simon de Montfort exercised the office of Steward. He had succeeded in convincing the exchequer that the stewardship went rightfully with the Leicester lands, although his claim was contested by Roger Bigod, the earl of Norfolk. It was Simon's responsibility to supervise the royal kitchen and arrange the banquet. During the feast, dressed in his robe of office, he presented the king with a basin of water to wash his hands. After it was over, the Steward had to pass his ceremonial robe on to the master-cook, for this was the cook's customary perquisite.[17] Certainly, during these years when Simon was in such great favour with the king and with him a great deal, Eleanor must have seen him at court under less formal circumstances. It is interesting to speculate whether she had already aroused his interest, or whether she seemed too rich a matrimonial prize.

Life at court does not seem to have been so pleasant for Eleanor after the arrival of her Provençal sister-in-law. After all, the queen outranked her and there is some suggestion that there may have been personal friction between the two Eleanors. In any case, she persuaded her brother of her need for a separate establishment, suitable to her position. In November of 1236, the king gave Eleanor the castle and manor of Odiham,[18] and the following year he added to the gift the park that went with it and its hunting rights.[19] Odiham was a valuable stronghold and the castle was quite new. As it was located between Windsor and Winchester, two of the king's favourite residences, it was also convenient. But the fortress seems to have been more utilitarian than elegant. The octagonal keep overlooked the river and the surrounding land was flat and marshy. The castle ditches were apparently used as fish-ponds, as well as for purposes of defence; a previous custodian had been allowed breams from the king's supply to stock the ponds. The main hall was the only room of the first floor and was about thirty feet high, with a great fireplace and pairs of small windows. Eleanor's chamber on the second floor also had a fireplace, which was no doubt a most welcome amenity in the damp surroundings.[20] King Henry must have been feeling particularly favourable to his young sister that November. Besides the castle of Odiham he gave her a splendid black palfrey which had been presented to him by the archbishop of York.[21]

While Eleanor was thus establishing herself as one of the great ladies of England, Simon de Montfort had been exploring the possibilities of marriage with a rich heiress from across the Channel. He had made two attempts to wed wealthy widows. One was Mahaut, the countess of Boulogne; the other Joan, countess of

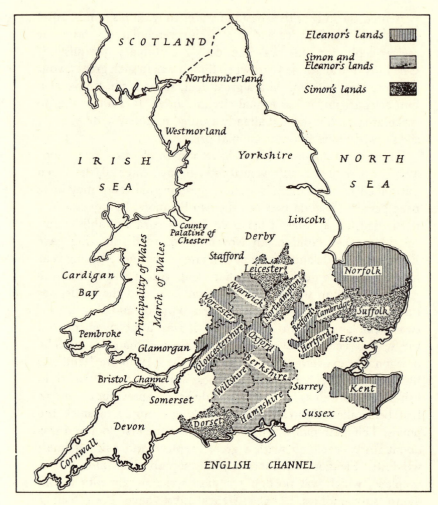

Counties of Simon's lands from the Earldom
of Leicester and lands of the Normans' and
Eleanor's Dower lands and gifts from the Kings

Flanders. The arrangements with Mahaut fell through for unknown reasons, but Queen Blanche, the regent of France, interfered in Joan's case. The lands of Flanders were so strategically located that the French queen was quite naturally unwilling to have them held by a powerful noble who had sworn fealty to the king of England. She may have been outspoken about her disapproval, for Guillaume de Nangis claimed that Simon fled from France because he feared that he had offended Queen Blanche.[22]

The failure of these French arrangements may well have endeared Simon even more to Henry III, for Henry was at this time on very bad terms with France. The king had become fond of Simon, who m ͘ have been a high-spirited and attractive young man. The English king often made sudden and very intimate friendships, especially among those who had little assured position of their own, and whose loyalty he felt he had purchased by generous gifts. Usually these friends were foreigners with whom he seemed to feel more at ease than with the English lords, especially as the "native-born" felt it was their right and duty to counsel the king and restrain his extravagance. Simon had been growing in the king's favour from the time that he was given the Leicester lands. He was frequently with the king, had been sent to York in 1237 as a negotiator in the agreement with Alexander II of Scotland, and generally seems to have been one of the king's trusted counsellors.

What sudden decision accounted for Henry's agreement to the marriage of his young sister to Simon de Montfort? The speed and secrecy with which the matter was handled were in sharp contrast to the years of debate which had preceded Eleanor's first marriage to William Marshal. Henry had been holding his Christmas court and council at Westminster and there, the day after Epiphany (January 6), 1238, the marriage was performed. Although it was solemnized by Walter, the chaplain of the royal chapel of St Stephen's, Westminster, the wedding did not take place in the relatively public St Stephen's. Instead the king arranged for the ceremony in his own private oratory in the corner of the Painted Chamber. This little chapel was planned for the royal convenience. There was even a window in the wall by the king's great bed so that he could follow the Mass without rising. But, on this occasion, the king himself placed his sister's hand in that of his French friend. Matthew Paris gives all the relevant details and tells us that Simon received her gratefully, as well he might. It was, of course, a marriage which brought him both prestige and riches far beyond his own position. The chronicler hints at the mixture of motives that incited Simon: love for her beauty; the distinction of marrying the sister of the king, the Scotch queen, and the empress; and even the possibility of having children who might one day aspire to the throne, since the king and queen had, as yet, no offspring.[23] Why did the marriage take place in such secrecy? Was Henry trying to provide the English magnates with a *fait accompli* which they would deplore but could not change? Or was there some truth in the king's later accusation that Simon had seduced Eleanor? There is no evidence to back up the one royal burst of vilification. Whatever the reasons, the result was trouble, both for the king and for Simon, on two separate grounds.

The clerics, especially the monks and the friars, were shocked at Eleanor's remarriage because it broke her vow of chastity. By many of them, this disrespect for her vow was considered to be the active cause of all her later misfortunes. The monastic annalist at Dunstable, the Augustinian priory in Bedfordshire, felt so strongly on this matter that he never referred to Eleanor except as countess of Pembroke, or as the king's sister – for him the second marriage did not exist. The most exaggerated and colourful embroidery on the facts comes from one of the northern chronicles, that of Lanercost, an Augustinian priory in the wilds of Cumberland. Its author seems, in several cases, to have abandoned the truth completely for dramatic effect. He gives a highly vivid and mendacious description of the affair, with Archbishop Edmund as the leading character. According to this chronicle, the archbishop was forced to flee the country because of his opposition to the marriage. On his way, he paused on a hill overlooking London and cursed the woman and all her progeny.[24] This kind of curse was very popular among medieval chroniclers, partly because curses and excommunications – often for the slightest of causes – were fairly frequent anyway, and partly because such a threat provided the ideal explanation for any later series of tragedies. In one thing the clerics were certainly right. Even if the vow had not been a solemn one, a dispensation should have been obtained. It would be wise for Simon to go to the papal curia in Rome as quickly as possible and ask for one.

Another much more dangerous matter for Simon was that he had roused the great lords of England against him. The king had disposed of his sister in marriage without the advice and assent of the council, which was an improper and much resented encroachment on the privileges of the magnates. Added to the other smouldering complaints against the king, this was the spark that caused a real explosion. Richard of Cornwall, the king's brother, was particularly incensed that he had not been consulted and he was joined by Gilbert Marshal and others of the barons. Henry, worried at the danger of revolt, wrote off to the barons of the Cinque Ports at the beginning of February, hoping to ensure their support.[25]

Already the pattern of baronial discontent exhibits the main lines which prevail throughout the reign. The barons were dissatisfied with the incurably personal rule of the king. He would not accept their advice. He squandered the lands and revenues of England on his wife's relations and favourites. They planned to remedy all difficulties by removing from the king's council the "foreigners not useful to the kingdom".[26] Since it was for this cause that Simon himself was to fight so vigorously in later years, it is ironic to see him in the position of a hated foreigner who should be dismissed. Ultimately the quarrel was smoothed over. Simon submitted to Earl Richard and, with the aid of gifts and some friendly intercession, obtained the kiss of peace from him. When Richard, its leader, withdrew, the baronial opposition fell apart. From then on, Earl Richard never joined the barons against the king. He became one of the most valuable of the royal supporters, for his shrewdness, wealth, and coolheaded advice were of tremendous value to his more hotheaded and vacillating brother.

This ill-advised marriage cooled the atmosphere of the court for the newly-wed couple. Earl Richard and the magnates were in violent opposition to Simon. The king, as usual, was angry with anyone who caused trouble for him, whether it was his own fault or not. The wrath of the church threatened the validity of the union. For Simon to go to Rome might serve two purposes. He could procure the needed dispensation, and he might improve the situation by his absence for a time. Matthew Paris over-emphasizes the natural difficulty of the situation by asserting that Simon wasted away with vehement sorrow and had to cross the Channel secretly with an immense amount of money.[27] Actually, the king gave Simon letters to the pope and cardinals, asking for a sympathetic hearing.[28] He never would have received these if the king had been irreparably angry with him. He certainly raised as much money as he could, including 500 marks seized from an unfortunate burgess of Leicester. Money would be essential if he wanted a speedy answer from the papal curia, for, like other courts of the time, the slowly turning wheels were speeded by judiciously arranged gifts to the proper people.

Simon left England around the end of March – his letters from the king were dated March 27th – and the urgency of his mission to Rome was increased by the suspicion that Eleanor was already pregnant. The dispensation was essential to validate the marriage and assure the legitimacy of the offspring. In his hurried trip he may have stopped briefly to see Emperor Frederick II, now his brother-in-law, for he seems to have obtained letters from the emperor favouring his cause.[29] But there was little chance for delay either with the emperor or at the papal court. The trip to Rome from London took around six weeks in those days – five at high speed. By May 10th, Simon's plea to the pope had been granted, for, on that date, Pope Gregory IX declared in a letter to Eleanor that nothing was to be presumed against the marriage contracted between her and Simon. The pope also ordered a copy of the privilege forwarded to the legate Otto in England.[30] Paris maliciously asserts that this dispensation was beyond the comprehension of many in England, but that the influence of money made the Curia take too "subtle" a view for the average Englishman.[31] After Simon had achieved his aim in Rome, he lingered a while in Italy and probably joined the English contingent sent to aid Frederick in his siege of Brescia. On October 14th he was back in England and was greeted with great joy by the king and the royal household.[32] Although the clouds of disapproval had vanished, Simon did not linger long at court but hastened to his wife at Kenilworth.

Apparently Eleanor remained at Kenilworth all the time that Simon was away.[33] The king made special efforts to see that she received the best in food and wine during these months, for the rolls are full of gifts of deer and wine, even, on one occasion, "six tuns of better wine".[34] If she was at Kenilworth, which was one of the royal castles, she probably had a fair amount of company. In March, the castle was offered to the papal legate Otto for his use during pleasure,[35] an arrangement which may have preceded Eleanor's use of it. However, Otto was not destined to enjoy a quiet stay in the Midlands. He spent Easter (April 4th) at Lincoln and then, after a few weeks, turned south to visit Oxford, staying at Osney Abbey there. Spring riots in the university seem to have been as much a pattern of the thirteenth century, as of later years, and legates and their foreign clerks were never popular. A squabble turned into a pitched battle, and the legate's brother was killed, while Otto himself, terrified for his safety, fled to the refuge of the church tower. The aroused clerks ransacked the abbey, shouting for "that usurer, that plunderer of revenues, who perverts the king and subverts the kingdom to enrich foreigners with our spoils".[36] Once rescued by the king, the legate retaliated with all the spiritual thunder at his command, and for a time studies at the university were suspended. If Otto did travel the forty-five miles to Kenilworth after this fracas, there is no record of it. He seems to have returned to the greater comfort of London, and probably the Countess Eleanor remained undisturbed in her occupation of the great castle, although the king himself spent a few days with her in September.

Simon returned to her before the arrival of their son on November 28th. It was an occasion for much rejoicing. King Henry seemed as friendly as before, and stood god-father to the boy whom he allowed to be named after him. Just at this time, Alexander Stavensby, the bishop of Lichfield, arrived at Kenilworth on the way to seek favour at court, and he baptized the baby. It was almost the bishop's last act, for he fell gravely ill and died at Kenilworth the day after Christmas.[37] But this cast only the slightest shadow on the joyful Christmas festivities. Henry was celebrating at Winchester this year and Simon, back from Italy, had resumed his place as one of the king's leading counsellors.[38] The king's Christmas present to his sister was truly a royal one. Besides a piece of the very rich baudekin cloth for a robe and supertunic with miniver to trim and line it, he gave her the same material for a quilt for her bed and a coverlet of grey fur lined with scarlet cloth. These most elegant furnishings were accompanied by the more utilitarian materials needed for the mattress. The whole thing was to be made and then carefully packed and sent in waxed canvas from Winchester to the countess at Kenilworth.[39] It was during these same festivities, it may be remembered, that Henry finally decided to give his brother-in-law his proper title as earl of Leicester, on the feast of Candlemas.

Even such an ambitious man as Simon de Montfort must have felt satisfied with life at the beginning of 1239. He had achieved the earldom of Leicester with what was, in reality, a rather tenuous legal claim. He had married the king's sister, who was much his superior in wealth and prestige. In the first year of their marriage they had had a son, who even seemed to stand in sight of the throne of England, for the king had as yet no children. But everything was not so perfect in reality. Already in 1239 the seeds of the conflict between the king and the earl of Leicester had been planted. The continuous controversy over Eleanor's dower lands; the complaint that Henry had given Simon his sister without lands or marriage-portion; the fact that no one could rely for long on Henry's favour; these troubles had not yet disturbed the placid surface of events.

4

Crusader and Warrior

The year 1239 promised good fortune for England, as well as for the earl of Leicester. Some years ago Simon had taken the cross, that is, he had promised to go on crusade, but no crusade was imminent since Pope Gregory IX had been busy dissuading the great English nobles from leaving to fulfil their vow. The pontiff was more concerned with the explosive situation developing with the Emperor Frederick and hoped to gain military support in Italy from those vowed to the crusade. Until the crusaders had papal permission to depart for the Holy Land they would gain none of the usual spiritual and temporal favours, especially the coveted forgiveness of their debts. In England, the summer of 1239 brought a happy event, for in June, Eleanor of Provence, Henry's queen, bore a son. There had been suppressed fear that perhaps the young queen was barren. At the infant Edward's christening at Westminster on July 16th, he was lifted from the font by three bishops and three earls, including his two uncles, Richard of Cornwall and Simon de Montfort.[1] This was a mark of great favour. But, as so often happened with King Henry, a halcyon period was ended by a wild storm of anger.

On August 9th, many of the nobles and their ladies came to London to be present at the solemn procession celebrating the queen's churching at the abbey of Westminster. When Simon de Montfort and Eleanor appeared, the king broke into a violent rage, implied that they had sinned before their marriage, and called the earl excommunicate. The reproaches multiplied, and the embarrassed earl and countess slipped down the river to their temporary lodgings at the house of the bishop of Winchester, which the king himself had loaned them for their stay in London. They hoped in this way to pacify the irate king, but with no success, for the king ordered them to be ejected from the house. They returned, weeping and begging forgiveness, but the royal wrath was still high. Again the king turned on Simon and accused him of having seduced his sister before their marriage, so that the king must assent to it to avoid scandal. He raked up the old complaint of the zealous preachers that Simon had corrupted the Roman curia with gifts and thus arranged the illicit dispensation of Eleanor from her vow, despite the contrary advice of Archbishop Edmund. Then, and here we come to what was probably the real cause of this tumultuous outburst, he accused his brother-in-law of having named him as security for his debts without the royal knowledge or consent. The earl grew red, and decided on immediate flight. That evening he and his pregnant wife, and their small household took a little boat down the Thames and crossed the Channel.[2]

The story as Paris tells it is sufficiently dramatic and agrees in most details with Simon's own recollection of the affair. Simon added that the king was so angry that he wanted to have the earl taken to the Tower immediately, but that Richard of Cornwall, always the voice of moderation, intervened for the time being. Simon agreed, too, that the quarrel arose over money. What was the debt that had driven Henry into such a fury of rage? It was, like so many other of Simon's financial transactions, a long-drawn-out and complicated affair. He had originally owed Earl Ranulf of Chester £200. On Ranulf's death the debt had been transferred to Peter Mauclerc, count of Brittany, who had taken the cross.[3] In September, 1238, the pope took a hand and ordered the bishop of Soissons to find out if the money, now over 2,000 marks, had been paid. If not, the bishop was to lay an interdict upon Simon's property and force him to pay, under the penalty of excommunication.[4] These threats did not achieve a settlement, but by May of 1239 Simon's creditor was Thomas of Savoy who occupied a strategic position for enforcing payment. Thomas was now count of Flanders by his marriage to the heiress Joan, whom Simon had unsuccessfully attempted to marry himself, and he was also one of Queen Eleanor's uncles, and, therefore, was received most favourably in England. He seems to have pressed his claim for payment vigorously. The result of the quarrel was that the king agreed to pay 500 marks of Simon's debt, and did so when the count of Flanders came to England in the middle of August. The rest – 1,500 marks – was raised from Simon's own lands "in a hard manner and of great harm to me for the haste".[5] The first great storm died down and, though it resulted in the temporary exile of the earl and countess, it did not yet affect the position of Simon as a supporter of the king. But the memory of the quarrel and its unbridled language sunk to the depths of the earl's memory to be revived for use as the first of the series of complaints about his mistreatment by the king. A proud, high-tempered man, Simon would neither easily forget the extreme language of his brother-in-law, nor easily forgive it.

For the time being he remained overseas with his wife. Quite probably he took her to Montfort-l'Amaury to stay at the family castle and perhaps to say goodbye to his eldest brother Amaury, who was about to leave on crusade. Caught up, as they must have been, in the flurry of preparation for the crusader's departure, Simon felt it essential that he, too, fulfil his vow, despite the lack of encouragement from the pope.

The thirteenth-century crusades were not like the great expeditions of the twelfth century which reunited the kings of western Europe in the common attempt to drive the infidel from the Holy Places. Crusading fervour had waned. The shocking misdirection of expeditions like the Fourth Crusade at the very beginning of the century, which Simon the Crusader had deplored, had tarnished the first purity of intention. Many of the western knights had settled down in the various castles and temporary Christian states of Palestine and Syria, such as Ascalon and Tyre, and there were relations and acquaintances to send back accounts of the fluctuating fortunes of the Christians and of the need for reinforcements. With the exception of the large expeditions of St Louis himself, the Crusade was a continuous, but minor, series of groups of knights going to the Holy Land to fight for limited periods of time. They were usually organized in rather loose n tional groups.

There was still true religious feeling and a fervent desire to free the Holy Places of Christ's life and death from the control of the Mohammedans, but it was a more limited ideal, which understood from sad experience the difficulties of campaigning in the hot and waterless terrain. This called for tactics very different from good fighting practice in Europe, and the sultans were not normally influenced by the same code of chivalry which governed the relations of Western knights. Joinville's chronicle, with its first-hand account of the first crusade of St Louis, puts in personal and intelligible terms the kind of difficulties, confusions, and jealousies, that beset the nobles of Europe when they tried to work together for the common cause.

We have seen how the disastrous attempt by Amaury de Montfort to cover himself with glory by a brilliant foray led instead to his immediate capture. From prison he had a chance to write to his wife telling of his capture. That letter was sent on by the countess to Richard of Cornwall, to encourage the king's brother as he gathered the English contingent together.[6]

In the spring of 1240 Simon came back to England. The king had forgotten their quarrel of the previous summer sufficiently to receive him with honour. Simon had not come to see the king, but to raise enough money for his "Jerusalem journey". This called for quite a large supply of ready cash, always a difficult commodity for most barons, and a perpetual difficulty for Simon. So he followed the usual practice of a baron in such a case. He sold off some of his forests and lands, and especially, he sold his "noble wood" of Leicester to the Hospitallers and canons of Leicester for about £1,000 – about four years' income.[7]

By the last week of May, Richard of Cornwall and his contingent were ready to depart. The English force split into two groups. One, headed by Earl Richard, went out through France, overland to Lyons, and then down the Rhone to Arles and Beaucaire. There Richard met the count of Provence, father of the queen, and probably made the acquaintance of the younger sister, Sanchia, whom he later married. Despite the discouragement of the papal legate and the archbishop of Arles, he insisted that he must carry out his crusade, so long projected, and arranged for at such expense. Finally, at la Roque, not far from Marseilles, he arranged and loaded his ships, and sailed off in the middle of September.[8] Simon, on the other hand, had taken some of the English knights with him and his wife, and they travelled down through Lombardy and Apulia, the territory of the emperor, his brother-in-law. The knights took ship at Brindisi, on the southern tip of Italy. Eleanor settled in a castle near Brindisi, lent to her by the emperor. She had two small sons with her, and was again pregnant.[9]

These years of Crusade form one of the maddening gaps in our knowledge of both Simon and Eleanor. Eleanor seems to have remained in Italy during her husband's absence in the Holy Land, and it must have been while she was there that their third son, Guy, was born. Perhaps she took advantage of her residence in the emperor's territories to try and see her sister Isabella, who was also pregnant and who was to die of a fever after childbirth in 1241. For the lonely Isabella, closed away from any society except that of her servants, the meeting would have been a happy reminder of her youth in England.

The English Crusade was not a very warlike affair. This is perhaps not too surprising, led as it was by Richard of Cornwall, who always preferred negotiation and arranged settlement to what he felt were unnecessary sorties. There is a fairly full account of the expedition in a letter he wrote to three of his friends: Baldwin Redvers, earl of Devon; the abbot of Beaulieu – where his first wife was buried; and Robert, his clerk.[10] In it he tells of his arrangements for the working out of a truce with the Saracens, and, most importantly, for the return of the French prisoners captured at Gaza. He also provided Christian burial for the nobles who had been slain in that disastrous rout, and, by both these actions, created a store of goodwill for himself in France, which was to serve him and his brother the king in good stead during the disastrous campaign of 1242 in Poitou. When he had achieved these concrete results, Richard embarked at Acre on May 3, 1241, on his way home. But the winds were contrary, and it was not until July 1 that he finally landed at Trapani in Sicily, in the dominions of his brother-in-law, the emperor Frederick.

Frederick treated him with great generosity, ordering triumphal processions as he passed through the imperial cities on his way to the emperor, and gave the earl's company horses and mules, because they had none. This display of generosity was maintained whilst the earl of Cornwall stayed at the imperial court.

There was a pleasant domestic side to Richard's visit, for he had the chance of seeing his sister Isabella, the emperor's wife. It is interesting to note from the tone of Matthew Paris's remarks on the subject, that her brother had to get the emperor's permission to see her. Apparently, too, it was only once in the whole four months he was there. The occasion was festive. They were entertained by games and musical instruments, and especially by two Saracen dancing girls, each dancing on two balls and singing and sounding cymbals. Matthew seems to have been much taken with the description he received of this event, for he has illustrated his account with a drawing of them in the margin, each standing on a green sphere.[11] Finally, Richard headed for England. He went overland through Italy and was again entertained by processions in the cities that touched his route. The most impressive was the spectacle at Cremona, where that notable curiosity, the emperor's elephant, was displayed in his honour. When they left the emperor's territories, the company broke up. The imperial proctor, who had served as their official host, retired. Many of the French nobles, who had travelled this far with Richard, went off to their own homes. They were well supplied with travellers' tales for their families and added to them the praises of Earl Richard who had freed them and sustained them by his gifts.

This group was only part of the English contingent, however, and Simon de Montfort was not in it. Although Richard got back to England in the first days of 1242, other nobles straggled back gradually. Simon himself seems to have stayed in the Holy Land much longer than Richard. There is a curious letter from the barons, knights and citizens of the kingdom of Jerusalem to the emperor, dated June 7, 1241. They asked that the emperor should appoint the earl as governor of their kingdom until young Conrad, the hereditary king, should reach his majority, and they promised to obey Simon as they would the emperor himself.[12] No such appointment was ever made, but it is interesting testimony of the universal regard in which the earl of Leicester was held. Undoubtedly, too, the fact that one of his cousins was lord of Tyre would have helped to make him known and valued by the predominantly French lords who had settled in the Middle East. Possibly he even spent some of this period with his cousin. At any rate, in 1242 he returned to France with the duke of Burgundy.[13]

Simon's only crusade was over. Although he was to take the cross again in 1247 – and so was his wife – his duties in Gascony interfered with any possibility of carrying out that vow. The very inconclusiveness of his crusading expedition, the general feeling of conventionality, of having done what was expected, even though not much was achieved – all these perhaps were a very real mirror of the general nature of crusades in the thirteenth century.

Meanwhile, King Henry had again become involved in hostilities with France. Here is another case which exemplifies the singularly personal character of so much of medieval politics. To disentangle the reasons for the conflict one must go back to the personal relations of the leading characters. The mother of Henry III had replaced her little daughter and married Hugh, the count of La Marche, in 1220, claiming that this was the only way to keep this important Poitevin noble loyal to the English king. Geographically, the county of La Marche was of extreme strategic importance. The count's territories protected the north-eastern flank of the English province of Gascony and lay in the middle of the now French lands of Poitou, which had been entrusted by Louis IX to his brother Alphonse. The Lusignan family, from which sprang the counts of La Marche, were distinguished and vigorous. Their mythical ancestress, the fairy Melusine, lent an air of other-worldly importance to a race that had already distinguished themselves in terrestrial affairs. Once the Crusades had begun, every head of the house of Lusignan was a Crusader, and the family supplied three kings of Jerusalem, as well as the dynasty which ruled Cyprus until the latter part of the fifteenth century.[14]

During the first half of the thirteenth century the counts of La Marche were attempting to set up a new independent principality, freed from the controls of France or England. But England's loss of Poitou under King John, and the growing firmness and control exercised by the royal government under St Louis, meant that the agents of the central power were becoming more aggressive. They impinged constantly on the vaunted independence of these strongwilled lords. The count of La Marche was required to do homage to the French king for his lands and accept the existence of Alphonse as the count of Poitiers. This was more than the countess could stand, for she felt her queenly dignity – as John's widow – very strongly, and reacted violently when insufficient honour was paid to her.

A townsman of La Rochelle, who was a secret agent for the queen-regent, Blanche of Castille, submitted a most vivid report in 1241 of Isabella's disgust, and of the conspiracy that she helped to engineer. Isabella was infuriated at her treatment by the French king and queen when they received the count's homage at Poitiers. She claimed that they kept her waiting three days before they would receive her, and then, when she did finally gain entrance to their chamber, neither the king nor the queen asked her to sit down, so as to abase her before all the world and treat her like a servant. She went back to La Marche in a rage, and stripped the castle of the hangings and chests, the mattresses and seats, even the ornaments of the chapel and a statue of the Blessed Virgin, and had them sent to Angoulême. When the bewildered count tried to get an explanation, she turned on him angrily: "Out of my presence, you have done honour to those who would disinherit you." At Angoulême, she shut the door on him for three days, until her anger and her tears moved the count to agree to whatever she wanted.

Her desire for vengeance, which was prodding her husband into revolt, was re-enforced by another of the Lusignans, Geoffrey, the count of Eu, in a conference at Parthenai. He called on all the independent spirit of the barons and painted the picture of their decline: "Today the least sergeant of the king does his will in Champagne, in Burgundy, and everywhere, because all the barons, like slaves, dare not move without his orders. I would like it better to be dead, and all you like me, than to be thus." So a confederacy of the Poitevin barons was formed against the growing might of the royal power, with the active assistance of the countess, and the general approval of the lords and citizens of Gascony, who feared the dominance of the active and near-by French much more than the nominal control of the distant king of England.[15] Hugh, count of La Marche, appealed to Henry, his stepson, for aid against the French who, he claimed, were about to dispossess him unjustly and for no cause. Much against the will of his barons, who reminded him of the futility of his last expedition against the French, Henry demanded a scutage, in this case, a payment of 20 marks on each knight's fee, called up his army, hired soldiers overseas, and put his ships in readiness to sail.

By May, the expedition was complete. The king's ships were arranged and thirty casks of the desired money had been loaded.* The king took the queen with him, and, together with Earl Richard and seven other earls and about three hundred knights, they set sail for Bordeaux. They crossed first to Finisterre in Brittany where they spent Sunday and the following day they arrived at Royan, on the mouth of the Gironde.[16] Meanwhile, a summons had gone out to Simon de Montfort to join the other nobles of England in the Gascon campaign. He came in obedience to the king's command, but told him frankly that he did not want to stay with him unless Henry was ready to redress some of the grievances which Simon felt he suffered. Henry agreed to repay him the sum which he had raised from Simon's land for Count Thomas of Flanders, and an extra hundred marks besides for the damage caused by the hurried levying of the sum.[17] On these terms, Simon was willing to serve and he fell back into his previous position of being one of the king's main advisers and supporters.

The Poitevin campaign, which had its birth in the deceit and treachery of the countess of La Marche, and the ambition of her husband, proved the incapacity of the Poitevin nobles to withstand the superior organization of the king of France. It also demonstrated, beyond any shadow of doubt, Henry III's military weakness. The English campaign was one of retreats and evasions,

---

* Since the only actual unit of money was the silver penny, the bulky problem of transporting large sums was a constant difficulty.

which did not even achieve a strategic advantage. Their position at Taillebourg was completely untenable. Save for the good offices of Richard of Cornwall, to whom many of the French owed their life and liberty, the English army might have been annihilated. Instead, they retreated ignobly to Saintes. They were followed by Louis IX and his army and the one real battle of the campaign took place in the vineyards just outside the city. The earl of Leicester and some of the other English nobles distinguished themselves in the skirmish, but the French king had won the campaign. Henry was unable to hold out at Saintes and fled south to Blaye.

The king's military incapacity at Saintes tried Simon's temper beyond the limits of discretion. Twenty years later, the king remembered that the earl had told him then that it would have been better if he had been taken and kept in one place, as Charles the Foolish had been. Indeed, the irascible earl had added in his disgust and anguish of heart, there were houses barred with iron at Windsor which would be good places to keep the king safely.[18]

Simon seems to have had contemporary reinforcement for his low estimate of the king. Dante put Henry in Purgatory among the negligent kings, whose great fault was inactivity. Even to the remote Italian, Henry was characterized as a "king of simple life".[19] Another Italian, Salimbene, the lively Franciscan, told a cruel story which reflected the same judgment. Once the royal jester compared the English king to Christ, before all his knights, and Henry, very flattered, asked him to explain the parallel. "Because," replied the jester, "Our Lord was as wise at the moment of His conception as when He was thirty years old; so likewise our King is as wise now as when he was a little child."[20] Even with a jester's freedom that was too much, and the angry king ordered him to be hanged. Fortunately, the royal servants merely pretended to carry out the execution and concealed the outspoken fool from the king's wrath. The king's weaknesses affected the good government of the realm; for as a politician, Henry was inept, as a soldier, he was hopeless, and his attacks of petulance and caprice alienated his best counsellors. This was of general concern, because ultimately all medieval government depended on the calibre of the king, and others besides the earl of Leicester despaired of the king's ability to lead and rule his kingdom.

The Poitevin allies, and especially the count of La Marche, the organizer of the revolt, melted away from the English army as they found a chance to settle on reasonable terms with the French king. Joinville gives a vivid story of the delight among some of the other Poitevin nobles when they saw the proud count of La Marche forced to sue for peace. One of the French knights at the court of St Louis in Poitiers was Geoffrey de Rancon. The common gossip was that the count of La Marche had done him some grave injury. Geoffrey had sworn on the gospels that he would not have his hair cut short, as a knight should, but would wear it long like a woman's, until the count was brought to justice. When he saw the count of La Marche and his wife and children kneeling before St Louis to ask for mercy, Geoffrey was overjoyed. Here was the fulfilment of his vow! Without wasting time, Geoffrey called for a stool and had the hateful woman's parting combed out and his hair cut short again in the presence of the king, the abashed count, and all the company.[21] Meanwhile sickness decimated both armies. St Louis himself fell dangerously ill. As both armies had no real desire to pursue the campaign and dissension was rife, a five-year truce was arranged. The English nobles became restive and asked permission to return home, while King Henry dawdled in Blaye, and the queen was delivered of a daughter, Beatrice, in Bordeaux. Permission was granted, and Earl Richard and many of the other nobles, including the Earl Marshal and Richard de Clare, left for England. They finally arrived after a stormy and difficult crossing.*

But though many of the English nobles returned to England, the king stayed on in Bordeaux – wasting his treasure, Matthew Paris says disapprovingly – and Simon stayed with him, as did William Lungespee, earl of Salisbury. The conditions were difficult. The king lacked food, supplies, clothes, and money to meet his obligations. He sent off to the archbishop of York, the regent of the kingdom, for the essentials, bacon, wheat, and oats; which

---

* It was so stormy and difficult that Richard made a vow to found an abbey if he should be delivered from the perils of the sea. The fulfilment of that vow created the great Cistercian abbey of Hayles in Gloucestershire.

the archbishop sent on to him with a multitude of pennies, "as if England was an inexhaustible well".[22] It was particularly difficult as the autumn was a very wet one. November was marked by a tremendous thunder-storm and by torrential rains which caused such flooding of the Thames that they could "swim boats in the great hall of Westminster".[23]

In Gascony, the old intrigues seethed below the surface. The count of Toulouse and the king of Aragon plotted to sow discord between Simon and the English king, because of their hatred of Simon's father who had fought so ruthlessly against them at the time of the Albigensian Crusade. But, for the time being, Simon was safe in the friendship of the king and was learning at first hand the conditions of the country which he was later to try and rule as the king's lieutenant. Much of the turbulence of the south would be part of his background, familiar from the household tales of his father's crusade. Then, too, the countess of Bigorre, ruler of the tiny county nestled in the foothills of the Pyrenees on the southern border of Gascony, was his sister-in-law. She had her small square in the chess-board of move and counter-move which was the constant pattern of the fluctuating political scene. Many of the local lords, such as Gaston de Béarn and his mother the countess, "a singularly monstrous woman and prodigious for fatness",[24] became known to him through their attendance at the king's court. All this was a valuable apprenticeship for the future, but it achieved nothing for the king's control of Gascony, and the king finally sailed home to England in September, 1243.

Henry had spent much time and treasure, and achieved no more than a five-year truce with the French, which could have been arranged at any time. His mother's intrigues and the claims of the Poitevin nobles to independence from the French crown had failed, imperilling in their failure the prestige of the English king and his always tentative hold over his independent and restive Gascon subjects. Two stories illustrate the incurably personal element in the whole campaign. The first is the epilogue to the violence and intrigues of the countess of La Marche. As the French chronicler tells the story, she was so furious at the French successes in Poitou that she begged two of her servants to poison the king and all his brothers, promising them knighthood and great lands if they were successful. When they attempted to find a chance to empty their poison in the king's food, the royal servants became suspicious, caught them, and took them to the king for judgment. His decision was swift and firm: "Let them have the reward of the present which they brought," and they were hustled off and immediately hung. When the countess heard of their failure and death, she was so upset that she seized a knife and would have plunged it into her heart, if her household had not stopped her. Frustrated, she tore her hair and her wimple and complained so vigorously that she was ill for a long time.[25] It is hardly surprising that public opinion hounded Isabella to retirement in the convent of Fontevrault. There she died in 1246, surrounded by the tombs of the equally violent-tempered Plantagenets, one of whom she had married.

The other story illustrates some of the considerations which loomed large in the minds of the medieval knights when it came to relations between nations. One of the English chroniclers tells of dissensions arising in the French army after the battle of Taillebourg, when the English strength was at its lowest ebb. The French knights argued among themselves:

> For some of them said it was not expedient for the French that the king of England be taken or confounded, nor England subjected to France, because if it should come about thus, even the most noble Frenchmen, if they were oppressed by the king of France, where could they fly for refuge, or the English if the same things should be born. We saw in the interdict of England how France was opened as a nest of refuge and protection to certain bishops and magnates of England, even Robert FitzWalter; and England to Reginald count of Boulogne. And those who said such things were of those whom Earl Richard had redeemed in the Holy Land; who when the other French heard them, accused them of treachery, and thus dissension arose, nearly to civil war.[26]

The personal ties of gratitude, self-interest and relationship, still overrode the larger conception of national unity and power. One of the guiding threads to the medieval maze is lost, unless this emphasis on the personal factor is followed to help unravel the tangled skein of politics.

Simon's return to England, after an absence of four years, brought him into the main current of English life. Now, he was not only the king's friend, but a noble of high position. The next few years were to be peaceful and fortunate, marked by the normal round of events which characterized the life of a great lord. Simon and Eleanor basked in the king's favour during this time, but they also began to develop the friendships, especially with ecclesiastics, which were to extend their interests and influence their actions.

5

The Peaceful Years

In the autumn of 1243 Simon de Montfort returned to England, probably accompanied by Eleanor and their children. There is no mention of her from the time of her settlement in the Apulian castle near Brindisi in the autumn of 1240, but there is also a complete gap in the list of courtesy presents of deer and wine which her brother, the king, was accustomed to send her when she was in England. Henry himself landed safely at Portsmouth in October and was greeted with presents by his nobles. Their courtesies helped him to put away the unpalatable thoughts of the complete failure of his Poitevin adventure, and the extravagant inroads it had made on his always confused finances. Now he could turn with real pleasure to the state visit of the countess of Provence, his mother-in-law, who was coming on his invitation, and at his expense, to bring her daughter Sanchia to marry Richard of Cornwall.

This was the sort of thing at which Henry excelled. The king's virtues were chiefly the private ones. He was pious, generous to the poor and to his old servants, and, above all, devoted to his wife and family. His generosity to his wife's relatives and his own Poitevin step-family was, in fact, a source of political weakness. With this strong sense of family feeling, the king had a real fondness for the spectacular side of the medieval king's function. He carried out well the great celebrations and feasts, such as these, and put England permanently in his debt by the buildings and works of art he encouraged and supported all over the kingdom, particularly in Westminster Abbey.

This second marriage of the king's brother is one of the few that seems to have been inspired by romantic attraction on the man's part. Richard had apparently been taken by Sanchia's beauty when he visited the count of Provence on his way to take ship for the Holy Land. The negotiations were begun soon after his return. There was no political or territorial gain for Richard, or England, in marrying into the same family as his brother. However, by now Richard was rich enough in his own right to be able to disregard the habit of marrying for money. The countess of Provence and her four daughters captured the imagination of the thirteenth-century chroniclers, because of their amazing success in achieving the most important marriages, as well as their generally accepted good looks. Marguerite, the eldest, married Louis of France; Eleanor married Henry III of England; Sanchia married Earl Richard and, when he was elected King of the Romans in 1257, she too became a queen. The youngest, Beatrice, married Count Charles of Anjou, younger brother of King Louis, and later king of Sicily. She carried the noble inheritance of the county of Provence to her husband, and it was later absorbed into the French kingdom.

When the Countess Beatrice arrived at Dover in November with her daughter, the king himself went to meet her with many of his nobles, and marked their meeting with all the visible signs of medieval politeness; gifts, the burning of innumerable candles, the ringing of bells, and the blowing of horns.[1] From Dover the ceremonial procession moved slowly on to London, where the king had ordered the citizens to decorate the city, and to clean all the mud and sewerage from view all the way from London Bridge to Westminster.[2] On November 23, the marriage of Richard and Sanchia was solemnized at Westminster. Apparently the wedding feast afterwards was of such scope and magnificence that even Matthew Paris felt that it defied description, but he added that the cooks had to prepare some thirty thousand places.[3] Even allowing for the notorious arithmetical exaggeration of medieval chroniclers, it must have been an enormous affair. All the great lords and their retinue would be present, for only a very pressing excuse would forgive the discourtesy of their absence, and then there would also be feasting for thousands of the poor. All December was a festive month and at Christmas the king went to Wallingford, the chief of his brother's Midland castles, just up the Thames from London, to celebrate the Christmas feast there with the newly married couple and many of the nobles of the realm.[4]

During this month of feasting and celebration, when the king was in such good temper about his brother's marriage, something was said about the lack of marriage-portion given to the king's sister when she married Simon de Montfort. Perhaps Eleanor herself brought the matter up, struck by the difference between this month of rejoicing over her brother's marriage, and the hole-and-corner ceremony that had united her to the earl of Leicester. The Countess Beatrice took up the matter, and begged the king to do something for his sister. The countess was much indebted to the king for his many generosities to her brothers of Savoy, but she felt that it was not fitting that he should give so much to other men, to whom he was not bound, and not to his own sister. Perhaps she reminded the king of the motto he had had painted in the gable of his great chamber at Westminster: "He who gives not what he has, obtains not what he desires". Whatever her arguments, he promised them 500 marks of lands or rents, at her request.[5]

Soon after the Countess Beatrice's departure, which was saddened by the news of the death of her husband, Count Raymond of Provence, the king began to make good his promises of favour to his sister and her husband. The quarrel of 1239 seemed to have vanished completely. During January, he pardoned them £1,000 for the debts of the earl, and the debts of the countess from the time of her widowhood.[6] Then he constituted himself surety for the annual payment of £400 owed to Eleanor by Walter Marshal for her dower[7] and also agreed to have all the countess's dower assigned to her the first time that the Earl Marshal defaulted in his payments.[8] This, of course, would have opened the door to the re-evaluation of the rightful amount owed Eleanor from the Marshal lands in Ireland. In February, Simon was excused £50 owing as relief for his half of the earldom of Leicester.[9] This meant that he was very far behind in his finances, because a relief was supposed to be paid when possession was taken of a fief. After all, Simon had had the lands of the honour of Leicester since 1231, and the title since 1239. At this same time, they were both pardoned £600 for an advance given them by the king on the dower payments.[10] In May, the king officially fulfilled the request made by the Countess Beatrice, by ordering the Exchequer to pay them 500 marks, yearly, until he should provide the same amount in lands for them, through escheats or wards. At the same time a similar grant of 300 marks was made to their heirs.[11] As the last of this series of financial manifestations of the king's generosity, Eleanor was pardoned, in June, a debt of £100 she owed to David, Jew of Oxford.[12] This particular mark of favour was a very painless proceeding on the king's part, since the only real loser was the unfortunate Jew. As all the Jews of the kingdom were directly under the control of the king and their legal status depended wholly on his favour, there was no hope of appeal from such decisions.

But the most striking, as it was to prove the most dangerous, of the king's gifts in this period of high favour, was the commitment to Simon de Montfort in February, 1244, of the custody of the castle of Kenilworth.[13] Four years later, the grant was confirmed to Eleanor for life.[14] It was truly a royal present. Kenilworth was one of the greatest of the Midland fortresses. It had originally been built by the chamberlain of Henry I, but had returned into royal control by the end of the reign of Henry II. In its twelfth-century state it did not rank as one of the most important strategic points, for its location was relatively weak. Geography had not given it the natural impregnability that the Normans looked for in their castles, but there were possibilities of improving on nature. The country between Warwick and Coventry, where Kenilworth stands, is gently rolling, and the square tower keep was built on the end of a low spur of sandstone and gravel between two brooks, which made the ground marshy. King John spent a good deal of money on building an outer curtain wall, but it was during Henry III's reign that the two brooks were dammed. What had been a slight pool became a great lake, covering more than 100 acres, and protecting the castle from attack on three sides. On the north side, where there was no water, a deep ditch was dug in the rock, and this weakest link in the defence system was overlooked by the keep. A series of dams, ditches and drawbridges, reinforced by stone towers, protected the lake from drainage by any attackers and rendered the castle almost impregnable to attack.

Even a brief description of the keep shows how thoroughly the place had been designed for defence. It was a large tower, 80 feet by 60, with two stories each about 40 feet high. The angles were reinforced with projecting square turrets, and the walls were 20 feet thick up to ten feet above the ground. This basement was filled in solid with earth, and the entry to the castle was through a forebuilding, a rectangular tower built against the west wall of the keep, with walls that were six feet thick and which went up to the second storey. The main door, protected by this forebuilding, entered the great hall. There was an inside staircase which connected the two floors and the battlements. Up on the battlements there were little chambers built into all the towers, a walk at the gutter level, and a series of arrow-slits provided for the use of the guards. The essential need for water was taken care of through a well in the south-east corner of the keep, with a small, square well-chamber built over the well pipe, and a pulley hung from the centre of the vault for working the bucket. Sanitation, too, was considered, the north-west angle tower being provided with three tiers of latrines, one for each floor and one for the battlements. Just outside the keep, but sheltered against its walls within the inner court, were built the kitchen and other domestic offices. Within this inner court, too, was the main chapel of the castle.[15]

Despite its strong defensive possibilities, Kenilworth seems to have had little attention while Henry was young, although in 1233 there was mention of repairs to its tower.[16] When the king came to inspect the castle himself in 1240 and 1241, the rolls immediately show what his observant eye and beauty-loving nature felt was lacking in this rather formidable dwelling. Apparently the wall of the castle was in great disrepair, for it threatened to fall into the fish-pond, and was to be pulled down and rebuilt. The jail and the shed where the king's bells hung were to be repaired. The porch of the tower, which had fallen, was to be rebuilt, and the gutters were to be repaired where necessary. A roof was to be put on the great chamber – whether this was an ornamental inside ceiling, or whether the roof had collapsed is not clear from the records. The king next turned his attention to items closer to his heart. The chapel was to be wainscotted, whitened, and painted; a wall was to be made to separate the chancel from the body of the chapel; and two seats, of suitably painted wood, were to be made in it for the king and queen. Another painted seat was to be made for the queen's chapel within the tower.[17] This would be a relatively small oratory, perhaps the one that seems to have existed on the groundfloor of the fore-building. These detailed orders to the sheriff in charge provide an attractive picture of the constructive side of Henry III, who hated to see palaces, castles and churches not properly kept up, or decorated in the newest fashion. From the minuteness of his orders, it is quite obvious that he spent a good deal of time inspecting the buildings himself, and that he had a very sharp eye for what needed to be done. Having given these instructions in February, 1241, he spent a couple of days there the following September, and fired off a few more commands to the sheriff about further improvements, and items which had been overlooked. This time the queen's chamber was to be wainscotted, whitened, and lined, and her windows were to be broken and made larger. The fire-places in both his and the queen's chambers needed to be repaired, and so did the queen's privy. A new porch was to be built in front of the queen's room. Outside, two of the castle gates needed to be repaired, and a new wall ought to be built between the inner and outer wall of the castle. A swing-bridge was to be erected, too, which perhaps means that the water-works were well under way by this time.[18]

It is easy to see that when the king entrusted the castle to the earl of Leicester it was in good repair. Perhaps it was not among the new and elegant residences of the kingdom, like the king's own Painted Chamber at Westminster, or that of the famous prison of Nicolette in the old romance:

> In a vaulted chamber cast,
> Shapen and carven wondrous well,
> Painted as by miracle.[19]

But the great mass of rosy sandstone, like Bishop Grosseteste's allegorical castle that was redder than any rose, had an impressive dignity of its own set in its great lake and thick forest. Indeed, the forest was so thick that the king had to give orders to have it cut back where it encroached on the main highway to Coventry and Warwick and might provide too convenient cover for the rogues who would break the king's peace.[20] In the possession of Kenilworth and Odiham, which Eleanor had been given before her marriage, the earl and countess of Leicester had acquired two of the most redoubtable strongholds in England.

These continuous marks of the king's favour to his sister and brother-in-law during the winter and spring of 1244 are particularly interesting when they are considered against Simon's share in the Candlemas Parliament. This February Parliament of 1244 has evoked much interest and controversy among the constitutional historians, for it was one of the notable occasions when nobles and prelates joined to counter what they both felt were the exorbitant demands of the king. When Henry came home from Gascony, he was empty-handed and he was anxious to force the nobles to refill his treasury. They were in no mood to do so, and with the clerical opposition encouraged by Robert Grosseteste, bishop of Lincoln, they refused to accede to his demands, unless he acceded to their complaints about the mismanagement of the government. This may or may not have been the year of the "Paper Constitution", an interesting document which in many respects foreshadows the Provisions of Oxford.[21] But whether this list of desired reforms belongs to 1244 or to the upheaval of 1238 – when Simon's marriage was one of the disturbing factors – the main points mentioned were the same. The prelates and barons assembled in council called for the king's acceptance of the English nobles, as his natural advisors, rather than foreign relations and adventurers. They sought to prevent the king from acting without the consent of his barons or a supervisory committee provided by general election from them. They wanted to control the machinery of government by the election and supervision of its greatest officers, the chancellor and the justiciar. In 1244, as is obvious from the continuous marks of the king's favour, as shown in the records, Simon de Montfort was not a leader of the barons in their demands, but rather a mediator for the king, trying to persuade the other nobles of the king's needs. Indeed, although 1244, as 1238, marked another milestone of opposition to the king's unbridled and irresponsible use of his power, there is no sign at all that Simon de Montfort had anticipated his later role of head of the constitutional opposition to the king. At this time, it was a matter of no concern to him.

This parliament of 1244 is interesting, too, for the testimony it gives of the status and political importance of the saintly bishop, Robert Grosseteste. He was one of the important formative influences on Simon's character, and one of his most revered friends. This friendship, and the friendship of the earl and the countess with the learned Franciscan, Adam Marsh, belong pre-eminently to these quiet years in England. It was a period when the earl of Leicester was exposed to the ideals and principles of two of the most brilliant and highly-regarded men of his time. Grosseteste was the finest example of the scholar-bishop; trained in the universities, anxious for reform, and steeped in the new spirit of the Lateran Council. He was an ardent upholder of the fullness of the power of the pope but an equally convinced opponent of those papal commands, which, he felt, negated the basic premise of the papal power, the salvation of souls. When Grosseteste was appointed bishop in 1235, he was already a man of over sixty-five and Lincoln was an enormous diocese that stretched from the Humber to the Thames. It would have been a tremendous load even for a younger man, but for nearly twenty years the bishop not only supervised his diocese most closely, he also continued his works of scholarship and translation. Such driving energy in a man of advanced years impressed his contemporaries, as it must impress us.

Grosseteste had been archdeacon of Leicester in the years when Simon had first taken possession of his Leicester inheritance, and had come into contact with him then. In fact, the first letter we have of their correspondence is a request of Grosseteste's to Simon that he should not deal too harshly with one of his burgesses of Leicester.[22] It was probably written in 1238 when Simon was gathering all the money he could lay his hands on, perhaps not too scrupulously, for his trip to Rome and the dispensation for his marriage. But even then the bishop was a good enough friend so that when the rift came with the king in 1239, Simon wrote him immediately asking his aid for his household, and his intercession with the king. The bishop wrote back suggesting, with biblical examples, that this tribulation should lead to spiritual health and even temporal glory, but he agreed to carry out the earl's requests.[23]

The knowledge we have of the relationship between the zealous bishop and the earl and countess is tantalizing in its incompleteness. Much of it is contained indirectly in letters of Adam Marsh to the bishop or to the Leicesters. The worthy Franciscan never dated his letters and tended to obscure their sense in a swirl of scriptural quotations and confused rhetoric, which gives little specific information. As the children of the earl and countess grew up, two of their sons were sent to form part of the bishop's household and to be instructed by him. Their relations seem to have been fairly intimate, for the bishop even borrowed the countess's cook on the death of his own. It speaks well for their friendship that the countess, instead of being annoyed, asserted that she would gladly concede her most necessary or her best servants to the bishop if he had need of them.[24]

The most puzzling and most often utilized of Adam's references to their relationship, however, is the friar's statement that he was returning to the bishop his treatise on kingship and tyranny, which had been loaned to Earl Simon and was sealed with his seal.[25] This famous vanished treatise was hopefully thought to have provided the theoretical basis for the later baronial government. Unfortunately for such a convenient hypothesis, it now seems sure that this memorandum was no more than one part of a long and closely reasoned case put before Pope Innocent IV at Lyons in 1250 by the bishop. Although it took as the starting-point for its argument Aristotle's discussion of monarchy and tyranny, it did not deal with secular politics, but with the supposed "tyranny" of the Archbishop of Canterbury who had been demanding excessive procurations – gifts and entertainment – while on his visitations of his diocese.[26]

The earl of Leicester does seem to have been genuinely interested, unusually so for a layman, in spiritual and intellectual affairs. He discussed with Adam Marsh Grosseteste's plan for freeing souls and was willing to assist, but was worried about the bishop's health and strength.[27] As to what this mysterious plan was and what it entailed, Adam is, as always, secretively silent. The earl and the bishop shared a lifelong tradition of friendship with the Mendicant orders and the earl seems to have shared too, at least to a degree, the scholarly tastes and friendships of the cleric. For example, John of Basingstoke, one of Grosseteste's successors as archdeacon of Leicester as well as his friend and scholarly collaborator, was also a good friend of the earl of Leicester, who was greatly grieved by his death.[28] John was himself an unusual and interesting person. One of the best Greek scholars of his generation in England, he had studied for some time in Athens, where his tutor, surprisingly, was an extremely learned girl, the daughter of the archbishop of Athens. When he came back to England he brought some Greek works to Grosseteste's attention.

Despite the fragmentary nature of our knowledge, it seems certain that Simon's friendship with the aged bishop, whose saintliness he revered and whose abilities he respected, was one of the best influences on his character. The practical effect his friendship had on his actions was limited, for Grosseteste died in 1253, before the real crisis between king and barons. But his influence would seem to have been exerted on the side of peace, for just before his death, he persuaded the earl to go and help King Henry in his efforts to pacify Gascony. Notwithstanding the earl's human tendency to stand aloof, since he had just been removed from the government of that province and his suggestions for its rule ignored, he agreed to go because of his reverence for the bishop, who reminded him of the many gifts he had received from the king.[29] Grosseteste might have been able, in the years of open strife, to convince both parties of their mutual duties. None of the other bishops were successful, but none had his enormous personal prestige, firmness, and acknowledged holiness. It would seem that the real friendship which existed between the indomitable bishop and the warlike earl was due to the fact that fundamentally they were the same kind of people. Both stood head and shoulders above their contemporaries in their abilities; both were concerned with the practical application of Christian principles to government, whether secular or ecclesiastic: this was their constructive side. Both lacked a genuine feeling for the individual and his rights, if by overriding the individual some greater cause was – or seemed to be – served. Neither knew the meaning of compromise on what they felt were their rights, but regarded the maintenance of those rights as a matter of principle. Perhaps it was this very unyielding steadfastness in their own beliefs that canonized them both in the popular eye and encouraged tales of their supposed miracles, for although such men are not successful politicians they inspire a great legend.

Their other great clerical friend was Brother Adam Marsh, whose letters, even at their most enigmatic, throw considerable light on the family life of the Leicester household. His name has barely survived the effacing shadow of the centuries, although his great friend Grosseteste stands revealed as scholar, scientist, translator of Greek, as well as bishop. To their contemporaries they were about equal in achievements. Roger Bacon, who was not much given to the praise of others, brackets Grosseteste and Adam as "the greatest clerks of the world, and perfect in divine and human wisdom".[30] Some of this praise, of course, may have been due to Brother Roger's very human desire to increase the prestige of his own order, and of one who was closely associated with it. Adam was rector of the Franciscan school at Oxford, and had a great reputation as scholar, theologian, and mathematician which was not only restricted to England. Salimbene, the lively and peripatetic Italian Franciscan, tells of hearing Brother Adam Marsh's lectures on *Genesis* from an English friar in Tarascon.[31] Except for his letters, all his works have vanished. We do not know how he earned the title "Doctor Illustris", which would seem to imply the English qualities of clearness and precision. His modern editor remarks rather tartly: "Justifiable as it might be when applied to his scholastic speculations, it is scarcely borne out by his letters."[32] They are, in fact, long-winded, rhetorical, and, in many cases, downright confusing. But behind the high-flown perorations, injunctions to secrecy, and scriptural quotations lurks some faded fragrance of the integrity of the man, the genuineness that inspired Grosseteste's tribute:

> I have found in you, in you alone, a truthful friend, a faithful counsellor, one who looks to the reality and not to the outward appearance, and who rests on a firm and solid foundation, not on a hollow and fragile reed.[33]

Adam's range of correspondents was wide and distinguished. He was a respected visitor at court, as well as the revered friend and counsellor of many of the bishops of his day. He was often spokesman, not only for the Franciscans at Oxford, but for the whole university. Indeed, his prestige and influence demonstrate most clearly the important position which the English Franciscans had won in contemporary life within twenty-five years of their arrival in the country, a footsore and homeless band.

Most of Adam's letters to the earl and countess of Leicester seem to belong to the period of the earl's seneschalship in Gascony, as when they were at home in England personal visits could be arranged. Although some of the letters clarify the earl's difficulties in Gascony or describe the impact of Gascon affairs on the English court, many of them are purely personal. For example, he urges the earl to look to the peace of his domestics and his own household, for "Better is a patient man than a strong man, and he who can rule his temper than he who storms a city".[34] His letters to the countess imply that she, too, was prone to high temper, for he warns her of the devilish furies of wrath and suggests that she lay aside all contentions and irritating quarrels, when it is necessary for her to counsel the earl in a spirit of moderation.[35] In a familiar vein of reformers before and after him, he scolded the countess – briefly, he says, although it runs to over three printed pages – for excesses in dress and the insanity and expense of superfluous ornament.[36] But his reproofs must have been taken in good part and the warm friendship continued until his death, for when Simon came to make his will, Adam was named as one of the executors. The exact date of Adam's death is unknown, but it was probably early in 1259, and because of his friendship for Grosseteste, he was buried near him in Lincoln Cathedral. Unfortunately for Simon, he had again lost, before the crucial period of his life, one of the few friends to whose reproof and good counsel he was willing to listen.

The tradition of ecclesiastical friendships was a strong one in the Leicester household. In 1245 Simon sent 20 timbers to the Friars Preachers at Wilton (Wilts) to help them build their church.[37] The Dominicans later discovered that they had made a mistake in their choice of a location for this convent and moved three miles into the faster growing new town of Salisbury. In 1246 the countess – who had to have a special permission from the pope – and the earl went on a personal visit to the abbey of Waverley with their two small sons. Waverley was the first Cistercian house in England and was even then over a century old. It was also the nearest important religious house to their castle at Odiham, being only ten miles away. On the Palm Sunday of their visit, they were there for a sermon in the chapter, High Mass and a procession. Eleanor had brought the monks a precious altar-cloth as a gift, and after her return home she gave them 68 marks as well. The chronicler of the abbey gave a very detailed description of the event. It was rare that the strict Cistercians were allowed to open their house to any woman, and a visit from the king's sister was an important event. Her generosity also allowed them to purchase another 150 acres of land, a reminder of the important role played by the Cistercian monks in the agricultural development of Scotland, especially in raising and marketing wool.[38] The abbot of Waverley seems to have remained on good terms with the family, as he was one of the visitors listed on Eleanor's household roll, when he came to visit her at Odiham in February, 1265.[39] Here seems to be the explanation for the strong bias in favour of Earl Simon and the barons in the annals of the monastery.

But the interests of the earl and countess of Leicester were by no means exclusively ecclesiastical during these years. They were filling a prominent place at court. The rolls are full of the incidental presents made them by the king: gifts of deer, both for food and for stocking one or other of the parks of their manors; wine, by the tun, to add to their own supplies; and oaks, from one of the royal forests, for the necessary rebuilding.[40] The king also completed the grant, which he had promised the Countess Beatrice he would give them. In Passion-week of 1245 Gilbert de Umfravill, one of the most important and wealthiest barons of the north of England, died, leaving a year-old infant as his heir. The king immediately bestowed the wardship of this child on Earl Simon, fulfilling the arrangement made at the Exchequer the year before. According to Matthew Paris, Richard of Cornwall, the king's brother and already the richest noble in the kingdom, was not pleased, as he had hoped to acquire the wardship for himself.[41] Simon, in turn, joined the king on his expedition to Wales in August of that year. It was not a very successful expedition and achieved little, but it provided a show of English force in the district around Snowdon. The relations between England and Wales during the reign of Henry III varied, depending on the strength of the leading Welsh prince, the alliances against him of the Marcher lords, and the amount of effort the king wanted to devote to the problem. It was Edward's task and achievement to subdue and control the Welsh when he came to the throne.

In England itself, king and barons were for once united in their opposition to the growing financial demands of Pope Innocent IV. The sorest point was the question of papal provisions, i.e., the system by which, under certain circumstances, the pope claimed the right to appoint his own nominees to livings that fell vacant. This arrangement aroused much indignation, both ecclesiastical and secular. The truly conscientious spiritual leaders deplored the handing over of the care of souls to foreigners, many of whom merely collected their revenues and never even came to England or provided for vicars to do their work. Even if these foreigners did come and live in the country and go through the motions of carrying out the duties of their office, they did not speak English and were not understood by their flock; again the care of souls suffered. This emphasis on the "care of souls" was the high-minded argument, the one that Grosseteste adopted and upheld even against the pope's express command. But benefices, in the thirteenth century, were not only spiritual duties, they were the accepted method of payment, and support for all clerics, whether in ecclesiastical, royal, or baronial service. Many less spiritual ecclesiastics than the saintly bishop of Lincoln deplored the system because it gave to foreigners the rewards that Englishmen deserved. Matthew Paris is the most typical and outspoken voice of this group. The secular lords objected also, partly influenced by anti-foreign prejudice, but also by the feeling that the pope was interfering with the prerogatives of king and baron, as well as bishop and abbot. Such a mixture of motives, good and bad, encouraged the rise of complaints to the papal court over its exactions and those of its collectors. Sometimes the complaints were quite vigorous, and one of the more amusing examples was the forced expulsion of Master Martin in 1245.

Master Martin had been sent over by Innocent IV the year before to gather more money for the pope's struggle against the emperor, Frederick II. He had been unpopular from the beginning because of his exactions and his reputation for arrogance. At the end of June, the troubles came to a head. Some of the barons had gathered at Luton and Dunstable, armed and ready for a tournament. Now a tournament in the thirteenth century was not the purely social event it later became. It was rather a species of sham war between two large groups of armed knights. Since even sham warfare often led to quarrels and conspiracies against the peace, the king had prohibited this one, as he did many times during his reign. But the barons, gathered together, had discussed this hated papal envoy and decided to rid England of him. They sent one of their number, Fulk Fitz Warin, to him ordering him to leave England immediately under the threat of imminent vengeance. Martin, terrified, hastened to the king, who was not in much milder mood than the barons. When the envoy asked licence to depart and a safe-conduct from the realm, the king, furious, shouted: "The devil give you a safe-conduct to hell!" Finally reason prevailed and the marshal of the palace was ordered to conduct Master Martin safely to the sea. It was an anxious trip for the fearful envoy. He dreaded attack so much, Matthew Paris says maliciously, "that if the earth had opened, he would have hidden himself under the turf". Thinking that some countrymen, who had gathered to buy trees from a wood put up for sale by the archbishop of Canterbury, were a force called to attack him, the trembling clerk clung to his escort and promised to get him a benefice for any of his relations or friends if only he would keep him safe. The marshal soon discovered the peaceful nature of the gathering, but put wings to Master Martin's flight by claiming that he had been hardly able to restrain them, and that it certainly would be the part of wisdom for him to depart and never return to England. This was counsel which Master Martin was more than willing to accept.[42]

During the great Christmas feast in London in 1245, the king invited many magnates who had been on the Welsh expedition with him, to be "sharers in joy as they were partners in tribulation".[43] The rumour circulated among the gathering that the pope was angry with the English and anxious to overthrow the kingdom. It was whispered that he had even suggested to King Louis that he should conquer the kingdom with the approval of the Holy See – an offer with which Louis would have nothing to do. Of course, neither Henry nor Louis were enthusiastic supporters of the papal policy of deposing and excommunicating the emperor Frederick, but they tried as far as possible to avoid the tangle. Frederick's death in 1250 helped to remove one of their great problems. Meanwhile in the parliament of March, 1246, the rumours, suspicions and opposition culminated in the formal complaints sent to the pope and the General Council, then in session at Lyons. There were three separate letters of complaint; one sent by the bishops, one by the abbots and priors, and one by the nobles, on behalf of the barons, clergy, and people of England.[44] It is interesting to note that Simon's name is put at the head of all the nobles, directly after that of Richard of Cornwall, the king's brother. His position was still emphasized as the king's brother-in-law. But the complaints achieved nothing. Pope Innocent IV was too deeply emmeshed in his life-and-death struggle with the emperor Frederick to be able to give up any source of revenue, unpopular though it might be. The military struggle and the growing bureaucracy, created by the effective centralizing of the church under the pope, called for constantly growing funds.

The last of the episodes that shows how close Simon de Montfort was to Henry III during these years is again one that tantalizes us by its incompleteness. In the summer or early autumn of 1247 the earl was sent abroad on royal, but secret, business. Was he trying to negotiate for the king – perhaps a further discussion of the land of Normandy or one of the other outstanding problems between France and England? King Louis was trying to settle any outstanding problems and injustices before he left on Crusade. Whatever the business was, nothing came of it. Simon was back in England by October 13th, the feast of Edward the Confessor.[45] This feast was always King Henry's favourite occasion of the year, as St Edward was a particular object of his devotion. When Henry rebuilt Westminster Abbey, special attention was paid to a suitably magnificent shrine, and it was solemnly consecrated at the very end of his reign.

In 1247, the feast of St Edward was to be particularly splendid for both religious and secular reasons. Henry had recently received from the Holy Land a portion of the Holy Blood. This relic was certified as authentic by the Masters of the Templars and the Hospitallers, the patriarch of Jerusalem, and a flock of lesser prelates. Since France had received the Crown of Thorns in 1241 and Louis was building the Sainte-Chapelle to enclose it worthily, Henry did not want to see England lag behind, either in the quality of its relics or the magnificence of their surroundings. On St Edward's day the king, in solemn procession and on foot, carried the precious relic all the way from St Paul's to the abbey of Westminster. Matthew Paris drew one of his spirited illustrations for his account of this event, showing the king, under a canopy carried by four men, met by three representatives of the bishops and prelates of England. They greeted the relic and its royal bearer with songs and rejoicing. The bishop of Norwich said the solemn mass and preached the sermon to the people who had crowded into the great open space of the unfinished nave. After the purely religious ceremony was over, the king put aside his humble garments and turned to more secular festivities. Clothed in a precious gilt brocade, with a golden circlet instead of his great crown, he knighted his young stepbrother, William de Valence, and his companions.

We know so many details about this occasion because the king saw Matthew Paris in the crowd at the Abbey and called him to the royal seat, bidding him sit there, on its step, so that he might see everything and fully and clearly write it down. When the ceremonies in church were over, the magnates – as well as Matthew Paris and three of his companions – adjourned to Westminster Hall for the great feast.[46] The quantities of food, especially meat, for such an occasion stagger the modern imagination. Although we have no exact report on what was used on this occasion, the orders for an earlier Christmas feast give some idea of what these ceremonial dinners demanded. At that time, the various sheriffs were ordered to deliver to Westminster: 7,000 hens, 800 hares, 500 rabbits, 1,500 lambs, 100 dozen partridges, 160 kids, 22 dozen pheasants, and 80 pigs. There were other items, too, which do not seem as digestible; 100 peacocks, 68 boars, swans, herons, cranes. A certain amount of fish was requested, but comparatively little, except for salmon, some of which was to be made into pies, and Henry's favourite lampreys.[47]

Simon hastened back from abroad to be present with his wife at this feast and the celebrations in the Abbey. This splendid occasion was both an end and a beginning. It was a fitting conclusion to the period when the earl had enjoyed the king's wholehearted trust and the royal favour. But the feast also marked a beginning, the rise of a new series of royal favourites – the king's Poitevin half-brothers and sisters, who flocked to England on the death of their mother Queen Isabella, to try and improve their fortunes. They were to displace Simon from his niche as counsellor and companion. In their arrogance and acquisition of a flood of royal gifts of money, lands, and rich marriages, they aroused the envy and fury of the responsible magnates, both the native and the foreign-born. The royal favour – like fortune – was fickle. Simon had discovered that before, he was to prove it yet again.

6

The Running of a Noble Household

Human curiosity is always whetted by the details of other people's lives. This is especially true when the people involved are so remote in time and circumstances. It is a happy chance when detailed records or fortunate excavations reveal that these remote strangers were plagued by the same daily problems, however differently these problems were stated. Suddenly there comes a stab of recognition that these are men and women, not just names in a history book. It is the excitement of that realization which lends zest to the search for material, and illumines the apparently dry detail of account book and treatise.

To run a noble household called for two separate kinds of accounts, one general, and one domestic. The general accounts were the returns from the system of administration which dealt with the honour of Leicester, which, it may be remembered, was a very mixed collection of lands, rents, jurisdictions, and privileges. It also dealt with the various manors, not part of the honour, which had been assigned to Simon and Eleanor as gifts, dower holdings, marriage portion, or in wardship. Of this fairly complicated administration, there are no surviving accounts of Simon de Montfort as the earl of Leicester. However, the accounts of other barons of the same period and the same type of lands have survived. From a study of them, it would seem that there were certain general lines which were common to all the great barons of Simon's day. Insofar as it is possible to judge, the nobles were establishing a system on their estates which was based on the system of royal administration. The earl would have had a permanent council, probably paid, made up of a nucleus of his officials and the knights who held from him. They were consulted on matters of importance, as the king consulted his council of his chief officials and the great barons of the realm. The baron's chief official was the steward, and he probably also had a receiver for the collection of moneys. The lord's local officials would have worn his livery and taken a special oath to him. They were controlled by his auditors, who would have formed part of his council, and would have been sent out periodically to check accounts. Such practice in local government gave the barons the knowledge and the experience which enabled them to judge the efficiency of the government of the realm.[1]

The seneschal, or steward, was the chief baronial official and himself a man of noble birth. He might well go on to the king's service and ultimately become a judge. The career of John La Warre illustrates the opportunities, and the type of man used as a baronial steward. John was steward of the earl of Warenne in 1261, and by 1265 was constable of Bristol for the baronial faction. In August of that year, he, with a body of archers, helped the countess of Leicester to garrison Dover Castle, and was paid by her for sixty-three days service. After Evesham, he joined the defenders of Kenilworth during the long-drawn-out royal siege. In fact, so vigorously did he fight on the baronial side that he was condemned by the Dictum de Kenilworth to buy his lands back at the rate of seven years rent, instead of the more normal five.

However, he was soon part of the normal life of the country again. In 1268 he became estates steward for Isabella de Fortibus, countess of Devon and Aumale and the richest widow in England, and remained with her for six years. When he left her service, he was given the manor of Whitchurch in payment for his work. From this he went on to a royal appointment as sheriff of Herefordshire. His son moved still further up in the world as the first Lord Delaware. The picture that emerges from this summary of the steward of a great baronial household is not that of a menial. He was a man of good family, a capable professional administrator, and a vigorous warrior.[2]

Under the seneschal were the bailiffs or the reeves, one of whom would be in charge of each manor. It is not surprising that a formal commitment was supposed to be made to the seneschal, in the presence of witnesses. The seneschal promised to keep trust and render proper account. Neither he, nor the bailiffs under him, should oppress the tenants by unlawful accusations, or fear, or the demand for presents, but rather do them justice.[3] As this contemporary description of his duties would suggest, the steward served as the representative of the lord, often presided over the more important meetings of the manorial courts, and was the symbol of ultimate authority to the average tenant.

The residence of the earl and countess of Leicester, when they were in England, was usually a great castle like Kenilworth or Odiham, but the source of their supplies was the manor. The manor was the fundamental economic unit of medieval civilization. Everyone agrees on this, but no one is quite sure exactly how a manor should be defined. The vaguest definition is probably the most useful, for the term manor was stretched to cover a great many things. It was a territorial unit, which varied greatly in size and importance, but which comprised the lord's own land and the lands of tenants who owed him rent and/or services. The actual description of one of the most valuable of Eleanor's manors, as it was assessed after her death, illustrates this better than any definition. The manor of Luton – between Dunstable and St Albans – was part of Eleanor's marriage-portion in her first marriage to William Marshal. When she died, it was valued at £85 8s. 6½d. It consisted of 97½ acres, 1 rood of arable lands in demesne, i.e., actually held by Eleanor herself and worked for her needs. There were 5½ acres of meadow with pasture and a wood: 39 acres, 1½ roods of demesne were let to tenants and there was £14 13s. 7d. in rent. Besides that there were a few shillings in rent and a little land held by "customers", i.e. villeins who performed services fixed by custom.[4] There is no mention here of milling rights, or advowson, i.e. right of choosing the local priest. These were often profitable manorial rights and usually specified. Luton is not a very big holding by modern standards, something less than 150 tillable acres. But from a group of manors like this all over England Simon and Eleanor drew the money for their expenses, and the necessary raw materials for feeding and clothing the household. It is easy to see why an efficient body of officials and an adequate set of records were necessary to keep such a far-flung enterprise in good running order.

What can only be assumed about baronial and manorial administration on the lands of the earl and countess of Leicester, because of a lack of pertinent records, can be stated without equivocation about their domestic affairs. There is an unusual amount of information about the way the countess of Leicester ran her household. The roll of her household expenses for nearly seven months of the year 1265 has survived. It is the earliest private household account of England still in existence, and it is a mine of information on purely domestic affairs. It also throws incidental light on the events of that turbulent summer. The contemporary *Rules of Seynt Robert,* written by Bishop Grosseteste, is a valuable commentary on the theoretical side of household and manorial management. It was written by the bishop for Simon's cousin and neighbour in the Midlands, the widowed countess of Lincoln, and was full of a great deal of specific, as well as general, advice as to how a great noblewoman and landholder should conduct her affairs. When it comes to the way that the foods mentioned in the accounts were actually utilized, there is no contemporary account. John of Garland, a learned Englishman living in France and in Toulouse at the time of the death of Simon the Crusader, wrote a book of vocabularies. When he talks of food-stuffs, he mentions the items used, including spices and things grown in the garden, but gives no recipes. The following century saw two notable cookbooks, *The Forme of Cury,* and the *Menagier de Paris. The Forme of Cury* was compiled at the very end of the fourteenth century by the master cooks of King Richard II. *The Menagier,* or the Goodman of Paris, was a treatise written by a bourgeois of Paris for his young bride and is, indeed, a fourteenth-century encyclopedia of household management. From their recipes it is possible to reconstruct the kind of meals that were provided from the raw materials mentioned in the household roll. Together they give a vivid picture of the work involved in running this type of complicated and far-flung operation. A noble household of the thirteenth century was such a large scale affair that the mistress of the house must have had great foresight, and the ability to choose good servants and oversee them carefully.

For example, one of the most important medieval domestic problems was to co-ordinate supply and demand. Since carriage of heavy and bulky goods was always expensive and sometimes impossible, it was of the utmost importance to know how to apportion the necessary supplies for the year. Grosseteste suggested some methods to the countess of Lincoln to aid her in estimating the year's harvest. Then at Michaelmas, when all the harvest would be nearly gathered, and the countess knew how much grain she had in hand for that year, she could make her plans. It was easier for a noble household to go to the supplies on the various manors than to try and have them stored in one central warehouse or barn. The countess had to plan how many weeks she should stay in each place; bearing in mind, not only the grain harvest, but the resources of fish and meat which were available at each manor, according to the season. Besides, there was some complicated calculation to be done about the amount of grain needed a week for the servants on each manor and the requirements for seed. There were also necessary allowances of bread and ale, both made from the local grain, and a definite amount to be put aside for alms to the poor.

After all these first charges on the harvest had been calculated then the surplus could be sold, preferably in times of scarcity when it would get the highest price. The proceeds of the sale, with the rents and other revenues, were used to pay the wages of the servants, the expenses of the kitchens, and the cost of the wines.[5] This type of leisurely sojourn, travelling from one estate to the other, was the recognized way of life for the upper class, from the king down. In fact, the king travelled even more than most of his nobles. But these well-regulated ways of obtaining and utilizing the necessary foodstuffs were often upset by the fortunes of war or unexpected events. The countess of Leicester, for example, in the fateful summer of 1265, could not peacefully peregrinate her estates. She must keep her household on a military footing, going from Odiham Castle across country to Porchester, Bramber, Winchelsea and finally Dover. Even in such disturbed circumstances, when she was hard-pressed to find enough supplies for her retinue, she could, and did, call on the stores of her closest manor to provide the essentials. The system worked almost to the end.

Before going into the details of daily expenditure, it is worth seeing what the roll was like on which they were listed. The countess's household roll was the statement of domestic accounts, all her daily expenses from February 19 to August 29, 1265. It consisted of a number of long narrow slips of parchment. On the front of the slip the clerk noted where the household was, and entered the normal, daily accounts of expenditure. When the slip was finished, he entered on its back the personal and miscellaneous expenses which had been incurred during the period covered by the entries on the front of the membrane, such as wages and items of clothing, as well as gifts and alms. Both the beginning and end of the roll are missing. It seems to have been taken to Montargis in France by the countess when she fled from Dover. It was recovered, during the French Revolution, from the ruins of the Montargis convent, in which she died, and ultimately brought back to England.

The format of the daily accounts is unvarying. The clerk – either Christopher or Eudes, for they give their names – first gives the day of the week to which the account applies. Then he mentions the presence of the countess, and gives the names of any of her important visitors. After this he gives the amount of grain used each day. The Latin word in the accounts is *panis*, but it needs to be translated here by grain or flour. The account also mentions whether it came from storage or was bought. After the grain, comes the supply of wine and then of beer, with the same note as to whether it was bought or came from storage. Beer was often brewed in the castle, and then the amount of grain required is listed. These supplies of bread and wine and beer were the direct responsibility of the household steward. The next item deals with the amount of supplies turned over to the kitchen. Sometimes it mentions where the meat or fish came from, but usually it is content to state whether they were from storage or bought. The last item was for the stables and included the number of horses that had to be fed. This gives a useful check on the fluctuating number of people in the household. The accounts for several days will show the pattern and illustrate some of the differences. As will be evident, the contrast between Lent and the ordinary meat day is quite striking.

Monday (Feb. 23),* for the Countess: Grain, 1½ quarters from stores. Wine, 2 sextaries, 1 gallon. Brewing, 5 quarters of barley, 7½ quarters of oats. *Kitchen* 400 herrings. Fish, by purchase, 7s. 9d. *Stables* For 33 horses, hay from stores. Oats, 2 quarters, 1 bushel.
Sum 8s.[6]

Wednesday (Feb. 25), for the Countess and the Abbot of Waverley: Grain 1½ quarters, from stores. Wine, 2½ sextaries. Beer, previously reckoned. *Kitchen* 400 herring. Fish, by purchase, 10s. 6d. Dishes, 15d. Peas, 23d. Napkins, 10½d. Onions, 6½d. Aples, 4½d. *Stables* Hay, from stores, for 32 horses. Oats, 2 quarters, from stores. Forge 12d.
Sum 16s. 5½d.[7]

Let us look first at the basic commodities and what the unfamiliar measures really imply. A quarter of dry grain would weigh from 400 to 600 pounds, but after milling there would not be more than 350 to 500 pounds of meal. A pound of flour could make a pound of bread. Grosseteste says that a quarter of wheat should make 9 score, or 180 loaves.[8] Roughly, then, a loaf of bread would be about two pounds, or a bit more. On this Monday and Wednesday, the amount of wheat provided would furnish 270 loaves, by this reckoning. That would supply both dinner and supper, and the remnants would be given to the poor. A sextary of wine seems to have comprised four English gallons. In this case, the daily issue was 9 and 10 gallons – very low compared to the amounts that were drunk when the earl came with his retinue, or when there were knights to be fed. Wine, of course, was only for the well-born in the household. The grooms and servants would have beer as their usual drink. Thirteenth-century beer was made indiscriminately of barley, oats, or wheat, or a mixture of them. Hops were not yet in use, so it was rather insipid and had to be used quickly because it would not keep, but it was flavoured with

* I have inserted the dates for convenience. They have to be calculated from the named feast-days.

spices, often pepper. The quantities used were enormous. The household brewed or bought beer at least once a week, and the average amount used would seem to have been in the neighbourhood of 200 gallons a week.

The difference in the types of supplies released to the kitchen on Monday and Wednesday demonstrate the extras which would be provided for an honoured guest like the Abbot of Waverley. Herring were always the mainstay of the Lenten diet. They were salted, and stored, and used by the hundreds. The problem, during Lent, of providing enough fish of different types and arranging for their delivery was often acute. For example, at the end of this week in February, the countess paid for two carts bringing 108 cod and ling, and 32 congers, and 500 hake from Bristol. Half was left at Wallingford to supply the stores there and the other half taken to Odiham. On this same load there seems to have been a porpoise, which was left at Wallingford, "except for two small pieces".[9] They also ate whale, while eels and lampreys were delicacies.

King Henry, like his father, had a passion for lampreys, which were best obtained in England from the Severn. There is a pathetic undertone in one order to the sheriff of Gloucester for the continuous provision of all the lampreys possible for, as he says, all fish but lampreys seem insipid to the king and queen.[10] Fish were often salted or smoked, baked or boiled in paste, or made into pies, to make them easier to keep and transport. Another staple that was easy to preserve was stockfish, which was cod that had had the head removed and had been gutted and dried in the sun and air, without salt or smoke. The Goodman of Paris suggests that when you want to eat it, it should be beaten with a wooden hammer for a full hour and then soaked in warm water for two hours or more. After that it could be eaten with mustard or soaked in butter, if it was not Lent. The left-overs, cut in small pieces, could be fried for supper and sprinkled with spices.[11] Since in Lent neither butter, eggs, milk nor cheese were used, the normal substitute was almonds. They were usually pounded and boiled to make milk of almonds, and it is not surprising that they would often use more than a pound a day.

Besides the everyday fish, the peas and onions were something of an extra touch. Dried peas were boiled to make a kind of thick soup or pottage. The onions were also boiled, then fried and often added to the purée of peas. This was one of those basic dishes which was made with bacon on meat days, or could be made with whale on a fish day. The apples were a great luxury, especially in February, and must have been specially provided for the abbot. Actually, very few fruits are mentioned in this account; only apples, pears, and once – in June – strawberries. The usual English dessert in the thirteenth century was dried or preserved fruits, such as figs or dates or raisins, eaten with nuts. These dried fruits and nuts do not come into the general accounts, but are listed in the special account for spices and were kept under lock and key in the countess's wardrobe.

The dishes and napkins mentioned in Wednesday's accounts imply that supplies were running short. The countess seems to have had to replace cups, dishes, and earthenware pots fairly frequently for the cook. No doubt the thirteenth-century kitchen was no more exempt from breakage than its modern successor. Cups of precious metal, such as silver and ornamented with jewels, were one of the visible signs of wealth, and often served as royal presents. In fact, the queen herself had once sent Simon two silver cups and a silver pot, worth 21 marks.[12] In times of financial need, such items were convenient security for loans with the money-lenders, Christian or Jew; but even a wealthy household would have only a few of these precious objects. The dishes were serving dishes, and possibly bowls for liquid food. Instead of individual plates, trenchers were used for solid food. A trencher was a flat piece of bread, about six inches wide and four inches high, from two to four days old, and thus hard enough to provide a solid foundation. After the meal, these trenchers and extra sops – i.e. pieces of bread used to sop up the gravies – were gathered and given to the poor with the other left-overs. Napkins were essential, since knives and fingers were the usual implements, although the countess seems to have had a few spoons. After the meal was finished, the servers brought round basins of warm water, perfumed with herbs, so that greasy fingers could be rinsed.

These two accounts for February give some idea of the basic pattern in Lent in a relatively small household. In March the earl came to spend two weeks at Odiham with a very large retinue, and left just before Easter. The impact on the household is measured in one day of the countess's account, the remaining two weeks were on the earl's own roll.

> Thursday (March 19), for the Earl and the Countess; Grain, 4 quarters bought, price 22s.; 1½ quarters from castle stores. Wine, 18½ sextaries. Beer bought, 240 gallons, for 14s. *Kitchen* 1,000 herrings from castle stores and 700 herrings. Sea fish, 26s. ½d. Sea-wolves, 14s. 7½d. Fish from Stanes, 10s. Almonds, 36 lbs, for the aforesaid expenses. *Stables* Hay for 334 horses, from stores. Oats from store, 18½ quarters; item, by purchase, for 9 quarters, 3 bushels; 18s. 9d.
>
> Sum 105s. 5d.[13]

The quantities and numbers are rather overwhelming. There is an amusing footnote to this provision of fish for the earl. Apparently, he was not satisfied with what Eleanor had been able to obtain, for she had to send several servants off to Farnham, eight miles away, where the bishop of Winchester had some very famous fish ponds. There they remained for eleven days, catching fresh fish for the earl.[14]

No matter how large or important the company, the Lenten fast was most rigorously observed. During the rest of the year the emphasis was on meat, although Fridays and Saturdays and most Wednesdays were fish days. Outside of Lent, though, butter, eggs, and cheese could be used to break the monotony of fish. Here are the accounts for two Sundays; exemplifying some changes in the pattern:

> Sunday (April 26), for the Countess and Sir Richard, chaplain of Kemsing, and Sir John, rector of the church of Catherington, and the household; Grain, 7 bushels. Wine, 2 sextaries, 3 gallons. Beer, previously reckoned. *Kitchen* 1½ ox, 3 sheep, 6s. Calves, 3s. 3d. Chickens, 3s. 8d. 2 kids, from the castle stores. Eggs, 150 from rents. Eggs bought, 8½d. farthing. Milk, 2d. *Stables* Hay for 32 horses. Oats, 2 quarters, 1 bushel.
>
> Sum 23s. 9½d. farthing.[15]

Sunday (July 12), for the Countess and the aforesaid, there being present the burgesses of Sandwich and Winchelsea, the wife of Lord Ralph Darcy, Lord Peter de Bourton and his wife, Master John of London and others; Grain, 1½ quarter, previously reckoned. Wine, 2 sextaries, 3 gallon of red, from the castle stores; 1 sextary, 1 gallon of white, bought, previously reckoned. Beer, for 45 gallons, 22½d. *Kitchen* Half an ox from Brabourne, not reckoned, and 2 sheep, previously reckoned; one pig, from the same, previously reckoned. Poultry, 2s. 8d. Peas in pods, 2d. Eggs, 16d. Milk, 3½d. *Stables* Grass for 27 horses. Oats, 1 quarter, 6½ bushels, previously reckoned.

Sum 6s. 2d.[16]

The account for the Sunday in April deals with an ordinary day and ordinary visitors at the countess's castle at Odiham. Kemsing was one of the countess's Kentish manors, part of her original marriage-portion, but recently made over to her son Henry. The chaplain of Kemsing may well have been appointed by the earl or countess. At any rate, he accompanied the countess when she left Odiham and went across country to Dover. Incidentally, the church at Kemsing has the remnants of a thirteenth-century wheel of fortune painted on its wall.[17] Was it perhaps a reminder, or an illustration, of the de Montfort reliance on that fickle lady? Catherington in Hampshire was in the hundred of Finchesden where Simon de Montfort held Chawton from the king. According to the inquisition regarding the rebels, taken after the war was over, the parson of Catherington was reckoned as an adherent of the earl of Leicester.[18] The bread and wine and beer follow the same pattern as during Lent. On this Sunday, 188 gallons of beer had just been bought the day before, so there was some on hand. The noticeable difference is in the extensive use of meat, no vegetables or fruit being mentioned. It sounds like a very heavy meal, but it must be remembered that many of the extras were issued from the wardrobe and only listed as a new supply was bought and paid for. For example, rice was reckoned as a spice and bought in large quantities. Gingerbread, too, was on the spice account, as well as the nuts and dried fruits previously mentioned. Then, too, if vegetables were grown in the castle garden, they would not figure on the accounts at all.

The dinner of July 12 represented entertaining with a purpose. The countess was staying in Dover Castle, which was officially committed to her eldest son Henry, and was trying to ensure that the leading townspeople of the Cinque Ports should remain favourable to the Baronial cause. Actually, the burgesses must have been relatively few in number, or very abstemious, for they consumed no more wine or beer than was used under normal circumstances. The meat which came from Brabourne was yet another example of that manorial economy which provided stores on each manor. Brabourne, about 18 miles inland from Dover, was also one of the countess's Kentish manors. During her stay at Dover Castle, its bailiff was kept busy bringing over stores from the manor to the castle for the use of her household. Ultimately, that supply was exhausted or unable to reach Dover, for, during the last two weeks of the account, much of the meat is simply listed as having been received as booty. These examples are sufficient to show the ordinary form of the accounts, and the type of entry which can be found for every day. Once the pattern has been established, there is little change.

Two important and expensive items had to be brought from outside the normal manorial economy, wine and spices. The wine trade was the commercial basis for the connection between England and Gascony. Under medieval conditions of transport, it was much easier and less expensive to carry heavy, bulky goods by water than by road. Thus, it was simpler and more profitable for the Gascon merchants to peddle their wares in the English market, which was always in need of wine, than to try and sell their goods in France which had other closer sources of supply. Both red and white wine were used extensively. The accounts from the household roll, during the period when the household was at Dover, tell how much was used of each kind, but during the earlier period no distinction was made. The phrase "bastard wine" is often used during August. This is the term applied to all mixed and sweetened wines which seem to have been given to the household when the usual supplies of beer ran short. In the summer of 1265 – when prices were probably high because of the disturbance in the land – wine cost about 5d. a gallon, or 2od. a sextary. This is considerably higher than during an earlier and more peaceful period of King Henry's reign. In 1237, for example, an order was sent to the sheriff of Warwick and Leicester forbidding the sale of a sextary of red wine at more than 12d., and a sextary of white wine at more than 10d.[19]

Using such large amounts as they did, wine was undoubtedly a source of major expenditure. It was usually bought in large quantities and laid down for the year at their various residences. For example, in 1247, Eleanor had purchased 24 tuns of wine from a Gascon merchant. When it arrived in London in November, the king ordered it to be delivered to her without any hindrance or extra duties.[20] At the ordinary rate of consumption, a tun, which was 252 gallons, might have lasted two or three weeks. During the worried days at Dover, when there were many soldiers to be considered, a tun was used almost every second day. When Simon was seneschal of Gascony, he imported wine on his own boat,[21] no doubt at most advantageous rates. It is easy to see that a royal present of a few tuns of wine to those in his favour, a frequent practice of the king's, was a real financial contribution.

Spices were the other great expense, and their purchase had to be arranged, either in London or at one of the more important district fairs. Being valuable, and treated accordingly, spices were kept in the wardrobe under lock and key and only distributed to the cook in small quantities. The largest accounting for spices in the countess's household roll was made in settlement of purchases made by William de Wortham, up to Palm Sunday, for the countess and her brother Richard of Cornwall, at this time king of Germany, who was the Montfort's prisoner at Kenilworth. As befitted his rank and importance, the imprisonment really consisted in keeping him safely under their eyes in one of their most powerful strongholds, so that he could not lead a movement against them. From the evidence of the spices and clothes that were sent him, he lived in considerable luxury.

For 2 lbs. ginger and 2 lbs. pepper, 4s. For 20 lbs. of almonds, 4s. For 1 quarter of saffron, 2s. 6d. For bags, 2d. For 2 kettles, for the use of the Lord Amaury, 23s. ½d. . . . Also, for 150 lbs. of almonds, 42s. For 100 lbs. of rice, 14s. For 10 lbs. of pepper, 8s. 4d.

For 6 lbs. of cinnamon, 5s. For 6 lbs. of galingale, 9s. For 1 lbs. of saffron, 10s. For ½ lb. of cloves, 5s. For 10 lbs. of ginger, 15s. For 10 lbs. of sugar, 10s. Item, for sacks, 2d. For one frail of grapes (Figs?), 12s. For 200 pieces of whale, 34s. From this spicery sent to the lord king of Germany; 20 lbs. of almonds, 6s.; 5 lbs. of rice, 9d.; 2 lbs. of pepper, 20d.; 2 lbs. of cinnamon, 20d.; half a pound of galingale, 9d.; 1 lb. of ginger, 18d.; 2 lbs. of sugar, 2s.; and 20 pieces of whale.

Sum £12 7s. 2d.[22]

Some further spices were bought after Easter, after Pentecost, and at the end of July. It is evident that the consumption of spices was high, even allowing for the size of the household. With the constant use of salted meat and fish, it is not surprising that the cook was required to spice foods highly, but it seems to have been the custom for fresh meats as well.

What kind of meat dishes did they make out of these spices and large amounts of flesh? In a list of customary privileges owed to one of the leading tenants of a manor in Somerset, there is included a detailed description of the Christmas dinner which must be given him. It is illuminating as an example of what an English feast day dinner might be like for the members of the household, or those below the rank of nobility. John, with two friends, was to have two white loaves, as much beer as he and his friends could drink in the day, a mess of beef and bacon with mustard, one of browis of hen, and a cheese. Incidentally, if he could not come himself, he could send for his bread, beef and bacon, and two gallons of beer – a generous allowance for one day's drinking.[23] A recipe from the Menagier's cookbook gives a vivid idea of the type of seasoning in this browis or brewet, which was a cross between a thick soup and a thin stew. A cinnamon brewet consisted of pieces of poultry or other meat stewed in water and wine and then fried. Then, says the Menagier,

> Take raw dried almonds in their shells unpelled and great plenty of cinnamon and bray (pound) them very well and moisten them with broth or with beef broth and boil them with your meat; then bray ginger, cloves, and cardamon, etc., and let it be thick and red.[24]

To many of the other brewets saffron was added, for this herb was highly regarded in the Middle Ages, both for the taste and as a colouring agent for food. Rice seems to have been used much as it is to-day. Either it was an accompaniment for the meat course, in which case it was flavoured with beef dripping and saffron, or it was a kind of pudding, prepared with pounded almonds and sugar.[25] Spices were used for fish, too, but in their preparation the emphasis was put on vinegar, mustard, and fennel, all of which the countess also bought.

These expenses for spices, as well as the occasional entry for wax for candles, for the chapel and the hall, are recorded on the front of the roll and simply fitted into the daily expenditures whenever settlement was made. The other main types of payments were listed separately on the backs of the membranes. These entries dealt, above all, with wages. The unnamed servants, who had occupations of lesser importance, were paid every week or two weeks. They generally received $1\frac{1}{2}$d. a day. This group included all kinds of miscellaneous occupations – they guarded the countess's greyhounds, watched the sick horses or were foresters, although the master of the foresters, being more important, received 2d. a day. The servants a notch above them were hired on a yearly basis. For example, Simon the Fisherman was paid 5s. the half-year, from Michaelmas to Easter,[26] but when Hande the servant from the mill, was paid off with two years' wages, he received only 10s.[27] The nurse of young Eleanor, the countess's daughter, was given 12d. in Easter week. She had already been paid 4s. two weeks before.[28]

Besides the money wages, it was up to the countess to provide most of her servants with a certain number of pairs of hose and shoes a year, and probably robes at Christmas as well. In addition, she paid their expenses when they went off to do her errands in other parts of the kingdom. It is interesting to see that many of these relatively unimportant servants were actually crisscrossing the country, from Odiham to London, to Dover, to Kenilworth, even to York, Hereford, and Cardiff. It is a striking tribute to the basic stability of the medieval population that, even in the middle of civil war, the peaceful use of the roads for commerce and travel seemed to go on much as usual. There was, in fact, quite a network of messengers carrying letters, and the amounts paid to them featured large in the accounts.

Obviously, during the spring and summer of 1265, it was most important that the countess of Leicester should be in close touch with her husband and sons, in order to follow the various moves in the political situation. So some of the well-trusted servants, like Slingaway and Gobithesti and Truebody, carried letters to the earl and her sons. Orders were sent, for purchases and other items, to her officials, like William de Wortham and Richard de Havering. In some cases a friend, like the Prioress of Amesbury, sought a favour from the king, who was in the earl's control, and the request was forwarded through Eleanor. But there seem to have been other less businesslike letters too. The countess corresponded with the countess of Lincoln and Gloucester and Isabella de Fortibus, and young Eleanor even wrote to the Lord Edward, her cousin, while he was still a hostage.[29] Payment was made to messengers at both ends of their trip, and these, too, are listed in the accounts. Again, the range of correspondence is surprising, and serves as a reminder of the wide scope of the Leicester interests. There were letters from Lourdes in Bigorre (the county on which Simon had a tenuous claim), from the Lady Loretta de Montfort, eldest daughter of Simon's brother Amaury, as well as a wide variety of English correspondents.

The evidence both of letters and individual travel demonstrate the ease with which people moved, and the wide extent of their connection. This, of course, is primarily true of a certain social class and their dependents, but travel was fairly widespread. Chaucer has shown us the extraordinary mixture of people found on the roads of England in the fourteenth century. Such household accounts as these make it obvious that the thirteenth century was almost as mobile as the fourteenth. A pilgrimage was a perennial medieval reason or excuse for travel among all social classes. Where the great noble would go on crusade or to an overseas shrine like Le Puy or Compostella, one of the countess's serving-maids would go the fifty miles from Odiham to Chichester, and have her expenses paid by her mistress.[30]

Another item which constantly appears on the back of the

membranes as one of the miscellaneous accounts is the amount spent on clothes. The countess seems to have worn undergarments of prepared sheepskin,[31] – winter garments, one would hope. Both noble men and women wore a tunic – the man's sometimes calf length, sometimes full length like the woman's. This was cut perfectly plain, bloused around the waist with a girdle, and had long sleeves. Often there was a super-tunic, a surcoat, which was sleeveless and only came to the knees. Over the tunic was worn an almost circular cloak, fastened with a clasp at the neck. The girdle and the clasp were particularly valuable, and were often given as presents on important occasions or to honoured visitors. For example, both Amaury de Montfort and his young sister Eleanor gave clasps to the son of Sir John de Haye when he visited them at Dover. Amaury's was much more valuable, as befitted his greater age and dignity.[32]

But apart from the splendour of their ornaments, what distinguished the dress of the wealthy was the luxury of the materials used. The finest cloths were linen, sindon – which was either satin or very fine linen – and the ultra-fashionable rayed, or striped, cloths which came from France or Italy. But the chief material for both men and women was woollen cloth, the manufacture of which was a flourishing industry in England during the thirteenth century. The different names for cloth, such as perse, scarlet, russet, described not always the colour, but the fineness of the cloth. Scarlet was the finest of all the wool cloths but it was not necessarily red. It was most used by the royal court, and Eleanor arranged for the purchase of some for Richard of Cornwall and his son Edmund, while they were in custody at Kenilworth, as well as for some rayed cloth and sindon for their summer wear.[33] Perse was a very fine deep blue cloth, died only with woad, one of the more expensive dyes. The retinue which accompanied young Richard de Montfort to Bigorre in September 1265 were given cloth of perse for their travels. The coarsest homespun-like cloth was russet, which was given as alms to the poor, as robes and hose for the least important servants, and was a visible sign of grief and poverty. Eleanor herself had worn it thirty years before in her first widowhood. When she heard of the death of the earl, she resumed it again, for the household roll mentions 34 ells of russet purchased for her own use.[34] When woollen cloth was new, the nap was very long. After it had been worn for some time, it was shorn, instead of washed. This was repeated as often as the material could stand it. Even the shearing seems to have been fairly expensive. In one case it cost the countess 12d.[35] Hicque the tailor was one of the countess's servants and was frequently sent up to London to buy cloth or have it sheared. Some washing was done, for there was a laundress in the household named Petronilla, and she received hose on one occasion. Besides that, there was one payment for laundry for 15d. in the spring.[36]

This discussion of the various items of clothing may sound frivolous. But, it seems evident that, even before the shock of her husband's death, Eleanor was much less absorbed in the love of fine clothes for which Adam Marsh had reproached her some years before. Certainly, the materials she ordered for her brother and his son were much finer than those on her personal account. It is only fair, too, to balance the record with the regular amount of alms given to the poor, which also appeared consistently in the accounts. They were sometimes given money; usually they received food and drink at the door; occasionally, they were fed in the hall. As soon as the news of the earl's death reached his wife, probably August 11th, there were offerings for his soul.

It is a temptation to linger among the other miscellaneous items that turn up in this household account, for they suggest so many new avenues of exploration. There is the boy who was paid 4d. for getting a crane out of the well.[37] Were they worried about the water-supply, and did they eat the crane? We know that cranes were a great delicacy at important feasts. There are four spoons that were repaired *with* eight silver pennies.[38] There are the 240 parchments bought at London through one of the friars for a breviary for the young Eleanor, and later the payment to the clerk at Oxford, for its writing.[39] Indeed, carefully analysed, the countess's household roll could serve as a text for a full discussion of many of the facets of medieval life, but that is beyond the scope of this chapter. Its various items will be mentioned later as they throw light on the mounting tempo of war and the shock of defeat.

There was the search for horses, the hurried cross-country trip of the household, the payments to William the engineer for improving Kenilworth's fortifications, and finally the messengers who went to plead the countess's cause with the restored King Henry and Richard of Cornwall. All these give evidence of the rapid fall of the Montfort fortunes.

Having looked at these details of household administration, let us try to make one coherent picture of the noble household at dinner in the hall. Grosseteste laid down a series of injunctions on how everyone should behave. The primary rule of medieval hospitality was that all guests should be received courteously and with good cheer. They were to be addressed courteously, lodged and served. Whether the lady of the house was there or not, her knights, chaplains, and servants should show honour to her friends. All the household was to gather for dinner and supper in the hall, and could only be excused for grave reasons.

This was true even of the countess. She was exhorted to eat in hall before her people, despite sickness or fatigue, to show herself and supervise her servants. The countess of Leicester observed this practice so consistently that it comes almost as a shock to observe her absence from hall during the black week in which she wrestled with her grief over her husband's tragic death. Once the countess was seated at the high table, the butler with the cup and the servant with the bread approached the table before grace was said. The marshal of the household was responsible for the smooth running of the meals. He appointed servants to wait on the high table, and the less distinguished side tables, with their drink of wine or beer. Also, he had to see that the lower members of the household were supervised. After the guests and the freemen had been seated, the servants came in. They were supposed to sit down together and rise together, as soon as they had finished, with no quarrelling among themselves. Meanwhile, the servers brought out the dishes of food from the kitchen. Normally, the household would be served with two meat dishes and two lighter dishes at dinner, and with one not so substantial meat dish at supper. Cheese might also be added at supper, and cheese pies seem to have been very popular. The countess's plate was to be so heaped that she could practise fully the medieval courtesy of sharing the choicest morsels from her own plate with her most distinguished guests, or with those whom she wished to honour. While everyone was allowed to eat as much as they wanted, the knights and gentlemen in livery were especially enjoined to watch their manners and keep their livery neat and clean at meals. The leftovers from dinner and supper were gathered and, in a well-run household, were distributed in an orderly fashion among the poor, the sick, and the beggars.[40]

The code of behaviour of the household was as much governed by rules as its accounting system. The household itself served as a tiny community, in which each had his own status, his own rights, and duties. It resembled in miniature the household of the king which, again, was supposed to be the pattern of the realm. This kind of loosely knit but efficient organization lay behind the activities of all the great nobles, and served them in England and beyond. For the members of such a household, life was neither as dull or as confining as has often been thought. As for the earl and countess, and their senior officials, they were indeed cosmopolitan. Their horizons were not limited by England, but by the ties of relationship, self-interest, and political manoeuvre which led them through England, France, Gascony, and Bigorre. Their household was enough of a unit to continue to function in much the same way, wherever the residence of the earl and countess of Leicester, be it Odiham, Bordeaux, or the castle of Lourdes.

7

The King's Lieutenant; Gascony

Since the earl of Leicester's return from crusade and his share in the unfortunate royal expedition in Poitou, Simon had lived the life of the typical great lord, putting down roots in England, extending and deepening his acquaintances and friendships. It was a peaceful interlude after the warlike activity of the previous years. England was more or less at peace, and King Henry revelled in the quiet years. They gave him the chance to carry out his many schemes for building and decorating. For example, Henry arranged with his master craftsman, Edward of Westminster, for a new royal seat in the great hall at Westminster Palace, made of marble and flanked with two brass leopards.[1] Then, as the king travelled the country, he left behind instructions for his sheriffs to provide improvements in the comfort or the beauty of the various royal establishments. At Geddington (Northants), he had several windows with glass put in, including one in the chamber "where the countess of Leicester lay".[2] The old mantel for the fireplace of the king's chamber at Clarendon (Wilts) was to be torn down and replaced with a more decorated one, adorned with a painting of the wheel of fortune. Typical of Henry's meticulous interest in these matters, his order specified that the paintings in his chamber were to be covered with canvas while the work was being done, so that they would not be damaged.[3]

But the king's life was unfortunately not bounded by these artistic concerns. These relatively quiet years saw difficulties with the pope, over his financial exactions; with the rebellious Welsh; and, above all, with Gascony. In 1247 began the Poitevin "invasion" of England, when the king's stepbrothers and sisters and their followers swarmed to the court of their royal relative like hungry locusts. All of these things meant further strains on the government of England.

Meanwhile, the recapture of Jerusalem by the Moslems in 1244 had caused great concern in the west. At the same Council of Lyons to which the great barons and clergy of England had complained over the papal financial exactions, Pope Innocent IV declared a general crusade, hoping to rally the forces of Western Europe to regain the Holy Places. King Louis of France answered the call with alacrity, but his preparations took some time. It was June of 1248 before he could lead the expedition away from Paris on the first stage of its long journey. King Louis's imminent departure from France aroused a wave of crusading fervour in England as well. Many Englishmen took the cross. Among them was Simon de Montfort who planned to lead the English contingent. Matthew Paris maliciously insisted on reviving the old matter of Simon's "ill-advised" marriage and Eleanor's vow of chastity.[4] But the earl of Leicester was not destined to fulfil his crusading vow nor to share the rigours of Louis's campaign. Another, and more difficult, mission was committed to his charge. On May 1, 1248, in a letter patent from Windsor, King Henry committed the government of Gascony to "his beloved brother-in-law and faithful Simon de Montfort" for a term of seven years.[5] The king considered this charge so important that it even superseded a crusading pledge.

Gascony was the last remnant of the great inheritance in Southern France which Eleanor of Aquitaine had brought to Henry II and tried to pass on to her sons.[6] Roughly defined, the duchy of Aquitaine ran from the river Loire to the Pyrenees and covered south-western France. This district was a seething caldron of shifting alliances among greater and lesser feudal lords, striving both to increase their own lands and to lessen their submission to any overlord. Gascony was merely the southern section of the duchy from the Garonne to the Pyrenees, and the title of duke of Gascony was merged in the larger title of duke of Aquitaine.

So long as the old Queen Eleanor lived – and she died in 1204 at the ripe age of 80 – she strove unceasingly to advance the

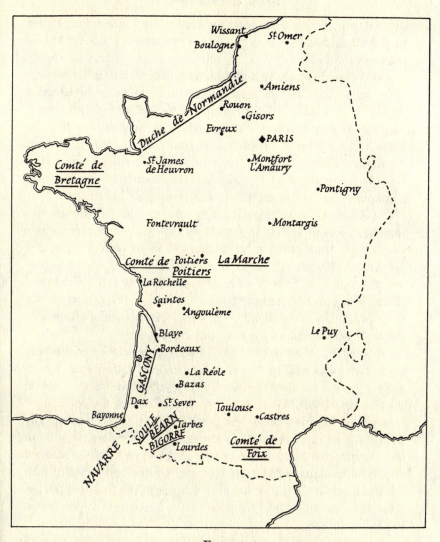

France

interests of her sons. Soon after her death, Aquitaine was involved in John's difficulties with Philip Augustus over his refusal to answer to the court of France, although summoned as a French vassal. When Normandy and Anjou were confiscated, by process of feudal law, the French king could, and did, enforce his decrees. Aquitaine was included, too, in this wholesale confiscation, but it was not so easy to carry out immediately the judgments of the French court there. However, gradually the northern part of Aquitaine, Poitou, was absorbed into the French kingdom, and slowly the quarrelling nobles, like the counts of La Marche, recognized the feudal suzerainty of the king of France.

But Gascony was linked to England by ties of commercial interest. Gascony's greatest export was its wine, and there was a much surer market for it in England than in Gascony's nearer neighbours, France or Spain. English grain was a valuable import and this bulky traffic was most easily handled by ship. The towns of Bordeaux and Bayonne, above all, relied on English trade for their prosperity, for Bayonne built the ships in which Bordeaux shipped the wine of all the surrounding districts.

Despite these commercial links, however, the relation of Gascony to England was seldom peaceful. Simon de Montfort had seen in 1242–3 how little trust the English king could afford to place in his Gascon vassals. Also he had learned a little of the continuous struggle for position of all the petty nobility of the duchy. The situation had not improved in the ensuing five years. It was, in fact, aggravated by sporadic revolts of the nobles, and continued efforts by the kings of France, Navarre, Castile and Aragon, who tried to assert their real or imaginary rights in the troubled duchy. This explosive situation led to the earl of Leicester's appointment in 1248.

The recent English seneschals in Gascony had been men of second rank, incapable of the task which confronted them. They were handicapped, too, by lack of power, for the Gascons refused to recognize the authority of anyone but the king himself. Discussing the matter nearly fifteen years later, Simon claimed that the king and queen had begged him to take up the government of Gascony. Certainly, he laid down some fairly stiff condi-

tions before he would agree to try and restore the duchy to peace
and quiet adherence to the king. He was to be the direct representative of the king, a lieutenant instead of just a subordinate
official, and his term of office was fixed at seven years. In other
words, he was not to be removable at the king's whim. The issues
and rents of the land were to go to him for the necessary maintenance of order, and the king was also to aid him with extra
knights and money to pay them. But in these very terms of the
agreement lay the seed of future difficulties. Simon felt that he
had a free hand to do as he saw fit. King Henry felt that he retained
the right of supervision, and if need be, of interference as the
overlord of the duchy.

During the summer months after his appointment, Simon was
putting his affairs in order at home, and building up supplies for
his new charge. As a matter of prudence, he immediately requested
from the king the postponement of all his debts until fifteen days
after Michaelmas, that is, the middle of October.[7] Then, while the
king was sending orders for the equipment of ships and the
provision of the promised contingent of knights, Simon crossed the
Channel and went to the court of France. From the tactical point
of view, one of the first settlements that had to be made to ensure
the peace of Gascony was to renew the truce with the French king
that was about to expire. This truce had been agreed upon after
King Henry's unfortunate and fruitless expedition to Gascony in
1242–3, but with King Louis away on crusade, the queen-regent,
Blanche of Castile, had no desire to embark on another war in the
south of France. The renewal of the truce was easily arranged and
with the pact concluded at Lorris at the end of September,[8] Simon
could travel south to the duchy with at least one of his problems
settled.

Before dealing with the independent and rebellious nobles of the
territory, he resolved to make his task easier by neutralizing the
king of Navarre. The kingdom of Navarre stretched north across
the Pyrenees into the southern sections of Gascony. It was a close
neighbour of the viscounty of Béarn, ruled by Gaston de Béarn,
son of the prodigiously fat Garsenda, and cousin of the English
queen. Béarn constantly asserted its independence from the

overlordship of the English king as duke of Gascony. It was also the centre of revolt and rebellion, often encouraged and assisted by Navarre.

The king of Navarre at this time had particular reasons for being interested in the affairs of the duchy of Gascony, for he was Count Thibault of Champagne, one of the most powerful lords of northern France, who had inherited Navarre through a failure of heirs in the main line. Naturally he was interested in affairs to the north of him. A man of many parts, he was a well-known poet as well as the commander of the French contingent on crusade in 1239. By the end of October Simon de Montfort had met with King Thibault at Ainhoa, a border town in the Pyrenees, and they had come to an agreement to submit all the disputes between the king of Navarre and the king of England to the judgment of arbiters.[9] This agreement was sent on to England for King Henry's ratification. In these first two moves Simon had succeeded in pacifying two of the four kings whose enmity was mentioned in his original commission. The other two, Castile and Aragon, were not at the moment a great threat.

The next, and more difficult, task of the king's lieutenant was to restore order among the turbulent Gascons themselves. The main city of Gascony, and the basis of its economic wealth, was Bordeaux, the great port and centre of the wine trade on the mouth of the Garonne. It was a very independent commune and had its own municipal government, but it was torn by strife between the two leading families, the Coloms and the Delsolers. During the early days of his rule, Simon found the two families at peace, for they had concluded a truce shortly before his arrival. The administration of the duchy was not, however, merely carried on from Bordeaux, and indeed, such a suggestion would lend an illusion of stability and settled government which was very much at variance with the facts. The feudal jurisdiction of Gascony was divided among four courts, whose centres were at Bordeaux and Bazas in the north, and Saint Sever and Dax in the south. These were the courts to which the king's lieutenant came. He received there the homage of the vassals of that area, swore to govern them according to the laws and customs of the country, and sat in judgment on the infractions of feudal law.

Simon followed the normal procedure of appearing at these courts, but he came re-enforced by a considerable part of that military force with which King Henry had provided him. Thus he was able to have his decisions carried out immediately, and many of the wild local knights, who were little better than armed brigands, found themselves imprisoned and their powers clipped. Such redoubtable characters as the viscounts of Soule and Gramont were put in prison and held for several years without trial, or put up at an extortionate ransom. The burgesses of the smaller towns also felt themselves aggrieved, as the earl of Leicester overrode their cherished custom of only having to go to Bordeaux to pay homage to the king himself. The king's lieutenant was supposed to come to them, but this Simon refused to do. If they did not send deputies to him at St Sever, they too would be held for fine or imprisonment.

But the greatest threat to the peace of the duchy was Viscount Gaston de Béarn. Here, too, Simon moved rapidly to consolidate his position, and in this case he was aided by family ties. The viscounty of Béarn was bordered on the east by the county of Bigorre, which was ruled at this time by the Countess Perronelle, who was Simon's sister-in-law, the widow of his elder brother Guy. The complications of Perronelle's five marriages and the involved tangle of events and disputed inheritances through which Simon, rather than Gaston de Béarn, acquired title to the county of Bigorre, must be dealt with in a separate chapter. But it is relevant to the earl's effort to gain control of the duchy of Gascony that he made an agreement with the aged countess Perronelle soon after his arrival in Gascony. He was to have the guardianship of Bigorre for a rent of 7,000s. (Morlaas)* annually. Thus he was placed in a commanding position on the east flank of Béarn. The viscount of Soule, Gaston de Béarn's neighbour on the west, was

---

* Morlaas was a town in central Béarn where most of the money current in south-western France at this time was coined. In giving sums the name of the place was normally given with the amount, because of the great discrepancies in value between coins minted in different localities.

held as a prisoner for ransom for not appearing at court. Despite the complaints of the burgesses of Dax, who had suffered heavily from the depredations of Gaston de Béarn, Simon found it wise to make a truce with his most dangerous enemy, rather than to fight with him. But the effectiveness of the truce was much enhanced by this planned campaign of isolation and containment.

Thus, the first three months of Simon's lieutenancy were a triumphal success. He came back to England with a good-sized retinue for the Christmas festivities, and was present for the celebration of another feast of St Edward the Confessor at St Peter's, Westminster, i.e. Westminster Abbey, on January 5th, 1249. Matthew Paris echoes the admiration of the king and council for the success of his achievements. The earl was flushed with the heady exhilaration of the submission of Gaston de Béarn and the disarming of less important nobles. It is easy to believe that Matthew's report of Simon's words is nearly accurate. The monk wrote that "if the king's council agreed, the earl returning to Gascony, would destroy all the enemies of the king".[10] But the Gascon problem was not to be so easily settled. For the moment, King Henry was pleased with the work of his brilliant, but brusque brother-in-law. As yet there had been no back-wash of complaints from Gascony, none of the quibbles over funds that so consistently marred the relations between the earl and his royal brother-in-law. Simon felt safe in remaining in England until the beginning of June, when he seems to have crossed at the same time as the English contingent for the crusade which he was originally to have led.

However, Gascony would not stay quiet for long, especially when the heavy hand of the king's lieutenant was removed. Simon had hardly got back to Bordeaux when real trouble developed. On the eve of the municipal elections, fighting broke out between the two main groups, the Coloms and the Delsolers. The news came to the earl in bed. Arming quickly, with a few knights, he rushed off to the fight. The Coloms – for whom he already was felt to have shown a preference – followed his lead. The Delsolers were gradually overpowered. Rostein Delsoler, as the leader of the family, was forced to admit defeat. The following morning Simon took hostages from both sides, but let those of the Coloms go, while he retained the Delsolers. Rostein, though honourably treated in his imprisonment in the castle of Bordeaux, died in custody. There were losses too among the earl's party, two of his knights and his standard-bearer were killed.[11] The Delsoler family felt themselves abused, both by the earl's repressive measures and by the reprisals of the "Columbines", as the party of the Colom were called. Their complaints and the replies of the earl form a large share of the depositions which figured so largely in the earl's trial three years later. But, as in many cases where anger had blinded the participants, it is almost impossible to find the full story. Certain things emerge, however. Since Simon had seized the vineyards – their most valuable asset – and other property of the Delsolers, King Henry forced him to restore them when the aggrieved parties sent messengers to him in England.[12] But messengers from the other party in Bordeaux soon gave the king a more balanced idea of the complications of his tumultuous duchy.

At the end of November, 1249, the king addressed a long letter to "his faithful and beloved Simon de Montfort, seneschal of Gascony" – the only time that he is given that title, surprisingly enough. The beginning of it was complimentary, praising the earl for his loyalty and his diligence, and promising him his deserved reward. But then the king went on to warn his lieutenant that there were troubles brewing again, and suggestions of treachery. The representatives of the Delsoler faction in Bordeaux were ordered to be sent back to Gascony for trial. But the king warned Simon that, though he should punish the criminals so that they would not start fresh troubles, the punishment ought not to be greater than the offence and that, while the trial was pending, they should not be treated as suspects, "that their judge himself be not suspected".[13] The repressive measures of the earl of Leicester had been very harsh, perhaps justifiably so, but they inevitably had aroused hated memories of the asperity and strictness of Simon the Crusader, whose uncompromising faith and ferocious battle tactics had terrified all southern France. Once again, Matthew Paris sums up the general English attitude.

However, the celebrated earl, desirous in all things to take after his father, and either to follow in his father's footsteps or to surpass him, subdued the insolence of the other rebels of the lord king at Bordeaux and in all Gascony.[14]

The year 1249 ended with Simon in control in Gascony, and the rebels, both among the nobles and faction-torn burgesses of the main towns, apparently subdued. There is outside testimony to this in a letter to Count Alphonse of Poitiers by one of his clerics. The count of Toulouse had died at the end of September, 1249, and Count Alphonse was the heir, through his wife. Since the count of Poitiers was on crusade with his brother King Louis, Alphonse's chaplain went to settle certain matters of litigation between Simon and the count. He also gives us a glimpse into the earl's domestic life. According to his letter, he was invited to visit the earl and countess at La Réole, and he describes for his master the state of the duchy. "Know that he holds Gascony in good estate and all obey him, and dare undertake naught against him."[15] This is the first reference to Eleanor's presence in Gascony. Although it is not possible to prove conclusively, it would seem likely that she was with him much of the time. There is a long gap in the presents of deer which the king was in the habit of giving his sister. The only reference is one in July, 1250, when she was given ten deer from the New Forest.[16] Then, too, many of Adam Marsh's letters to the earl and countess were written while they were in Gascony, but they are, unfortunately, undated. While Simon was away from England, he had entrusted two of his sons to the household of the bishop of Lincoln. During these years in Gascony, the earl and countess had a daughter who died very young and was buried in the Dominican convent at Bordeaux. In her memory the earl gave them money for the construction of an infirmary.[17]

But while affairs in Gascony seemed so favourable to Simon's efforts, the undermining of his power began in England. In the usual fashion of all feudal rebels, those accused and punished by the earl of Leicester sought redress in the court of their overlord, the English king. Above all, Gaston de Béarn, fortified by the ties of kinship, sought to be restored to his old position of independence. King Henry could never maintain a single policy for long, especially when it ran counter to the claims of relationship. Just after Christmas, 1249, he pardoned Gaston de Béarn and his followers together with Arnold Segin, who had abetted him, and returned them to favour.[18]

Meanwhile, Simon had been planning to return to England in June, going first to France about the business of the truce, which was to be extended for another five years,[19] and dealing with the English king's affairs at the *parlement* of Paris. But by Easter eve (March 26th) he had heard of trouble brewing in Gascony and wrote a long letter to King Henry about his problems. When the king had pardoned Gaston, he had aroused the hopes of the lesser Gascon nobility that they would get their lands back from the hands of the king's lieutenant. Since this had so far proved impossible, they decided to try and seize them by armed force. Simon insisted, as he reiterated in his later defence of his government of Gascony, that the great lords hated him because he upheld the king's rights and those of the poor men. This was probably a fair claim. Certainly it was the poor and the lowly in England who later treated him as a saint. His description of the type of warfare also explains why it was so difficult to keep the country quiet for long. It was conducted as guerrilla warfare, where the plundering barons rode by night "in the manner of thieves", pillaging, and seizing the crops and goods of the lands that lay in their way. Simon announced his arrival in England for Whitsuntide – the middle of May – and gave notice of his need for money, as the king of France had detained all the rents which Henry had sent him. However, he felt that the state of the duchy and the armament of the castles was sufficient until he got back to Gascony, especially as he had sent one of the best of his lieutenants, Vital de Caupenne.[20]

Simon arrived in England at the beginning of May and settled with the king for the money he needed. In January the king had ordered that all the Irish revenues should be delivered to him for use in strengthening the king's castles and cities in Gascony. As well he was to have 1,000 marks, half from the taxation of the Jews, and the other half from perquisites and rents in the city of London. All these moneys were to be sent out to him by Richard de Havering, his steward,[21] and it was probably these that he claimed the king of France was holding. So in May, the king arranged with one of the foreign merchants for a loan of 1,800 marks to Simon, payable at the Exchequer the following Michaelmas, and also for £803 from his own pocket, to substitute for the knights which he was supposed to have provided.[22] Although Simon left England after the middle of May to see what had been happening in Gascony, he had managed to impress on the king the need for further sums for the defence of the castles which he had fortified and garrisoned for the king. In September, a further £1,000 from the money of the Jews was to be paid to Simon de Montfort's messenger at the New Temple, for strengthening the castle of Cussac, but only for that purpose.[23] Already in July, two of the king's officials had been appointed to go to Gascony by the feast of the Assumption (August 15th) to audit his accounts and see the use made of the money sent him by the king.[24]

But soon after the earl's return to Gascony, in a letter reminiscent of affairs the previous year, the king warned him that there were again rumours of plots against the peace and security of Gascony, led this time by the viscount of Fronsac and certain officials.[25] Simon, for the moment, felt himself secure. He had again subdued Bordeaux, and had control of most of the strategic castles of the duchy. But his confidence was premature. One of the lesser nobles made an alliance with Gaston de Béarn and handed over to him the strategically valuable castles of Bazas and Caseneuve.[26] The Gascons, whose appreciation of authority was only increased by the distance of its effectiveness, rose with enthusiasm against the harsh and thorough rule of the king's lieutenant. This time Simon had neither the men nor the supplies needed to quell the uprising. Flight to England for aid seemed the only possibility.

On the feast of the Epiphany (January 6, 1251), the earl arrived in London with only three men-at-arms, "hurried and inglorious", to beseech the king's aid against the Gascon rebels. He reminded the king of the treachery of the Gascons during the campaign of 1242–3 and of their lack of compassion for the queen when she was pregnant and sick. The king was moved by the earl's reminder and promised him the necessary aid, but he warned him that the complaints from Gascony about his conduct were coming thick and fast. The main item was that Simon had improperly imprisoned and put in chains those who came to him peacefully, or whom he summoned to his courts as if in good faith.[27] In other words, the harshness of Simon's tactics had put him beyond the pale of feudal regulations, and in the manner of his rule the Gascons had a legitimate complaint. But, despite the implied rebuke, the king gave him money from the treasury, and the earl raised more from his earldom of Leicester and the lands of Gilbert of Umfravill, which he had in wardship.

Returning to Gascony with a large company, including a force of Brabant mercenaries, Simon found the conspiracy against him ready to blaze into active war.[28] He was armed with a papal indult which protected him from any sentence of excommunication or interdict proclaimed by any cleric in Gascony without a special papal mandate – a valuable privilege when bishops had been known to excommunicate their diocese for affairs as trifling as a lost falcon. At the end of January Pope Innocent IV also sent a letter to the bishop of Agen encouraging him to make peace between Simon de Montfort and the nobles of Gascony.[29] Simon made war against the league of disaffected citizens so successfully that the confederation was forced to make peace with him by the end of May and by midsummer the duchy was once again firmly under his control.[30] Even the uprising of the Pastoureaux – a group of French shepherds and common folk – who were plaguing much of France did not particularly disturb Gascony. Although they had attacked the University of Orleans, burned books and had thrown many in the Loire, when they came to Bordeaux they were resisted by Earl Simon and were, as the chronicler says, "dispersed, conquered and confused".[31]

By this time, though, King Henry had lost much of his enthusiasm for the vigorous methods of his brother-in-law. Although he wanted a submissive Gascony, which he already had in mind to turn over to his son Edward, now in his thirteenth year, he detested the stream of complaints which the rebellious Gascons constantly addressed to him. When Earl Simon and Countess Eleanor took ship for England at the end of 1251 they sailed from

Wissant in the company of Guy de Lusignan, the king's step-brother. They were driven back at first by a contrary wind in the Channel and, according to Matthew Paris – a malicious witness in any matter that concerned the king's French brothers – the French wits at the inn in Wissant, where they had to take refuge while they waited for the wind to change, mocked them over the great number of the king's brothers in England. They all went there just to fill their pockets, but finally even the sea threw them back.[32] The king went to meet them on their way from Dover to London, not out of respect for the earl of Leicester or his sister, but only because he wished to do honour to Guy de Lusignan. However, the earl was enough in favour to be taken to York for the Christmas festivities, and the marriage of Alexander of Scotland to Henry's daughter Margaret. But this time, there was no easy solution to the problem.

While the king was in York, he decided to appoint a commission of arbiters to settle the continually vexed question as to whether he owed Simon money, or Simon owed it to him. On January 4th, a commission of notable bishops and magnates were appointed to deal with the question. They included Walter Cantilupe, the bishop of Worcester and one of Simon's staunchest supporters, as well as Richard of Cornwall, and three of the Lusignan half-brothers.[33] Yet within two days – perhaps influenced by further complaints from Gascony – the king had changed his method of dealing with the question. He adopted one far less favourable to the earl. First, he appointed Henry de Wingham, one of his confidential clerks and later chancellor and bishop of London, and Roscelin de Fos, the master of the Temple in England, to go to Gascony. They were to investigate the situation and report on it to him. On the way they were to stop in France and deal with Blanche, the queen-regent, concerning complaints about infringements of the truce.[34] On the same day King Henry wrote to all the important individuals and leading men of the main towns to send their representatives to England in the octave of Easter so that he could hear their complaints. In other words, the king was arranging for a commission of enquiry into Simon's behaviour in Gascony.[35] These letters were given to the two commissioners to deliver as the opportunities presented themselves.

Neither Henry of Wingham nor the Master of the Temple delayed much on their mission. In a long letter, written from Gascony on March 6th, they gave the king a detailed description of the result of their efforts so far. They had stopped to see Queen Blanche at Melun, but hurried to get on to Gascony because they had heard rumours of much trouble there. They met Geoffrey de Lusignan, another of the king's half-brothers, at Tours on their way south. He had been begged by William Pigorel, Simon's lieutenant, to bring horses and arms to his aid, because the burgesses of La Réole were besieging the royal castle there. So the commissioners joined this armed force and met Pigorel and his army at the town of Gironde, near La Réole. They went on from there to deliver the king's letters to the archbishop of Bordeaux and the other notables to whom they were addressed.

The Gascons refused to come unless they could be assured of an effective truce, and unless they could also be assured that Earl Simon would be in England and not on his way to Gascony. The commissioners announced that a truce had been made till June 24th (St John's day) and that the Gascons had promised to appear in the king's court if they were sent the proper safe-conducts and it was clearly recognized that going to England was not a precedent. All this was done in the presence of Geoffrey de Lusignan. The messenger was sent off with this interim report because, as they said, "Gascony is so upset, that we cannot tell you anything certain either now or later."[36] Immediately, upon hearing from Gascony, the king wrote the earl, obviously in high temper, as there are none of the usual polite phrases. The letter was merely addressed "to the earl of Leicester". It commanded him to be present before the king a month after Easter to hear the Gascon complaints and warned him that grave harm might arise if he went to Gascony.[37] The stage was set for the great trial.

A good deal is known about this trial of the earl of Leicester, for there are the reports of several witnesses, varying in their partialities. First, there are the group of complaints by the various groups and individuals in Gascony, which were presented before the king and have been kept in the family archives.[38] Then, Simon's great friend, Adam Marsh, was present at the trial, and wrote a long account of it to Bishop Grosseteste.[39] And, of course, Matthew Paris had a long and colourful account of it in his chronicle.[40] There are other accounts of Simon's government in Gascony – the king's own complaints and Simon's replies – but these belong to a period ten years later and are more interesting as showing what the chief protagonists brought forward to justify their actions, rather than for the exact facts.

The period after Easter was one of the normal meeting times for the great assembly of the king and the magnates which transacted the most important business of the realm. It was not a parliament, in the modern sense of the term, although the chronicles called it that. There was no such legislative body as yet, but this gathering represented all the magnates of the kingdom, both lay and ecclesiastical. In this particular case, the meeting had more than overtones of the judicial functions which were the original core of parliament. Around Ascension Day – in this year, May 9th – the discussion began, and ran on till almost the middle of June. Certainly, from the account of both the chronicler and the Franciscan, the Gascons were given favoured treatment.

The refectory of the abbey of Westminster was rocked by a continuous stream of charges and counter-charges. To add strength to Earl Simon's claims that all he had done in Gascony was to ensure the king's honour and the keeping of his peace, he was supported by some of the greatest nobles of the realm: the earl of Gloucester, the earl of Hereford, the king's uncle, Peter of Savoy, and the king's brother, Richard of Cornwall. These were not all men who were normally favourable to the earl, and with the exception of Richard of Cornwall, they had no personal interest in the affair. Earl Richard certainly was more than glad to see the Gascons humbled. Gascony had been nominally given to him by his brother. Now Henry had changed his mind and was making ready to give the duchy to his son. Understandably Richard was not a prime supporter of his brother's policies at this moment. Besides, he had had enough experience of the Gascons to doubt their zealous protestations of unimpeachable loyalty and unblemished innocence.

After some weeks of pleading and discussion of the affairs of Gascony, a decision had to be made. The king and the magnates having weighed the merits of the case on both sides, the king finally gave public sentence, and asserted his confidence in the earl and his men. This declaration of confidence was received with acclaim by Earl Richard and the other nobles and prelates, and even by the king's counsellors. But the solution was not to be so easy as this. Twenty-four hours after the public sentence the king again changed his mind, and returned to his threats and reproaches of his lieutenant in Gascony. Like all petulant people, the king lost his temper easily, although he did not indulge in the towering rages of his Angevin forebears. Nor was Earl Simon one of those who believed in the soft answer when provoked. Adam Marsh says that the earl had to stand insults and reproaches from the king, screamed before the assemblage. Matthew Paris goes further and gives us the details of what must have been some very violent sessions. The king implied that the earl was a traitor. This was the ultimate insult to a medieval knight. Simon replied that if the king was not protected by the kingly authority, "like an umbrella", this would have been an evil hour for him. He went on in bitter rage: "Do you believe yourself to be a Christian? Have you ever confessed?" Brushing aside the royal rejoinder, the earl claimed that if the king had ever confessed, it would not be adequate, since he was neither repentant nor gave satisfaction. This was too much for Henry. "Glowing with rage, he shouted: 'Never have I regretted any deed so much as I regret that I ever permitted you to enter England or to possess honour or anything in this land.' " And, with the quarrel reaching such violence, their friends stepped in to break up the dispute.[41]

The king would accept neither of Simon's suggestions; that he should renounce the custody of Gascony, if the king would promise to keep him and his from loss and disgrace; that he should return to Gascony and again pacify the land, either peaceably or by military efforts. The final decision as to the disposition of the affair called for a firm truce till the following February when the king himself, or Edward, would go to Gascony and settle all the disputes themselves. Meanwhile, the king would send a deputy to Gascony to deal with the most immediate affairs. But, in a final sarcastic fling to Earl Simon, the king taunted him: "Return to Gascony, so that you who are an inciter and lover of war may find enough war, so that you may bring back its very worthy rewards as your father did!"[42] The earl was pleased enough to have his leave, even in such ungracious terms, and left immediately for France, taking his eldest son Henry with him. The countess Eleanor remained in England. She was, for the time being, at her manor of Sutton in Kent awaiting the birth of her daughter. Adam Marsh had gone there after the trial, and from there he wrote his long descriptive letter to Grosseteste.

Meanwhile, the Gascon problem developed on both sides of the Channel. In London, the king ordered all the Gascons who were still in London, including the archbishop of Bordeaux and his companions, to witness his bestowal of the duchy of Gascony on Edward, just reaching his thirteenth birthday. They swore fealty and did homage and received valuable presents from their new duke. Then they all settled down to feast while the Gascons boasted that Earl Simon would be cut to pieces or driven away from the country as an exile.[43] Long before Cyrano de Bergerac appeared on the scene, the Gascons were inclined to extravagant claims. After this they sailed home.

Meanwhile Simon had landed at Boulogne. He marched through the lands of the Ile-de-France where he could recruit mercenaries from his kinsmen and friends. Having acquired a fairly strong force, the earl headed for Gascony. There the Gascons were waiting for a good opportunity to oppose him. Neither side was being particularly solicitous of the truce which had been imposed by King Henry. Several times the earl of Leicester was in great danger, especially when he was besieged in the castle of Montauban, but, aided by his own fighting abilities and the devotion of his troops, he succeeded in battling his way free. From there he went on to take vengeance on his enemies by besieging La Réole to win back his own supporters imprisoned there. He cut the vines – the greatest possible damage in that wine-producing country – and ravaged the surrounding lands. Just at this time the commissioners from England, again the Master of the Templars and Nicholas de Meulles, arrived with the king's strict orders that the truce must be observed. Simon replied that it was impossible, since he could not observe the truce while the Gascons warred against him.[44] The commissioners then told him that, under the circumstances, the king had removed him from his charge and freed the Gascons from the duty of obedience to him. Simon replied that the terms of the king's original commission to him ensured that he could not be dismissed until the king had fulfilled his obligations towards him. Once more there was an impasse.

Back in England, the nobles, gathered for the October parliament, supported the cause of the earl of Leicester, while the king inveighed against him. The magnates had a pretty good idea of just how difficult the government of Gascony was, and felt that the earl should be left to finish out his seven-year term. The king, acting as always on impulse, was annoyed with his brother-in-law, for his opposition to his orders. At the back of his mind he even seemed to have entertained the idea of declaring Simon a traitor and thus making all his lands forfeit. Simon felt that the king wanted to be able to enrich one of his step-brothers or one of the queen's relations with the Leicester lands. But even Henry was forced to see that this was inadvisable and the dispute moved once more into the possible grounds for compromise. The earl's friends in England – Adam Marsh especially – kept him in touch with the various negotiations.

Finally, a settlement was reached. A covenant between the Lord Edward, as duke of Gascony, and Simon de Montfort arranged for the quittance by Simon of all his claims in Gascony for the remainder of his seven-year term in return for the sum of 7,000 marks. Simon was to surrender to Edward all the castles which he held from the king and all the newly fortified castles which he himself had acquired and strengthened during the term of his lieutenancy in the duchy. The prisoners taken inside Gascony were to be set free for a ransom, the others were to remain in the earl's hands. Half the money was to be paid by Easter of 1253, and the other half by the following Michaelmas.[45] On these terms, Simon withdrew into France and left Gascony to the growing turbulence of those royal vassals who had been so vigorously asserting their utter fidelity. The archbishop of Bordeaux, always a trouble-maker, had declared the earl excommunicate, despite the privilege exempting the earl from such a sentence, without the assent of the Holy Father. In April, 1253, Pope Innocent IV ordered the Bishop of Clermont to investigate the dispute and gave him the authority to settle it. As a suffragan of the Archbishop of Bourges, he was remote enough to be less involved in the local politics of the case than the last negotiator who had been the bishop of Agen, a suffragan of the fiery Archbishop of Bordeaux.[46]

Simon had now withdrawn from the inflamed politics of Gascony, but the duchy did not immediately become pacified, as the king had naïvely supposed. Indeed, the rebels were even more rebellious than before. To add to the complications of the situation, Alfonso of Castile took advantage of the departure of the redoubtable earl to assert again his old but extremely vague claims to the suzerainty of Gascony. The Castilian king summoned Gaston de Béarn and many of the other magnates. Resentment had been brewing among the Gascon wine-merchants over the way the English king had seized their shipments and deprived them of their profits, so many of these joined Alfonso as well. The party in Bordeaux which remained faithful to the English king was outnumbered and badly in need of help. They hurriedly demanded aid from King Henry if he wanted to retain Gascony.[47] By now King Henry was beginning to have more sober second thoughts on having dismissed the earl, and some lingering doubts about the complete credibility of the Gascon witnesses against him. However, he called for aid from all those owing knight service for an expedition to Gascony. He further decided to raise money by enforcing the old requirement that everyone who owned more than fifteen librates of land* should be made a knight.[48] This power, known as "distraint of knighthood", was not very frequently practised in King Henry's reign, but it was an extra source of revenue. Those with the required amount of land who did not want the rigours and expenses of knighthood paid for the privilege of remaining untroubled. Finally, at the end of August, six months after they were supposed to have arrived, Henry and his expedition reached Bordeaux and headed immediately for La Réole, which was the centre of the rebellion. Encamped at Bénauges, north of La Réole between the Garonne and Dordogne rivers, the king wrote to his ousted lieutenant, both begging and commanding him to come to his aid in Gascony. He agreed that the earl could withdraw if it seemed necessary for his honour or the king's and that the king would not then be angry with him. He sent a strong guard; the earls of Norfolk and Hereford, Guy de Lusignan, William de Cantilupe, John de Balliol and Stephen de Lungespee to conduct him safely to the king.[49]

This was very different language from the tone of the king's letters to the earl in the previous year. How did the earl answer the summons? Simon seems to have shown nobility and generosity, tempered as always by a very shrewd eye for the main chance. His position was not as uncomfortable as might have been thought. Although he had been dismissed from his post in Gascony, his return to France brought him among friends and kinsfolk. So great was his reputation in France that the story goes that at the end of 1252, when Queen Blanche, the queen-regent, died, and Louis was still on Crusade with Queen Marguerite, the French offered him the guardianship of the realm. Matthew Paris is so much impressed with this story that he tells it twice, with slight changes in wording; but it is clear that the French made him a good offer, trusting in his faithfulness and abilities, and influenced by his father's renown and the fact that he was a born Frenchman. They seem also to have promised him suitable rewards. But the earl, influenced by his oath

* That is, land worth more than £15 a year.

of allegiance, refused "lest he seem to have acted as a traitor".[50]

This command of King Henry's seemed like a good way to avoid an unpleasant situation. Immediately the earl set out for Gascony, bringing an army of his own, chosen and paid for by him. He may, too, have had a more high-minded motive, for Bishop Grosseteste had always insisted that he should rather remember the benefits that the king had given him, than his sudden angry words.[51] Grosseteste had recently died and the earl's sorrow for the loss of his friend would have heightened his respect for the good bishop's wishes. However, quite characteristically, Simon took advantage of the king's need to require some deeds in his favour. Most importantly, he was given a writ of *liberate* for the money still owing him for the Gascon settlement which was deposited in the house of the Hospitallers in Paris.[52] He was also given £500 for his losses and expenses in Gascony, and another rent of 600 marks until it could be translated into land.[53] At the same time, the castles of Odiham and Kenilworth were confirmed to the earl and countess for the duration of their lives.[54]

During the three months that Earl Simon spent with the king he was in high favour, and there were many acts of reparation for the losses that he had incurred during his years in Gascony. He seems to have left the king at the beginning of February and is known to have been in London by April. Earl Simon had once more saved the king's reputation, and enhanced his own position after a period of quarrels. When Earl Simon left Gascony in February he was to return only briefly to the turbulent province, where his reputation for military ability had been much enhanced, but his reputation for justice had been more than a little tarnished.

The earl's term as king's lieutenant in Gascony was over, and superficially all was well; but although the damage was patched up for a while by the king's grants and the earl's willingness to obey the royal summons, the rift between them was to deepen. The testimony of both king and earl, in the attempt to arbitrate their differences in 1262, demonstrates clearly that the real beginning of the trouble between them was Gascony. This controversy arose not only from events, although they sharpened the difficulties, but from the essential dissimilarity of the two men's personalities and the very different concept each had of what were the basic terms for the government of Gascony.

8

Simon de Montfort, Count of Bigorre?

Separate from Gascony, yet frequently entangled in its concerns, the little county of Bigorre was utilized by the earl of Leicester in his struggle for power and position. Its history was exceedingly complicated. The multiplicity of claimants to the county, in the middle of the thirteenth century, and the vigorous disputes over the possession of its feudal homage illustrate most vividly the medieval passion for lengthy and involved legal squabbles. The attempt to untangle some of the complications involved in the inheritance and overlordship of even such a tiny county gives a clearer insight into the complications of feudal law. So many political moves of this time depended, not necessarily on long-range planning, but rather on a tangled complex of personal ambitions and private motives which no charter can eloquently describe.

The part that Simon and Eleanor played in this long-drawn-out process has not always been clear. The complications arose from the five marriages of the Countess Perronelle, who ruled the county of Bigorre during the whole first half of the thirteenth century. Her series of matrimonial adventures puts one in mind of the Wife of Bath, who much enjoyed the pleasures of matrimony and the subduing of her five husbands. But Perronelle's marriages were a matter of necessity, rather than of choice. Any heiress to lands and political power in feudal times had to have a strong-armed husband to maintain her rights and protect her territories. The countess survived all her husbands, and died peacefully in the convent of l'Escale Dieu in 1251, leaving a flock of claimants to contest the possession of her county. It is not surprising that there was so much dispute over Bigorre, and Simon de Montfort became involved because of his position in Gascony, and the ties of relationship.

The early history of that little county, which nestles in the foothills of the Pyrenees, is obscure. The district was created an hereditary county in the ninth century, and given to a remote descendant of Clovis, the great king of the Franks. The early counts are nameless, faceless figures. The first notable ruler who emerges from the mists of early history is Count Bernard I, a wise and strong man, fervently pious. Unfortunately, his piety was to complicate the future feudal position of Bigorre. In 1062, the count and his countess Clemence went on pilgrimage to the famous hilltop shrine of Our Lady of Le Puy, in Velay, the mountainous region of the Massif Central. There, as a sign of their devotion, they put the county of Bigorre under Our Lady's care and protection. As a token of this occasion, Count Bernard promised that he and his successors would annually place the sum of 60s. (Morlaas) on the high altar of the church. The phrases of his charter, describing this gift, are heavy with fear of the impending doom of the Day of Judgment, which seemed so imminent to many religious minds in the eleventh century. But the charter is clear that the gift itself was purely religious in nature, with no thought of feudal obligations.[1] As the sixty shillings was paid continuously over the years, the simple gift of the eleventh century became something much more precise and binding to the legalistic minds of the thirteenth century. To them, this was not a spiritual token, but rather the recognition by the counts of Bigorre of the feudal suzerainty of Our Lady, and thus of the bishop and chapter of Le Puy as her earthly representatives.

This rather prosaic story of how the county of Bigorre fell under the overlordship of the church of Le Puy cannot, of course, compare with the legend for colour. According to tradition, when Charlemagne was journeying towards Spain in that great expedition which inspired the *Song of Roland*, he besieged the castle of Mirambel. It was held by a redoubtable pagan lord, Mirat, who refused to submit to any mortal man, not even to the great emperor. The bishop of Le Puy, travelling in the emperor's train, persuaded the pagan that it would be no disgrace to surrender his castle to the Queen of Heaven, Our Lady. Mirat and his men agreed, and went to Le Puy, bearing bundles of straw on their lances. They swore homage to Our Lady and were baptized. Mirat himself took the name of Lorus, and changed the name of his great stronghold to Lourdes, a surprising anticipation of the connection of Lourdes with Our Lady. Gradually, tradition believed, the ceremony of the counts of Bigorre and their followers bringing straw with them when they swore homage to Our Lady of Le Puy was changed to annual payments of money.[2]

Whether it was based on legend or fact, it is undoubtedly true that, by the middle of the thirteenth century, the bishop and chapter of Le Puy felt that they had the right to be regarded as the overlords of the county of Bigorre. They argued their claim against other lords whose assertions were based on earthly, rather than heavenly, sources. The counts who succeeded Bernard, for example, found themselves more closely linked to their Spanish neighbours in Aragon than to any French overlord. Count Bernard's sister married the king of Aragon, which added the tie of relationship to the concrete fact that Aragon was nearer and more powerful, and thus could help to protect Bigorre from the depredations of greedy lords. The counts of Bigorre rendered homage to the king of Aragon and he, in return, made them some gifts of territory.[3]

At the end of the twelfth century, the king of Aragon asserted the feudal suzerain's right of wardship and arranged the countess Perronelle's first marriage to Gaston VI of Béarn. In the treaty settling the marriage the place of the king of Aragon as overlord of Bigorre was specifically and completely recognized.[4] Although Perronelle's second marriage was also arranged by Aragonese influence, this marked the end of Aragon's claim on Bigorre. Probably this abandonment of claims was due to the suspicion with which Aragon was regarded by the orthodox during the Albigensian Crusade, for its king supported Count Raymond of Toulouse, the political leader of the heretics. Since both

Simon the Crusader and the orthodox clergy were particularly zealous to preserve the small principalities of the south of France from religious heresy and political intrigue, they decided to provide the young countess with another, more correct, husband. Consanguinity provided the convenient excuse, but, to add to later confusions, there was no formal annulment.

Perronelle's third husband was Guy, the second son of Simon the Crusader, who thus cloaked personal gain under the mantle of religious scruple. As count of Bigorre, the impecunious younger son gained position and power, though he was not to hold them for long. Killed at the siege of Castelnaudary in 1220, Guy left the countess with two young daughters, Alice and Perronelle. The countess married twice more, but had only one more daughter, by her fifth husband. This daughter, Mathe, married Gaston VII of Béarn, the great-nephew of the Gaston who had married her mother. Even the marriages of Mathe and her step-sister Alice added to the inherent confusion because they brought on quarrels over lands in northern Poitou. It is easy to see the clouds of conflict gathering on the horizon even before Simon de Montfort came to Gascony as the king's lieutenant. The old countess's death would bring an era of discord and confusion in Bigorre.

By 1248, the time of the earl of Leicester's arrival in Gascony, Countess Perronelle was old and tired, and quite ready to hand over the responsibility for her county to someone else. She feared the growing vehemence of the claims of Gaston of Béarn, and it seemed natural to turn to the might of her brother-in-law, re-enforced as he was by the support of the king of England. So, in the autumn of 1248, she handed over the county to Earl Simon for protection. He was to pay an annual rent of 7,000s. (Morlaas) in return. As usual, the earl was a poor financial risk. By the time the countess died, three years later, he was already much in arrears. But, during those three years, Earl Simon had used his possession of Bigorre to aid him in his struggles with Gaston of Béarn, and the situation remained relatively peaceful.

The countess's will, in 1251, really unleashed the controversies.

THE COUNTESS OF BIGORRE AND HER DESCENDANTS

Perronelle, c. of Bigorre, d. 1251

m.

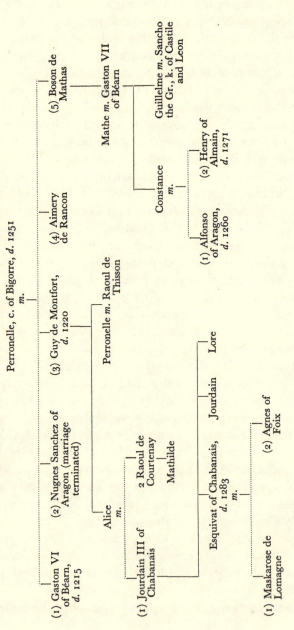

(1) Gaston VI of Béarn, d. 1215

(2) Nugnes Sanchez of Aragon (marriage terminated)

(3) Guy de Montfort, d. 1220

(4) Aimery de Rancon

(5) Boson de Mathas

Alice m.

(1) Jourdain III of Chabanais

(2) Raoul de Courtenay

Mathilde

Perronelle m. Raoul de Thisson

Esquivat of Chabanais, d. 1283

Jourdain

Lore

m.

(1) Maskarose de Lomagne

(2) Agnes of Foix

Mathe m. Gaston VII of Béarn

Guillelme m. Sancho the Gr., k. of Castile and Leon

Constance m.

(1) Alfonso of Aragon, d. 1260

(2) Henry of Almain, d. 1271

It provided that the county of Bigorre was to go to Esquivat de Chabanais, the eldest son of her eldest daughter by her third marriage to Guy de Montfort. If he died without direct heirs, then it was to pass to his brother, Jourdain. But, if Jourdain should also die without direct heirs, then, by substitution, the county should pass to Mathe, daughter by the fifth marriage, and her heirs direct or otherwise.[5]

Trying to satisfy the children of different marriages is always difficult, but these provisions suited no one. Mathe, with her belligerent husband, Gaston de Béarn, argued that the Countess Perronelle's marriage with Guy de Montfort was invalid, because there had been no annulment of the second marriage. If this was so, then Perronelle's children by Guy were illegitimate, and therefore incapable of inheriting. The county of Bigorre, according to Mathe's view, obviously belonged to her immediately. The descendants by the third marriage were not happy either. The right of substitution, which the countess had invoked in transferring the inheritance, if necessary, from Jourdain to Mathe, was recognized in southern France as a means of preserving intact the inheritance of a family. But Lore, the sister of Esquivat and Jourdain, did not see why she should have been passed over. Neither did Perronelle the younger, Alice's younger sister and the aunt of Esquivat and Jourdain. To add to an already complicated situation, the last clause of Perronelle's will begged her brother-in-law, Simon de Montfort, to pay the sum he owed, so that her own debts might be settled. She added that so long as he held the county – and no definite term was mentioned – he should pay the debts and deal with the creditors.[6] Thus the claims of still another individual were added to the flock which already besieged the small county.

During the ten years after the countess's death, the problem of Bigorre resolved itself into a struggle for power between Gaston of Béarn and the more or less shadowy figure of Esquivat de Chabanais, vigorously supported by Earl Simon, who was, after all, his great-uncle. Simon was glad to help maintain Esquivat in the county of Bigorre, because it helped him to almost encircle Gaston of Béarn – a perennial thorn in his side –

and also assisted him in his efforts to pacify Gascony. Naturally, there was enmity between the earl of Leicester and the viscount of Béarn. It was only increased by the earl's actions in Bigorre, which Gaston felt infringed his ancient prerogatives. He complained to the English king, from his favoured position as one of the queen's relatives, that Simon had re-routed trade from Bigorre through Gascony instead of through Béarn, that he refused to recognize the competency of the courts of Béarn in cases that concerned men of Bigorre.[7] In other words, Simon had hurt Gaston's pride and damaged his pocket-book, and the viscount of Béarn's complaints mirror the general tone of all the Gascons in their grievances against the vigorous lieutenant sent them by the king. By June of 1253, two years after his grandmother's death, when Simon de Montfort had withdrawn to France, Esquivat was given control of Bigorre. By that time the young count was fairly deeply in debt to his great-uncle and ceded him his rights to certain territories in northern Poitou, until the earl had been repaid for his expenses and loans.[8]

Almost immediately, another complication was introduced. When King Henry came to Gascony in the summer of 1253, after Simon's departure, he discovered that controlling Gaston de Béarn was just as difficult as Simon had always insisted. The king also proceeded to try and protect Gascony's flank by securing Bigorre. His method was to offer to buy the rights of the bishop and chapter of Le Puy. In November, 1253, he offered them £3,200 of the money of Pau for the homage and "*dominium*" of the county of Bigorre and the castle of Lourdes, with all the services, usages, obligations, and obediences owed them.[9] However the king never seems to have been quite sure just what he was purchasing, for he arranged with Esquivat for messengers to be sent to Le Puy to find out exactly what were the usual rights of the church of Le Puy.[10]

Despite the uncertainty, the English kings claimed the homage of Bigorre as their right, until the end of the century, and based their claim on this sale. The only person who seems to have recognized the change effected was young Esquivat, now the count of Bigorre. He was willing to acknowledge the English king's claim, because he badly needed English help against the continued depredations of Gaston de Béarn. During the next few years, Esquivat did homage to King Henry for the county of Bigorre and the castle of Lourdes.[11] He also went to fight with the king in Gascony. But King Henry and Count Esquivat had different aims. The king was interested in seeing how much could be made out of the feudal claim on Bigorre, and also in obtaining the lease of certain well-fortified castles to improve his military position in Gascony. He was not really concerned about giving aid to the count of Bigorre against his rapacious neighbours, while this was, naturally enough, what Esquivat wanted. King Henry was also at a low ebb financially when he returned home from this second expedition to Gascony. He had not the money to fulfil the many promises of financial aid he had distributed so lightheartedly among the lords of southern Aquitaine. By 1255, the king owed Count Esquivat £1,000 for the lease of his castles, as well as 1,000 marks of arrears for the time that Esquivat was in the king's service in Gascony. To further complicate the accounts, since Esquivat still owed money to Simon de Montfort, the young count named the earl and countess of Leicester as the receivers of the king's debt to him.[12]

Unfortunately, this sum remained unpaid, and thus compounded the financial grievances that already divided the changeable king and the headstrong and exacting earl and countess. By July of 1256, the king was plaintively admitting that he owed his beloved sister Eleanor much money for arrears of dower in Ireland and for the county of Bigorre and that he would try to collect it from various sources "so that our sister may not remain unsatisfied".[13]

But while the king was getting into further financial difficulties with his sister and brother-in-law, Esquivat still needed help against Gaston de Béarn. It was most natural that he should turn again to the great-uncle who had supported him before, and who certainly knew by sad experience the problems with which he had to deal. Earl Simon's reputation, in France as in England, was that of a singularly efficient and formidable warrior, who would be able to keep even the aggressive Gaston de Béarn in check.

At the beginning of August, 1256, the bishops of Tarbes, the count of Bigorre, his younger brother Jourdain, and the barons and estates addressed a formal and desperate appeal to the earl of Leicester, begging his help against the ravages of Gaston de Béarn. They did not dare to emerge from their strong castles or fortified towns. If Earl Simon did not aid them, they would have to leave Gascony.[14] We do not know the earl's answer, but a few days later, Esquivat, with his younger brother Jourdain, gave the county to Simon.[15]

Perhaps the gift was Simon's price for help to his great-nephew. This original charter of donation was repeated and confirmed in 1258, and the terms of the charter certainly seem unequivocal. Esquivat said:

> I make it known to you that, since Gaston of Béarn would have devastated all my land so that I could not defend it; I give, concede, and, by this present charter, confirm to lord Simon de Montfort, earl of Leicester, my dearest uncle, and to his heirs or assigns, all the county of Bigorre with all its appurtenances, in sane mind and of free will.[16]

Now this would appear clear enough. But, in this matter of Bigorre, no charter seems to agree with the events which follow. Although Esquivat apparently gave Simon the county of Bigorre in August of 1256, September saw him acting again as independent count. In that month, he submitted, with Gaston de Béarn, to the arbitration of Roger, count of Foix, one of the lesser lords of the county of Toulouse. The settlement which the count of Foix gave provided that Gaston should have the district of Marsan, which had been his wife's dower, undisturbedly. He was also to have the northern part of Bigorre from the city of Malborguet towards Armagnac. Esquivat was to be untroubled in his possession of the rest, and in his northern lands, Chabanais and Confolens.[17] This was a compromise between the warring parties, and the count of Foix may have had a personal interest in seeing that Esquivat was treated reasonably well. His daughter Agnes married Esquivat only a few months later. Certainly he did his best to make the settlement binding. There was a very strict clause for the maintenance of the sentence, in which the consenting parties renounced the aid of any law, human or divine, any pact or obligation, which might break the arbitral sentence.[18] If this had preceded the gift to Simon, it would have rendered that gift invalid, but it came after. Here again, there is another case where there are too many documents, and it seems impossible to fit them all coherently into the passage of events.

During the next few years, the situation remained confused and contradictory. King Henry had bought the homage of the county of Bigorre from the bishop and chapter of Le Puy, but was not the undisputed overlord. Esquivat had given the county to his great-uncle – under what pressure we do not know – and both he and Simon were trying to act as counts of Bigorre. In 1259, when Simon was busy at the courts of France and England with the negotiations for the treaty of Paris, he thought enough of Bigorre to constitute Philip de Montfort as its guardian.[19] Philip was a cousin of the earl's, and lord of the seigneury of Castres, just south of Albi. This was territory which had been acquired by Philip's father during the Albigensian Crusade and added to the family holding of La-Ferté-Alais in the Ile de France. He was in a good position to keep an eye on his cousin's interests in the south, and the closely knit ties of relationship again worked to Earl Simon's advantage. Meanwhile, during the summer before the publication of the treaty of Paris, Simon agreed to lease the county of Bigorre to King Henry for seven years for a rental of £1,000.[20] Since, by the treaty, the question of the rightful owner of the homage of Bigorre was to be subject to arbitration, the king naturally wanted to have it in his own hands.

Once more, an arrangement was duly made for someone to hand over the county to someone else. The next fact that emerges is that the original owner was completely disregarding the settlement. Simon obviously maintained his grasp on Bigorre, despite this arrangement with the king. In May, 1260, Esquivat's father-in-law, the count of Foix, urged Gaston of Béarn to denounce all truce between himself and the earl, because Simon refused to render the county to Esquivat. Gaston argued, in a most unusually high-minded way, that according to the arrangement of 1256 Simon was only meant to pacify the county and then return it to Esquivat. He was never meant to keep it for himself.[21] Hostilities continued until October, when the bishops of Lectoure and Oléron arranged for a truce between Simon and Esquivat for a year. Simon was told to hold peaceably until Christmas, 1261, the castle and the surrounding districts of Lourdes, and the city of Tarbes. Before the truce expired, these places had the right to declare for Esquivat – a kind of medieval "local option".[22] In fact, the inhabitants of Tarbes did declare for Esquivat, leaving only the castle of Lourdes in Simon's possession. Whether or not Esquivat had intended to give away his county in 1256, he was practical master of it again by 1261.

During these years, Simon de Montfort was busily engaged in his own quarrels with King Henry and with the larger struggle of the barons. He had little time to devote personally to the question of Bigorre. But it would not have been like Simon to let any possible claims lapse. He had appointed Raymond Bodin of Aurillac, near Le Puy, as his proctor at the English court in the matter of Bigorre, and Bodin was active in his lord's behalf.[23] He made the original agreement for the leasing of the county to King Henry, and on July 20, 1262, this clerk deposited 60s. (Morlaas) on the high altar of the church of Le Puy, in the name of his master, Simon de Montfort.[24] The gesture is intriguing, but its significance is puzzling. It was not inspired by ignorance of the claims of King Henry and the proposed arbitration. Perhaps Simon's continued irritation with the English king sought this opportunity of undermining his position in Gascony. The dramatic gesture, with its appearance of piety, and its undertones of political opportunism, is quite in keeping with Simon's character.

In the last three years of his life, the earl of Leicester was too busy in England to have much time for the problems of Bigorre. But it is worth remembering that, even when Simon was the *de facto* ruler of England, the earl and countess continued to have contact with Bigorre. In Eleanor's household accounts, for the spring and summer of 1265, there are several references to messengers to and from Lourdes. It was to Bigorre, too, as a safer part of their lands, that young Richard de Montfort properly equipped with shoes of cowhide and hose of russet, was hurriedly packed off after his mother had received the dreadful news of Evesham.[25] His hurried trip to Bigorre is almost the last thing we hear of young Richard before he disappears completely from the records of history.

By October, 1265, when the rout of the baronial forces at Evesham had been re-enforced by the continued successes of the king's son, the widowed Eleanor and young Simon decided to hand over their claims to Bigorre to a stronger prince. They ceded their rights in the county of Bigorre and the castle of Lourdes to Thibault, king of Navarre and count of Champagne.[26] It was a last show of defiance to the king of England. Thibault promised to maintain the rights of the church of Le Puy. In his first agreement with the bishop and chapter in January, 1267, he duly promised to pay homage for the county of Bigorre and the castle of Lourdes, to pay annually 60s. (Morlaas) as a feudal due, and to fly the flag of Our Lady of Le Puy over the castle of Lourdes upon a change in lords and every fifty years.[27] He was also to pay the expenses of the legal proceedings between the church of Le Puy and the English king over the disputed homage, which was being argued in the *parlement* of Paris.

This cession ended the Montforts' connection with Bigorre. Here is a brief summary of the conclusion of the matter. The king of Navarre maintained his legal claim, but, in actual fact, Esquivat remained in uneasy control of the county until his death in 1283. By his will, he tried to leave the county to his sister, Lore, who had not been mentioned at all in the original will of his grandmother. Her possession was naturally disputed by a flock of claimants, especially by Constance de Béarn, the daughter of Gaston and Mathe. Constance was the rightful heir by the terms of the Countess Perronelle's will. Meanwhile, Thibault de Navarre had died childless. His brother, Henry, succeeded to the throne of Navarre and Navarre's claim on Bigorre, acquired from the countess of Leicester. Henry's daughter, Jeanne, married King Philip the Fair of France, who was already using every possible legal subterfuge to extend the power and borders of the French kingdom.

Under such conditions, the end was inevitable. King Philip, through the *parlement* of Paris, recognized the bishop and chapter of Le Puy as the rightful owners of the homage of Bigorre and threw out the English claim. The sale was considered invalid, because it was supposed to have been extorted from the bishop of that day by the threat of force. Immediately, the proctors of Queen Jeanne did homage to the church of Le Puy in her name. Since it was accepted feudal law that the king could not do homage to anyone in his kingdom for lands, and the husband normally did homage for the lands of his wife, Philip had really decided for himself by deciding in favour of the bishop and chapter of Le Puy. By 1307, the county of Bigorre had become an integral part of the kingdom of France, through a claim which was traced from the possession of the county by Simon de Montfort, earl of Leicester.

It is an odd and interesting footnote to history that the mission of the earl of Leicester as king's lieutenant in Gascony should lead, by such circuitous paths, to the English king's removal from this small section of southern France, which was a valuable protection to his position in Gascony. The main elements of what happened can be worked out, but why it happened that way is still a mystery.

9

The King's Envoy; France

Although Simon de Montfort had been removed from his appointment as king's lieutenant in Gascony before the expiration of his term, and there were several financial settlements disputed between them, the earl remained fairly close to the king. The brothers-in-law were not the intimate friends they had been in the halcyon days of Simon's first settlement in England; that position had been usurped by the Poitevins. Besides, an inherent clash of personalities and divergent views on policy separated Henry and Simon more and more. But between 1254 and 1259 the earl of Leicester was frequently employed on diplomatic missions for the king, for Simon's skill and prestige were still used to serve the aims of the English monarch in foreign affairs. Unfortunately the part of Simon, and Eleanor, in delaying the treaty of Paris, which was the most important and long-drawn-out of these diplomatic missions, added still another item to the long list of grievances and complaints that lay unresolved between the king and the earl.

Henry had been called to Gascony in 1253. There was general turmoil in the province, once the earl of Leicester's strong hand was removed from the reins of government. The threats of Alfonso of Castile, bent on inspiring revolt among the volatile Gascons, worried Henry, who was also concerned about the activities of that notorious time-server, Gaston de Béarn. The king soon decided that the best way to protect the duchy from any threat from the south was to arrange a marriage alliance with Castile. At the beginning of 1254 his secret negotiators were sent to the Castilian court to work out a marriage treaty between Edward, the king's eldest son and titular ruler of Gascony, and Eleanor, the stepsister of King Alfonso. It is typical of the always devious manner of Henry's dealings with his subjects that no premature knowledge of these negotiations was allowed to slip back to England. In fact, when Earl Simon returned to England for the Easter parliament of 1254, the barons were being asked for military and financial aid to repel a threatened invasion from Castile. Simon brought the most recent news from Gascony, and told the gathering that he knew of no Castilian invasion. This encouraged the barons to turn down the king's demand, which was based on an urgent need for money, although not for the reason he gave. In fact, although even the earl of Leicester did not know of it, the marriage treaty had already been signed in Spain. It united Edward and Eleanor in one of the happiest of royal marriages, and ended any Castilian threat to the duchy of Gascony.

When the news of the impending marriage was sent to the queen, she set off for Gascony, accompanied by Edward and his younger brother, Edmund, as well as her uncle, Boniface of Savoy, the archbishop of Canterbury. Simon de Montfort also returned to see the king during the summer. At the end of August – when Edward had already departed for Burgos and the various celebrations surrounding his marriage and solemn knighting by the king of Castile – Simon was sent off on a secret mission to King Alexander of Scotland. No clue is given as to the nature of the mission, for nothing was committed to writing. The royal letter specifically says that a certain secret was put in Simon de Montfort's mouth, to be told only to the king of Scotland.[1] A further suggestion of complicated and secretive manoeuvres is heightened by another letter of September 16th, also from Bordeaux, which mentions Simon's mission, and adds that the archbishop of York and John of Lexington, a king's clerk, had also been sent to the king of Scotland and his council on certain arduous affairs touching the honour of both kings.[2] Whatever this most private business may have been, Henry had tried to put the Scottish king in a receptive frame of mind by restoring to him the honour of Huntingdon a few days before the mission was ordered.[3] Probably Simon carried this grant with him on his travels.

During the rest of 1254, there is no reference in the documents or the chroniclers to the whereabouts of the earl of Leicester. He is not mentioned as being with King Henry and he certainly was not involved in the beginnings of the "Sicilian affair". Like the Castilian marriage, this was a personal scheme of Henry's by which he secretly accepted the pope's gift of the kingdom of Sicily for his younger son, Edmund. The alliance with Castile was most successful, but the Sicilian project was a very different matter. This visionary and ill-fated commitment was to cause the king great expense and trouble, indirectly bring on the flare-up with the barons, and come to nothing in the end.

The pope had been deeply involved for some time in the affairs of the troubled kingdom of Sicily. It formed part of the territories of the Emperor Frederick II, once the pope's most feared and dangerous enemy. Innocent IV had excommunicated the emperor and declared Sicily, which was a fief of the Holy See, forfeit. After Frederick's death in 1250, his heirs kept possession of Sicily, but were opposed by the pope. As the kingdom included the land around Naples, and thus bordered on the papal domains, the pope was particularly anxious to find a rich and docile noble who would accept the royal title and then finance the expensive papal campaigns against Frederick's heirs. Innocent IV first offered Sicily to Richard of Cornwall, who was far too shrewd and too thrifty to embark on a venture which promised so much expense and so little success. The earl of Cornwall's reaction to the extremely stringent papal conditions attached to the offer was that the pope was really saying: "I sell or give thee the moon. Go up and take it."[4] The pope then turned to Henry, who lacked his brother's coolheaded ability to count the cost. The king quickly accepted the offer, overjoyed at the prospect of such prestige for his son.

The first charter conceding the kingdom of Sicily to Edmund was dated March 6, 1254, and was witnessed by only the inner circle of King Henry's advisers. It included John Mansel, always the king's most trusted clerk; Peter Chaceporc, the Poitevin keeper of the royal wardrobe; two of the queen's uncles, Count Thomas of Savoy and Peter, his brother; and the notorious alien bishop of Hereford, Peter of Aigueblanche.[5] The point to be noticed about these witnesses, which helps to explain much of the later trouble over this matter of Sicily, is that they included none of the barons of the realm. Even though the king was in Gascony, the barons felt that they had a right to be consulted on a matter of such importance for the whole kingdom. From 1254 on, the Sicilian affair hung like a millstone around King Henry's neck. Perennially short of money, he became hopelessly indebted to the pope, who insisted on astronomical sums in payment of the cost of the campaign against the vigorous Manfred, Frederick's illegitimate son and the practical ruler of Sicily. Like circles on the water, the repercussions of the Sicilian affair spread to other problems in the government of the realm. The papal demand for heavier taxation of the clergy and the rapacity of the papal collectors inflated the continuous murmur of complaint to a loud chorus of protest against papal exactions. The magnates, profoundly distrustful of this latest expensive scheme of their impulsive monarch, grudgingly offered some of the financial assistance required, but only on their own terms.

King Henry's part in this Sicilian adventure also affected his relations with France. There had been no real treaty of peace with France since the condemnation of John in 1204 by Philip Augustus, and the subsequent confiscation of most of the English lands in France. This unsettled state of affairs was now fifty years old. During Henry's reign, relations between the two countries had been quite peaceful, although they were handled by a series of truces, constantly re-negotiated and extended. In fact, there had only been three periods of real hostility during those fifty years, including, most recently, Henry's disastrous campaign in Poitou in 1242-3. Since relations between France and England were more friendly than they had been for years, or, actually, than they were to be for centuries, it was a good time to conclude a definite treaty of peace, particularly as all the weight of King Louis's prestige was thrown on the side of peace and the settlement of any outstanding quarrels.

Louis IX of France was, for his own time, as for later centuries, the ideal man of his age. His passionate devotion to justice and burning desire to re-conquer the Holy Land were joined to a hatred of vain display and a truly charming sense of humour. But his virtues did not make him a weakling. He maintained the rights of the king in France as sturdily as he protected the rights of others, and did not hesitate to refuse even the pope when he trespassed on uncertain ground. The tall slender king "having an angelic look and a gracious face"[6] was a familiar figure throughout his realm in his sombre clothes, for after his first Crusade he no longer wore the elegant silks and fine cloths that were the usual garb of kings. Family affection warmed his feelings towards England and gave impetus to his desire for peace. Louis and Henry had married sisters, their children were cousins, and thus the French king felt they should be friends. Louis wanted the formal recognition of the fact that Normandy, Anjou, Poitou, Touraine, and Maine had been absorbed into the kingdom of France. In lands where the possession was still disputed, the French king was more ready to honour the English point of view than the peers of France thought wise or necessary. Despite the retention in the English royal style of the resounding, but empty, titles of duke of Normandy and count of Anjou, Henry was willing to recognize formally the French expansion into his overseas lands. It seemed the strategic moment to try for a treaty. Besides, the pope was anxiously pressing the kings to make peace. He felt that once a settlement with France was achieved, King Henry would be freer to devote his interest and resources to a more vigorous prosecution of the Sicilian affair.

These latent pressures for the conclusion of peace between the two countries received a powerful impetus from the state visit of King Henry to King Louis at the end of 1254. Henry had stayed in Gascony almost all the year. He had arranged Edward's marriage and given him the duchy of Gascony. By a policy of appeasement and compromise he had tried to soothe the Gascon tempers, so exasperated by the heavy-handed tactics of the earl of Leicester. Now the king wanted to go home through France. He proposed to stop at the abbey of Fontevrault where his violent-tempered mother had sought refuge at the last, and where she lay buried in the churchyard. Her son felt that her tomb should be properly placed within the church with the other royal dead, for Fontevrault was the burial place of his redoubtable grandparents,

Henry II and Eleanor of Aquitaine, as well as his uncle, Richard the Lionhearted. Once this deed of filial piety was accomplished, Henry was anxious to swing far to the east for a pilgrimage to Pontigny. At the Cistercian abbey there was the tomb of St Edmund, the archbishop of Canterbury who had died in voluntary exile at Pontigny not so many years before. Henry had a passion for pilgrimages, and St Edmund dead was a far stronger magnet than Archbishop Edmund living. Louis's permission for the trip across France was graciously granted, and his invitation to stop in Paris was gladly accepted.

Louis and his queen had recently returned from six years on crusade, and the French king no doubt thought that the two sisters would welcome the chance to meet again. The whole affair became a combination family party and sightseeing tour. The countess of Provence, the mother of the two queens, was there, and so were her two younger daughters with their husbands, Richard of Cornwall and Charles of Anjou. Henry's love of beauty and passion for building were inspired by Paris, where he was particularly anxious to see the Ste-Chapelle which Louis had been building to house the precious relic of the Crown of Thorns. So fascinated was the English king by its beauties that a popular song claimed that he would have liked to roll it off in a cart.[7] The king's stay was punctuated by banquets of more than usual splendour, with the nobles of England and France trying to outdo each other. Matthew Paris concludes his most circumstantial account of all the glories of the highly-coloured occasion by remarking smugly that: "there was never so noble or famous a banquet celebrated in the time of Ahasuerus, or Arthur, or Charles".*[8]

When the two kings parted after a week spent in exploring the wonders of Paris with its glorious new churches and elegant plastered houses, of exchanging the feasts and the valuable presents that medieval etiquette demanded, they had laid the foundation of personal affection and mutual interest. It is not too extravagant to believe the chronicler's remark that King Louis felt that they would have been indissoluble friends except for the

* Charles, for these centuries, always referred to Charlemagne, and needed no more introduction than King Arthur.

enmity of the peers of France.[9] A favourable climate had been created for the making of permanent peace, although nothing was done immediately.

Matthew Paris, and the chroniclers who copy him, are so detailed in their information about this visit because King Henry himself came to visit St Albans soon after his return home. The king spent almost a week there, and the abbey's historian had a magnificent opportunity to enliven his narrative with details gathered directly from the lips of the central figure. One of the new curiosities the king described tickled Matthew's inquisitive mind particularly. King Louis had given Henry an elephant, which the French king had brought back from the crusade, and the beast was brought to England in February, 1255.[10] It was housed in the Tower of London, where the king had started to build up a private zoo from the gifts of his fellow monarchs. There were three leopards from the Emperor Frederick II, and also a camel.[11] Perhaps Richard of Cornwall also kept there the buffaloes which had been sent to him only a couple of years before.[12] The poor elephant did not survive the rigours of the English climate for very long, but Matthew Paris immortalized it in one of his lively marginal drawings.

The earl of Leicester does not seem to have formed part of the king's retinue during the leisurely trip through France. Probably he stayed in England after completing his mission to the king of Scotland in the previous summer. Now Simon was anxious to return to the continent as soon as possible, and sought the king's permission as soon as he landed. Henry reached Dover on December 27, and the next day ordered the warden of the Cinque Ports to allow the earl of Leicester and his household to leave England, despite the general prohibition.[13] The next few months Simon spent in France on his private affairs, but there is no record of what he was doing.

The question of a permanent peace with France seemed for a time to be in abeyance. In May, 1255, Peter of Savoy was appointed by King Henry to join Simon who was already in France. They were given power to arrange another truce with France for three years.[14] Within a month the negotiators had completed their task, and the new truce was made to run for three years from the feast of St Rémi (October 1).[15] Not much was done about any serious attempt at peace in 1256. In January, King Henry sent Peter de Montfort* to the French court about certain breaches of the truce charged by Simon and Peter of Savoy.[16] A few days later John Mansel and Bertram de Crioll were given full powers to continue the truce.[17] The earl of Leicester devoted most of the year to his own interests. There was the matter of his being given the county of Bigorre by his hard-pressed nephew and, in England, the earl and countess obtained promises from the king on the payment of the arrears of Eleanor's dower.[18]

Not until 1257 did the real negotiations for peace begin. Much of Earl Simon's time and energy for the next three years was consumed by the thorny question of the treaty with France. It must be remembered that Simon was more than just a negotiator in this affair. Although he served continuously as the king's envoy and, with Peter of Savoy, was the main architect of the terms of the treaty, he also had a vital personal interest in its contents, both for himself and his wife. It may seem odd that two private individuals should be so intimately concerned in a matter of public policy. First of all, it must always be remembered that the strict distinction between private and public affairs did not exist in the medieval mind. A settlement like the treaty of Paris was a mixture of national policy, feudal law, and hereditary rights. To make such a treaty binding, it was essential to include and satisfy the greatest lords who might be capable of upsetting its terms. Besides, Simon and Eleanor were not really private individuals. The son of the Albigensian crusader who had conquered the whole south of France and the daughter of an English king had claims on the lands of France which had to be respectfully considered.

Simon de Montfort had the shadow of a hereditary claim to the lands which his father had gained in Toulouse, Beziers, and the other Albigensian territories. Amaury, the eldest son, had surrendered the lands to King Louis VIII when Simon was still under age. But Amaury was dead and as the eldest remaining heir

* Peter de Montfort was a neighbour of Simon's in Warwickshire and his staunch supporter, but no relation.

Simon might dispute the original cession. Then, too, there were a few family claims to the Montfort lands in Evreux and Normandy. These formed part of the recently acquired territory of the king of France, and were to be included in the treaty. Thus, King Louis could rightfully demand a renunciation from Simon which would reinforce the royal legal title.

Much more complicated, and important, than any possible rights of Simon's were the claims of the Countess Eleanor. Eleanor, as the only surviving daughter of King John, might have an hereditary claim to a share in the English lands in France once held by her father. If a renunciation of such claims was to be required from King Henry and his sons, and also from Richard of Cornwall, then a formal renunciation could be required of her too. Much to Eleanor's pleasure, this placed her in a strong bargaining position. Her consent was needed to complete the treaty, and she and her husband had no intention of giving it until their claims on Henry were fully settled.

The basic issue between the king and his sister was the dower from her first husband. When William Marshal the younger had died, leaving her a widow of sixteen, the king had made the dower settlement for his sister with the Marshal heirs, accepting a money payment of £400 a year as the value of her dower lands in Ireland and Wales. Eleanor and Simon had always felt themselves aggrieved by this. They claimed that the settlement was inadequate, that her dower rights were worth much more than this, and that Eleanor had suffered grievous financial loss by the arrangement made in her name by the king. Then, to complicate the matter further, outside affairs intruded into this domestic issue. King Henry ran into debt with his sister and brother-in-law, not only over private matters, but over Bigorre. The English king owed money to Esquivat de Chabanais for Bigorre, and Esquivat himself was in debt to his great-uncle, the earl of Leicester. So, Esquivat transferred the money owing him from the king to the earl and countess of Leicester, in the attempt to settle his accounts. This intrusion of the confused Bigorre question into the accounts of the dower settlement only made things more difficult. Another disturbing factor was added, in the midst of the negotiations, by the barons' new scheme of government, proposed in 1258, which fettered the king's power through a ruling Committee of Fifteen. Naturally, Henry was opposed to this change. Since Simon de Montfort was one of the prominent baronial appointments to that committee he shared in the king's disfavour. The earl's uncompromising character, as well as his share in the baronial opposition to his fickle brother-in-law, further entangled the problems between them.

Matthew Paris has an illuminating story of an encounter between the king and the earl of Leicester in the tense summer of 1258. It illustrates very clearly the volatile king's distrust, and latent fear, of his sister's inflexible husband. In July, the king was at Westminster and, as it was a warm and oppressive summer day, Henry had gone down the Thames by boat to enjoy his dinner out-of-doors. Suddenly, a thunder-storm swept up, with lightning and heavy rain. Henry was terrified of thunder-storms, and ordered his boatmen to seek the nearest shelter. That happened to be the riverside palace of the bishop of Durham, where the earl of Leicester was staying while he was in London on business connected with the baron's new scheme of government. The earl went to greet his unexpected royal guest with proper respect, and asked the king why he was fearful, as the thunder-storm was already over. But the king answered seriously, jolted by the two perils he encountered: "The thunder and lightning I fear beyond measure, but, by the Head of God, I fear thee more than all the thunder and lightning in the world."[19] The earl tried to soothe his distraught sovereign, assuring him of friendship and fidelity, but the king was not really convinced. Personal mistrust added its weight to the domestic and political problems which already separated the king and his brother-in-law.

All these complications of personal and public rights lay behind the long months and years of bickering over the terms of the treaty of Paris. February 1257 marked the real beginning of serious negotiations for peace. Simon and Robert Walerand, steward of the household and one of the king's most trusted officials, were sent to King Louis to treat of peace.[20] During the ensuing years of negotiation Simon was intimately connected with all the manoeuvres and played the leading part in the settlement. He was, of course, in a particularly favourable situation. As the brother-in-law of the English king and the earl of Leicester, he was one of the leading English magnates and could be expected by King Louis to know the mind of his royal brother-in-law. But, at the same time, King Louis never forgot that the Montforts were one of the great French families of the Ile-de-France, and that Earl Simon still shone in French eyes with the halo of his father's prestige. The earl of Leicester was not only an English noble, but a man of European reputation. The election of Richard of Cornwall to succeed William of Holland in the Holy Roman Empire, in January, 1257, increased the French desire for peace. The pope had pushed Richard's candidacy, to further his own schemes, and the election was disputed by Alfonso of Castile. Even though Richard was never officially crowned and normally used only the title of king of the Romans, his rather ambiguous position heightened English prestige and extended English influence on the continent. It was time to settle the French affair.

Simon's first letters of appointment carried the information that Henry had authorized Simon to receive any or all of his French inheritance that the French king might be prepared to give him.[21] The earl had again taken good care that he did not neglect his own interests while he laboured for the king. Nothing much came of the first mission, and, at the end of June, a new group of negotiators was appointed by King Henry to serve till August 15th, with the assent and counsel of Simon and Peter of Savoy. They included Hugh Bigod, the capable younger brother of the earl of Norfolk, and two clerics. One was Adam Marsh, probably the most intimate spiritual adviser of the Leicester household; the other Walter de Cantilupe, the bishop of Worcester.[22]

Walter was the outstanding prelate in England since the death of Grosseteste, and of a very different type from that saintly scholar. He typified a great class of medieval bishops. Genuinely religious, he was an excellent administrator of his diocese, but he was jealously conscious of his temporal importance and bitterly resented any limitation of benefices which would deprive clerics of their income. His father had been of the lesser nobility, a royal seneschal under King John, and Walter had served in his youth as an itinerant justice before his appointment to Worcester. From 1257 on he played a steadily more important role in the political history of his time and became, ultimately, Simon's staunchest clerical supporter. Walter's particular duty at this time was to go and report to Richard of Cornwall in Germany, and to obtain his counsel as soon as the ambassadors had heard and understood the intentions of the king of France. Henry, quite wisely, recognized Richard's greater shrewdness and coolheadedness and relied implicitly on his counsel.[23]

While negotiation went on with the French, the Sicilian problem was also bothering King Henry. As the pope's terms became steadily more onerous, the two issues became more and more entangled. Only a few days after the appointment of the negotiators for France, the pope was notified that Earl Simon, Peter of Savoy, and John Mansel, as well as the archbishop of Tarentaise, had been given special instructions to beg the pope for a legate who would treat of peace with the king of France.

This was only part of their mission; they were also given power to treat of the business of the realm of Sicily, and even, if necessary, to renounce it.[24] In less formal language, they were to try and make the pope lessen his demands so that England could be freed from the debts into which she had been plunged by this affair. The veiled threat that they would give up the whole business and leave the Sicilian problem in the pope's own hands reinforced their requests. A week later a further note was sent to Simon and Peter of Savoy in Paris. To corroborate the king's offer of withdrawal, Henry was sending to them in Paris the original charter of Innocent IV, marking the gift of Sicily to Edmund. If Simon and Peter of Savoy could not go to the Roman curia personally to deal with the matter then the king wanted the charter returned safely to England by one of his trusted officials.[25] Despite all these elaborate preparations, there was no change in the status of the Sicilian affair and no legate for the French peace.

After the expiration of the term of these envoys in August, another group was commissioned in the autumn. It included Simon, Peter of Savoy, and the bishop of Worcester, and, if Matthew Paris is to be trusted, Roger Bigod, Robert Walerand, the abbot of Westminster, and Aymer de Valence. Apparently, these envoys were most intransigeant in their demands, clamouring for the restoration of all the ancient rights of the English king which they claimed had been unjustly detained. Perhaps they were encouraged in this extreme behaviour by the knowledge of a shortage of grain and wine in France and the illness of the French king's brother, but it proved no asset to bargaining. King Louis met their extravagant statements with polite restraint, but the French magnates denied them harshly. Most of the embassy went back to England to report their lack of success, probably around Candlemas, 1258, but the abbot of Westminster stayed on in Paris. The French magnates gathered in parliament at mid-lent – this year towards the end of February – and the abbot seemingly remained to hear their discussion and decision, and to transmit it to England in person.[26] There is no extant draft of the terms suggested by the French at this time, although they were probably not far from those of the later agreement. They were not as favourable as King Henry hoped.

However, events in England were forcing the king's hand. In the Hoke-tide* parliament, all Henry's troubles descended on his head at once. The Roman envoys renewed the papal demands for military and financial aid for the business of Sicily. They insisted that the king must make peace with France, so as to be free to devote his energies and finances to this pressing matter, and they suggested that perhaps the French king could be persuaded to contribute to the support of some knights. At the same time, the English barons completely refused any subsidy for the Sicilian affair, and left Henry struggling in the inexorably closing vice of the papal financial demands.

Nor was this parliament free from personal outbursts. A violent quarrel broke out between the earl of Leicester and William de Valence,† another of the king's Poitevin stepbrothers. William had

* Hoke-tide was the Monday and Tuesday of the second week after Easter. In the year 1258, it fell on April 1st and 2nd.

† William, as also his younger brother Aymer, took the name of Valence from the place a few miles south of Lusignan where he was born. He is not to be confused with William, bishop-elect of Valence (on the Rhone), who was an uncle of Queen Eleanor and a prominent counsellor of the king some years earlier.

married the heiress of the Marshal lands in Pembroke, and he was much concerned by the Welsh encroachments on his lands. Naturally, he wanted aid, but, in the present state of the kingdom, both the earl of Gloucester and the earl of Leicester were opposed to sending an expensive expedition to Wales. William was so angry that he lost all discretion. There had already been trouble the previous year between Simon and William, over the depredations of William's officials on the earl's lands. They had had such a furious quarrel that the king himself had had to separate them.[27] When William saw himself balked once again by the earl of Leicester, he turned in fury on Simon, in the presence of the magnates, and called him a liar and an old traitor. The earl, equally angry, reproached the young Poitevin with the disreputable conduct of his father, the count of La Marche, saying: "No, no, William, I am not the traitor or the son of a traitor. Our ancestors were not alike." The two came so close to blows that the king had to come between them.[28] For the time being the affair died down, but the enmity between the two nobles was permanent.

From the April parliament dated the barons' scheme for the reform of the realm, for they were pushed to the edge of revolution by Henry's ineptitude. The political changes also speeded up considerably the tempo of the French negotiations. When parliament had concluded, on May 8th, a new set of proctors was appointed. They included Simon and Peter of Savoy, as usual, as well as Hugh Bigod and two of the king's stepbrothers, Guy and Geoffrey de Lusignan. They, or any three of them, were to negotiate the treaty and swear the required oaths. They were also empowered to swear that the king would do his best to procure the necessary renunciations of claims from Eleanor and Richard of Cornwall.[29] This delegation started off immediately for Paris, accompanied by some of the Roman envoys, who were to attend the negotiations and then take a report to the pope. When they arrived in the French capital, the Whitsun *parlement* was sitting and matters proceeded speedily. Within eight days the envoys from England had reached basic agreement on the terms of the peace with the count of Eu and the lord of Nesles, who served as negotiators for the French. A copy of the agreement was sealed with the seals of the archbishop of

Tarentaise, one of the pope's envoys, and of the archbishop of Rouen, and placed in the Temple at Paris.

The English envoys agreed to the surrender of English claims to Normandy, Anjou, Touraine, Maine, and Poitou, and called for a personal act of renunciation to be made, not only by King Henry and his two sons, but also by Richard and Eleanor and her two sons. Here was the major stumbling-block that was to delay the final ratification of the treaty for another year and a half. King Henry later complained bitterly that Simon had used his privileged position as one of the negotiators of the peace to have this clause about Eleanor inserted. No such renunciation was required of the king's daughters, or of the heiresses of the Empress Isabella, Eleanor's elder sister, or even from Richard of Cornwall's younger son. Simon, in return, asserted that it was none of his doing, but the will of the king of France.[30] Whatever the truth of the matter, the clause provided a very strong bargaining position for the earl and countess of Leicester in their demands upon the king.

The first formal ratification of the agreement took place in Paris on May 28th, just three weeks after the appointment of the envoys. Simon, Peter, and Hugh Bigod swore, on King Henry's behalf, that he would keep the articles, and the French envoys did the same for King Louis.[31] In the Middle Ages a king never took an oath in person with his inferiors, except at his coronation. Thus, a king never swore personally to keep the terms of a treaty except when his brother monarch was there. Otherwise, the solemn oaths were taken by the official negotiators on the king's soul, in his presence and that of the envoys of the absent king.

Unfortunately, the final conclusion of the treaty was not to be arrived at so simply. The envoys had arranged that the French and English kings and Richard of Cornwall, king of the Romans, should meet at Cambrai at the end of November to formally ratify and publish the treaty. Pope Alexander IV was to be requested to send a legate. Both these arrangements fell through. The pope could not send a legate at the time. The committee of barons, who were in virtual charge of the government during the summer and autumn of 1258, would not risk letting King Henry leave the country, and their surveillance. Instead, they sent the most distinguished of the magnates to the planned meeting. As well as the earls of Leicester and Norfolk, there were the bishop of Worcester and the recently consecrated bishop of Lincoln, Richard Gravesend. But King Louis refused to meet these envoys. It was only too apparent to him that the English barons had fettered King Henry's movements, and Louis always had a very lively idea of the proper respect and freedom owed a monarch. Hampered by the royal disapproval, the envoys returned to England having achieved nothing.

The time fixed for the treaty to come into force was Candlemas, 1259. At that time, King Louis sent messengers to England to make sure that Henry was negotiating in good faith. Indeed, he felt it was necessary to have a new oath from the English king. After all, the men who had been busy arranging the treaty at the French court were mainly ardent baronial supporters, and Louis was not sure that Henry agreed with the actions of his envoys. February, 1259, saw the negotiations for the treaty move another step forward. A solemn oath was sworn in Henry's presence, and before French envoys, that the English king would maintain the provisions of the peace. Richard of Cornwall, and his elder son, Henry, made solemn renunciation of their claims to Normandy and the other English lands absorbed by France. A few days later, the king's younger son, Edmund, also made the necessary surrender. Finally, on February 24th, King Henry himself, in the presence of the French envoys, renounced his claims to Normandy, Anjou, Touraine, Maine, and Poitou.

Only two problems remained, the acquiescence of Edward, and Eleanor, in these renunciations. Edward was rather reluctant, but finally capitulated, and fulfilled the necessary form by the end of May. From February till December, 1259, however, the treaty was held up by the intransigeance of Simon and Eleanor. They absolutely refused to make the required renunciation until their grievances were assuaged. For a while it looked as if it might be impossible to get Eleanor to agree at all. A new approach was attempted, with one ratification of the treaty supposing Eleanor's agreement, and the other omitting it altogether. Naturally the chroniclers had uncomplimentary things to say about the countess of Leicester's tenacity, although they did not know of the pecuniary demands that bolstered it. Thomas Wykes suggested that the real reason for her refusal lay in the earl's ambition, dreaming that the kingdom of England – and these French claims – might succeed to his sons or heirs by hereditary right.[32] The suggestion was born of malice and Wykes's hatred of the earl, for Henry's two sons and Richard of Cornwall and his two sons obscured any dream of the throne for the earl of Leicester's heirs.

During the spring and summer of 1259 the problem of satisfying the claims of Simon and Eleanor occupied the French and English kings and the barons. There was intense diplomatic activity at the court of the French king. Simon himself spent most of the summer in France with the other envoys; the earl of Gloucester, Peter of Savoy, and the king's trusted officials, John Mansel and Robert Walerand. They were trying to iron out such disputed sections of the treaty as the amount of money due for the 500 knights whom Louis had agreed to subsidize for his brother-in-law for two years; also the complicated questions of holdings in Cahors, Quercy, and Perigord.

There seems to have been continual discussion between the English and French negotiators. For example, in August Simon dined with Archbishop Odo Rigaud of Rouen at the stronghold of Néaufle-le-Chateau (Eure), not far west of Paris. The learned Franciscan, who played such an active part in the negotiation of the peace, seems to have spent much of that summer serving as King Louis's intermediary. In this case, he had come from the king at Gisors to meet Simon, and then returned immediately to Gisors to report to the king on the business they had discussed.[33] Probably the earl and the archbishop had dealt with the possibilities of settlement of the troubled question of Eleanor's renunciation. Louis knew that Archbishop Odo was not only a valuable royal servant, but also a good friend of Simon, who had been recommended to him by his fellow Franciscan, Brother Adam Marsh.

Meanwhile in England, Eleanor was proving recalcitrant. Various groups of arbitrators were appointed and laboured fruitlessly to arrive at a satisfactory conclusion. Always the countess repeated her main claim, reinforced by her husband; King Henry had accepted a settlement of 600 marks a year in his sister's name, for all her dowry, when it was worth 2,000 marks a year or more. She wanted the arrears of this difference for the last twenty-seven years,[34] a formidable sum even for a king less financially embarrassed than Henry. In July King Henry tried to pacify his sister and brother-in-law with the gift of ten manors, scattered throughout England. They were to replace the annual payment of £400.[35] The earl's officials did not delay in taking possession of these manors for their master. In Bere Regis (Dorset), for example, the king had to intervene, at the petition of the abbess of Tarrant, to restrain Simon's bailiffs in their attempt to seize the early crops which belonged to the abbess.[36] But even this gift was not sufficient to satisfy the earl and the countess. In exasperation and despair at ever achieving a settlement with the tenacious couple, a peace treaty was drawn up in October which omitted the controversial article of their renunciation. This peace was immediately ratified by the prelates and barons of England.[37] The final meeting for the publication of the often delayed peace treaty was arranged for Paris at the end of November.

With the end of the negotiations at last in sight, King Henry proposed to make his trip to Paris a leisurely and pleasant one. He took the queen with him, and a large retinue of nobles and prelates, including the earl of Gloucester, Peter of Savoy, and John Mansel. Simon himself, and probably Eleanor, were already in France. The elegant cavalcade left Westminster on November 6th, and ambled slowly through the English countryside, stopping at Canterbury and Dover. They did not cross the Channel till November 14th, and from Wissant – the favourite cross-Channel port in those days, about twelve miles north of Boulogne – they proceeded by very easy stages towards Paris. They finally arrived at St Denis on November 24th where King Louis and Archbishop Odo Rigaud had been waiting to welcome them since the previous day. The monks of St Denis greeted the English king with a solemn procession in their church, in the presence of King Louis and the archbishop, as well as the surrounding retinues. On the following day the glittering assembly moved on to Paris where the formal reception was repeated by the citizens of the city.[38]

But, before the final publication of the treaty, King Louis

Manors in the Counties

Herefordshire:
Dylwin: Lugwardin: Marden

Nottingham:
Gunthorpe: Kingshawe

Derby:
Melbourne

Yorkshire:
Esingwald with Hoby

Dorset:
Bere Regis

Counties of manors given to Eleanor and Simon
in 1259 during the negotiations for the
Treaty of Paris

159

decided on one last attempt to embody in it Eleanor's renunciation. He encouraged his royal brother-in-law to agree to the further discussion of the countess's claims, which the French king, in view of his unparalleled reputation for justice, may have felt had not been considered seriously enough. Finally an accommodation was worked out. On December 3rd, King Henry agreed that 15,000 marks sterling of the money to be paid him by Louis under the terms of the treaty should be retained by the French king until the quarrel between Henry and the earl and countess was settled. This was to be done according to the witness of the bishops of Lincoln and London, or one of them, and once settlement was achieved, the money was to be delivered to King Henry. At the latest, the matter was to be completed within the next two years.[39] The next day, the very day of the publication of the treaty, the earl and countess at last made the necessary renunciations, reassured by the support of King Louis. Eleanor swore to renounce any claims she or her heirs might have in Anjou, Touraine, Poitou, and Normandy. Her oath was made with the authority and agreement of her husband, in his presence and that of the two kings and many members of their courts.[40] Simon, in his turn, renounced any claims he might have to his father's conquests in Toulouse, Beziers, and all the Albigensian territories, as well as any claims through his brother in Evreux and Normandy.[41] With this last stumbling-block cleared away, after three long years of negotiation, they could proceed to the final formalities. In the garden of the king's palace in Paris, on December 4th, Archbishop Odo of Rouen recited and formally published the treaty, in the presence of the two kings, and a multitude of French and English barons and prelates. Immediately after this ceremony, the king of England did homage to King Louis for the English lands in France, and was then recognized as a peer of France.[42]

The final terms of the treaty mainly legalized the already existing situation. Henry, and his family, renounced to the king of France all rights in Normandy, Anjou, Maine, Touraine, and Poitou. In return, Louis gave the king of England the Agenais, Quercy, the part of Saintonge south of the Charente, and much of the dioceses of Limoges, Cahors, and Perigord, subject to certain limitations. For all these, as well as for Gascony, the English king was to do liege homage as duke of Aquitaine and peer of France. The disputes over the homages of Bigorre, Armagnac, and Fezansac were to be held over for further legal investigation. Besides the territorial provisions, the French king agreed to give Henry the sum necessary to support 500 knights for two years.[43]

It was not a perfect peace, but it was reasonably fair. Both sides complained. Many of the English chroniclers complained that their king had surrendered more than he should. Joinville says that the French councillors were angry with their king for giving away rights unnecessarily. King Louis did not look on the matter in this light, and he had his own motives:

> I know quite well that it was with complete justice that the King of England's predecessors lost the possessions which I hold; and the territory which I am giving him I am not giving because I am under any obligation to him or his heirs, but simply to foster love between his children and mine, who are first cousins. Moreover I think that I am obtaining this advantage from my gift, that before the king of England was not my liegeman, but now he owes me homage.[44]

In fact, Henry had only surrendered claims he could not enforce. The generosity of the French king, too, in the disputed territories to the south, was more apparent than real, for they never really came into the hands of the English despite years of legal quibbles. The provision which was of immediate and practical advantage for Henry was the one by which Louis agreed to pay for the 500 knights. Although these knights were supposed to be devoted to the service of God and the church and had been included in the treaty with the idea that they would be used to bolster the papal troops in Sicily, they proved instead a valuable reinforcement for the royal cause in England. Henry was struggling to break away from the tutelage of the barons, and such a sizeable force of knights – equal almost to the whole fighting strength of the baronage of England[45] – was of enormous value.

Now that the problem of peace with France was settled at last, Henry had to turn back to England to try and deal with the even greater problem that awaited him there. During much of the time that the treaty of Paris had been under discussion, the king's hand had been forced by the barons' control of the government. Simon de Montfort was not only the king's envoy during this complicated time, which brought conflict between him and his royal brother-in-law over Eleanor's claims. The earl of Leicester was also one of the committee of barons who were imposing a new form of government on the realm of England. To see how political events in England meshed into foreign affairs, we must turn back to the spring of 1258 and the remarkable programme of reform as the Provisions of Oxford.

The Common Enterprise

Mutterings of discontent had been heard throughout the realm for some time, but, in the spring and summer of 1258, natural bad luck and the results of the king's poor judgment swelled their volume to an unbearable pitch. Nature herself added to the chorus of complaint. The weather and harvests for 1257 and 1258 were extraordinarily bad. Most of England was threatened with general famine, far worse than the frequent local shortages. Since medieval man never lived in an economy of abundance, but existed almost from hand to mouth, the result of a general crop failure was disastrous. Grain, the staple of the poor man's diet, was so expensive as to be prohibitive, when it was available at all. Many died of hunger in the fields and on the roads, searching vainly for food. To add to the disaster, heavy rains in June caused the river Severn to flood from Shrewsbury to Bristol, inundating the fields and drowning people and farm animals.[1] Under the stress of such conditions, upheaval was not surprising. But the revolution of 1258 which created the Provisions of Oxford, and the whole system of government which flowed from them, was not the product of the unreasoning and despairing revolt of the poor, but calculated decision of the great barons.

When Simon de Montfort travelled back from Paris to share in the Hoke-tide parliament of 1258, more was at stake than he at first realized. This momentous April session did accelerate the pace of the negotiations with France, as we have seen, but there was more important business than the treaty Simon had been negotiating. In that April assembly the barons joined together to control their king and reform the state of the realm.

A series of factors impelled them. After the Welsh successes in 1257, Llywelyn had temporarily united the chiefs of north and south Wales to wage concerted warfare on the baronies of the Marches. These depredations inspired the violent quarrel between Simon and William de Valence. There were also the obvious difficulties over the French treaty. None of this was new. The troubles merely added powder to the explosive charge of the pope's final and excessive demands for Sicily. The papal demands from Henry for money and troops were far beyond any power of the king to fulfil personally. The king had to turn to his nobles for help and aid. Since Richard of Cornwall's election as king of the Romans in January, 1257, and his virtual removal to Germany, King Henry had lost one of the few counsellors whom both he and his nobles trusted. Richard's wealth had reinforced his brother before, but now it was the less sympathetic barons with whom Henry had to deal. In his effort to get the money to meet his commitments, the king had started a reform movement which he did not desire and could not control.

For the barons, the "Sicilian affair" epitomized all they most disliked about their king. Henry had involved himself – and the realm – in this wild affair without any consultation with them. It should have been part of the "business of the realm", in which the major nobles had a recognized right to give advice. The barons mistrusted, as the old aristocracy had always mistrusted, the growing centralization of the government. They deplored the continual inability of the king to make ends meet on his own customary revenues, refusing to recognize his higher costs and greater expenses. They disapproved of the presence of the royal clerks – the civil service of the thirteenth century – among the trusted counsellors of the king. Above all, they disapproved of the Lusignan half-brothers of the king, and of the train of penniless Poitevin adventurers they had brought to England. The arrogance of the king's step-brothers and their lion's share of the available wealthy marriages, lands, and pensions angered many besides the barons. The chroniclers attempted to ascribe the Provisions of Oxford and the ensuing civil war to no more fundamental cause then the evils wrought by these interlopers. The disgusted chroniclers over-simplified the issue, but the hated aliens were an ever-present irritant.

When Henry's mother, Queen Isabella, married Count Hugh of La Marche after the death of King John, she established a connection between England and Poitou which was to plague her son until the end of his days. After the death of their father and mother, the king's impecunious step-brothers and step-sisters had descended on England, to improve their fortunes. Henry was genuinely fond of his relations, and over-indulged these adventurers. This royal virtue of family feeling did not appeal to the English barons and people who saw these interlopers loaded with wealth. William de Valence's marriage to Joan of Munchesney, heiress of the Pembroke lands, has already been mentioned. The youngest brother, Aymer de Valence, was pushed into the see of Winchester by royal pressure, although he was still under the canonical age for consecration. Aymer, an acute man of business, was in no particular hurry to be consecrated, for until he took that step he could enjoy all the revenues of his see, the wealthiest in the kingdom, and yet not resign any of his other many profitable benefices. The chroniclers described him as haughty, belligerent, and uneducated, but they paid reluctant tribute to his business abilities which enabled him to accumulate a large fortune and tuck it safely away in various parts of England.[2] Two other step-brothers, Guy and Geoffrey de Lusignan, had lordships in France and never really settled in England, but they often came to visit their royal relative and were loaded with gifts of money and fees. Equally favourable arrangements were made for the girls of the family. One step-sister was married to John de Warenne, the earl of Surrey, and a seven-year-old niece was married to the nine-year-old Robert de Ferrers, heir to the wealthy earl of Derby.[3]

This outpouring of wealth on foreigners aggravated the English, but the arrogance of the Poitevins and their belief that they were immune to the laws of the land irritated them beyond measure. One tale from the chroniclers explains their wrath. Once Geoffrey de Lusignan was angered at one of the king's chief cooks – the chronicler does not say why – so he carried him off to Guildford. There Geoffrey amused himself by torturing the poor wretch, suspending him naked and ordering each hair of his head to be pulled out one by one. The cook died during this treatment, and the master of the cooks complained to the king, but Henry merely made a face and refused even to reprimand his brother.[4] In contemporary opinion such treatment could only be meted out to Jews without some shadow of legal justification.

When such irresponsible conduct was added to greedy claims on the king's disposable wealth, it is easy to understand the barons' fury with the Poitevins, and their general anti-foreign bias. The financial exactions of the papal agents had previously aroused this same insular prejudice, on the grounds that they, too, were foreigners who had already been too richly rewarded from the resources of England. The excessive collections made by the pope for the Sicilian affair sharpened this opposition immeasurably; but in this case there was also a principle at stake, the disputed principle of the rightful share of the barons in the government of the realm.

In most cases the thirteenth-century king or lord was not particularly adept at abstract thought. He expressed in action, rather than in theory, his assumptions about the nature of government. It was left to the articulate clerics and lawyers to formulate the vague general beliefs into specific terms which caught, more or less accurately, the flavour of their times. But it is essential to realize that these almost unconscious assumptions of both king and barons are of the utmost importance for a genuine understanding of the situation. The unexpressed beliefs of the protagonists profoundly affected their behaviour, and were as important, if less obvious, a factor in the situation as the personal clashes and the struggles over property rights. Each side felt, with some reason, that they had right on their side, and their convictions added bitterness to the struggle.

Fortunately there are two excellent sources for the basic theories of the opposing parties during these troubled years. One is that great summary of English law, Bracton's *De Legibus*, or, to give it its full English title, *Concerning the Laws and Customs of England*. It is the most comprehensive treatise on English law of its time and is a mine of information on the theories generally accepted by the lawyers and judges. Henry de Bratton, or Bracton as he was called after his death, was a Devonshire man with years of experience as one of the king's judges. He served on the assize, and also on the central court which was coming to be called "king's bench". Apparently he came into the royal service as a *protégé* of William Ralegh, another Devonshire man, who was one of the great judges of his day and ultimately won promotion to the bishopric of Norwich and then of Winchester. Besides the *De Legibus*, Bracton also compiled a voluminous *Notebook* which dealt, not with the basic ideas behind law and government, but with the actual conduct of specific cases. Bracton's great work was written not long before the years of the baronial rebellion, so that, both by training and by circumstance, he was ideally placed to sum up the general theory of his time while also conscious of the changes that were being worked. His book was so useful and so widely known that one scholar has called it "an embodiment of the experience and legal conscience of his age."[5]

It is, of course, difficult to deduce Bracton's exact position on many issues. Like most medieval writers, he felt that the argument from authority was the most telling. The authors of the Middle Ages truly believed that it was far more effective to quote from a number of respected sources than it was to state boldly their own original opinion. This did not necessarily mean that they lacked originality. Instead they rearranged and reapplied their quotations to fit a very different set of facts, so that they cloaked the new under the borrowed garments of some authority. Bracton was a man of great learning and penetrating intellect, and he quoted from all the best writers in his field: the Bible; Gratian's *Decretum;* Justinian's *Code* and *Digest*; John of Salisbury's twelfth-century treatise, the *Policraticus*; and that wonderful mine of miscellaneous information which was the Encyclopedia Britannica of the Middle Ages, the *Etymologies* of Isidore of Seville. But Bracton endeavoured to make his quotations and authorities fit into the set of facts with which he was familiar in thirteenth-century England. His statement that the king ought not to be under man, but under God and under the law, can be accepted as the generally recognized theory of the time. His contemporary, the great Dominican philosopher Thomas

Aquinas, put the same theory in philosophical terms. To this uncompromising statement of the royal power Bracton added that the law was not merely what the king willed, but rather what the king had decided and defined with the counsel of his magnates, which was then enforced with the royal authority.

Thus Bracton balanced the opposing claims of king and barons; the theoretical unmeasured supremacy of the king against the practical necessity for the co-operation of the barons in the process of government. The hard core of the problem, for which Bracton had no real solution, was what action to take if the king refused to follow the law. The justice of God seemed remote, and the thirteenth-century lawyer refused to go as far as John of Salisbury and admit that it was lawful to kill a tyrant. It was to solve this problem, probably, that some unknown hand added to the Bracton text the suggestion that the earls and barons served as the partners of the king and had the right to restrain him if he acted without law. This addition is undoubtedly not Bracton's, and does not agree with the body of his thought. It seems to have been the work of an isolated thinker, for it appears on only one of all the many Bracton manuscripts. Though it suited very well the beliefs and practices of the reforming baronial party, it is not indicative of a generally accepted idea.[6]

An interesting bit of special pleading, the *Song of Lewes*, expounds the barons' position.[7] This long Latin poem in two parts, full of Biblical parallels, was undoubtedly written by a cleric, probably one of the extravagant Franciscan admirers of Simon de Montfort. The first part is devoted to the description of the events leading up to the battle of Lewes and the battle itself. Everything that Simon had done was wonderful, he was the flower of nobility and good faith, and his victory in the battle was truly miraculous. In the second part of the poem, the author summarizes the theoretical position of the barons, and underlines an idea which was continually growing in importance – the place of the "community" in administering the affairs of the realm. This cleric agrees with Bracton that the law is superior to the king, but in the *Song of Lewes* it is pre-eminently the barons who are the supporters of the law by which the king is ruled. The king must turn to the barons for their advice and be guided by them, or suffer the consequences of disobedience.

> For every king is ruled by the laws he makes; King Saul is rejected because he broke the laws, and David is related to have been punished as soon as he acted contrary to the law; hence, therefore, let him who makes the laws learn that he cannot rule who observes not the law.[8]

Fundamentally then the controversy lay in the disputed understanding of the king's position. If Bracton's estimate was correct, a weak or a bad king could not be forced by his subjects to obey the law. The only real sanction was the judgment of God. Any attempt by the barons to enforce the law or extend their right of consultation to the actual management of the government of the country was, in fact, a derogation from the royal power. Such a derogation was inadmissible, because it limited and circumscribed the actual rights of the crown. So, both the pope and King Louis were acting within the theoretical framework of their time when they denied the validity of the barons' scheme of government. On the other hand the barons, by acting on their conviction that they had a right to have some control over the actions of their monarch, were in fact helping to develop a theory of limitation on the unbridled power of the king which was to bear fruit centuries later. However, their attempt to ensure their unquestioned right of advice and counsel and participation in the business of the realm served a more immediate purpose. It reminded later kings that it was imperative that they should so order their affairs that their government was satisfactory to this important class of the governed, if they did not want the barons to meddle in what was properly the king's business. Edward, in particular, learned this lesson superbly well from his observation of his father's uncomfortable situation and the efforts of the barons led by Simon de Montfort.

All these varied factors; theoretical, practical, and personal, worked together to provoke the explosion of 1258 and brought about the Provisions of Oxford. It is difficult to determine the exact part Simon de Montfort played. Some claim that he was the conscious innovator and political theorist, actuated by the highest motives and consciously designing a new form of government for England; others that he was a somewhat unprincipled adventurer, led by ambition and the lust for power. Neither of these claims can be accepted wholeheartedly. They are too simple to fit the complex personality of the earl of Leicester. The answer lies in the part that Simon played during the next agitated years; but the same set of facts can provide very different interpretations, a truth which has been abundantly illustrated by Simon's previous biographers.

During the early years of the barons' rule the earl of Leicester spent the major part of his time in France during 1258 and 1259, where he was busy with the negotiations for the treaty of Paris. Naturally, he returned to England frequently and he certainly formed one of the group that drew up the Provisions of Oxford; however, he was not the leader in its activities and could not, because of his absence, be intimately connected with its day-to-day work of reform. Nevertheless, as a strong and competent man with his own financial grievances against King Henry, he deplored the king's weakness and extravagance. Like the rest of the barons, Simon had a personal interest in seeing maintained the safeguards which had been won by Magna Carta, and supposedly guaranteed by its reissues, but as the chronicler remarked wistfully: "That so oft was ere granted, and so oft undo".[9]

During these early years of the revolt the dual nature of Simon's position was demonstrated more clearly than ever. His work in France emphasized his importance on both sides of the Channel and his influential friends at the French court. As yet, though he shared in reform with the other English barons, he was not totally committed to England. It was only in 1263, after King Henry had aired his complaints against the earl in both the English and French courts, reaching no solution and intensifying the bad feeling between them, that Simon finally determined to take control of the movement. His fellow barons might fall away from the oath they had all sworn to uphold the Provisions. Whatever happened, he would carry the movement to its logical conclusion, even though it meant opposition to the king himself in the name of the king's government. His motives were undoubtedly mixed, but they included a genuine, almost mystical, belief in the sanctity of his oath, as well as human exasperation and disgust with King Henry's vacillations and evasions.

The upheaval began with the Hoke-tide parliament of 1258.[10] Faced with the exorbitant papal demands and the dangers of the marauding Welsh, the assembly flared into controversy. The great nobles decided to take matters into their own hands. On Friday, April 12th, Richard de Clare, earl of Gloucester and Hertford and the richest and most influential noble in the kingdom, formed a confederation. His partners were Roger Bigod, the earl Marshal and earl of Norfolk; Hugh Bigod, his brother; Simon de Montfort; Peter of Savoy, one of the queen's uncles but for awhile a member of the moderate reforming group; and Peter de Montfort and John Fitz Geoffrey, less important but devoted followers of the earl of Leicester. These barons pledged to stand together in all things, saving only their faith to the king and the crown.[11] The royal demands for money were met with determined resistance. The clergy withdrew and planned for a further convocation at Merton to map their opposition to the king's requests. The barons themselves were aroused and determined. This time the king's empty promises and reaffirmations of the charters would not be sufficient. What was needed was the total reform of the realm, organized and controlled by the leaders of the chief barons.

In the beginning of May, the barons appeared at court, in full armour and wearing their swords, at nine o'clock in the morning. Although they took off their swords and greeted the king with proper courtesy, Henry was startled by their warlike appearance. "What is this, my lords? Am I taken captive by you?" Earl Roger Bigod spoke for all the barons and outlined their scheme:

> No, my lord king, no. But the intolerable Poitevins and all aliens should flee from your presence and ours. . . . Swear total observance to our counsels. . . . Swear, touching Holy Gospel, you and your son and heir Edward that you will not act without the advice of twenty-four good men of England, namely, the elected bishops, earls, and barons. . . .[12]

The king fearfully agreed. In his letters of May 2nd to the leading magnates Henry bound himself and Edward to carry out this plan, and agreed to the election of the Twenty-four who would reform the state of the realm.[13] This vital committee, whose powers were not circumscribed by their terms of appointment, were chosen by the beginning of May. The king's nominees showed the weakness of his position. They included three of his step-brothers, a nephew, and the husband of his niece. Then there were four of his clerks and confidential chaplains. The only individuals with independent status among the king's appointees were Fulk Basset, the bishop of London, and the earl of Warwick. Neither was of primary importance among the nobles of the realm. To oppose this uninspiring group the barons had such determined men as the earls of Gloucester, Leicester, Hereford, and Norfolk, Hugh Bigod, Roger Mortimer, and Hugh Dispenser.

The great experiment began. What had seemed at the time merely a concession by the king to the complaints of the barons became a legislative programme with far-reaching effects. Another parliament met at Oxford in the middle of June, and the barons in attendance came in military array to hear the first suggestions on the items to be reformed. The Petition of the Barons contained a memorandum of grievances.[14] In this time of high feelings when the barons were in the first flush of their power, the Provisions of Oxford were drawn up. Now, the Provisions, as they have come down to us in the annals of Burton, are not a public document or a permanent record. They are merely a series of memoranda, probably compiled during July, as a guide for the Council of Fifteen which had been ordained at the Oxford Parliament. Nevertheless, they provide a valuable guide to the work that was done during June and July. Essentially, they record the turning over of the supreme power in the kingdom to the Council of Fifteen. The Fifteen had been chosen by electors from the original group of twenty-four to control the king and supervise the royal organization. The reality of power remained with the Fifteen, and they were to give a report of their stewardship in parliaments to be held regularly three times a year. To these arrangements the "community of England" swore at Oxford. They added that final clause to their oath which was to provoke so much mischief, that if anyone acted against this they were to be regarded as a mortal enemy.[15]

This revolution was not achieved without opposition. The Poitevins objected to most of the changes decreed by the barons and three, which touched them most nearly, provoked them to defiance. The most painful was the order that all aliens should give up any lands and revenues granted them by the king – this was ostensibly to help Henry pay his debts – and, for the greater security of the realm, restore any royal castles they held. Secondly, any oppression proved against the bailiffs was to be punished and the lord was to make reparation. Finally, the aliens had to join in swearing to uphold the Provisions.[16] Among the Poitevins opposition hardened into defiance, and when that, too, proved unsuccessful the king's relations took to flight. One evening at the end of June they eluded the barons' watch and rode pell-mell from Oxford to the castle of Aymer de Valence at Winchester. They were soon pursued and besieged, while the court and council moved on from Oxford to Winchester. But their impetuous flight had sealed their fate. Although the Poitevins later agreed to take the oath, the barons refused the concession and insisted on their exile. Even William and Aymer de Valence, who were denizens of England, had to go with only 3,000 marks each from their various hoards throughout the country. When they were finally seen across the Channel in the middle of July, Henry de Montfort, Simon's eldest son, and some of the other young hotheads followed them and penned them in Boulogne. Finally King Louis freed them and gave them safe-conduct across his lands to their native Poitou.[17]

While the barons continued their deliberations at Winchester they suffered from what seems to have been a poison plot, perhaps by the Poitevins. The earl of Gloucester barely escaped death, and his brother William did die, as well as many others of lesser importance.[18] From Winchester the council went on with hardly a break to London. They wanted to secure the support of the city of London to the new oath, and then continue their discussions "upon the changing for the better the uses and customs of the realm."[19] Simon was among the lords who went to interview the Londoners at the Guildhall and he shared in the discussions at the New Temple. It seems possible that some of the meetings were held at the house where he was staying – the town house of the bishop of Durham, near the present site of Charing Cross. It was during his stay there that Henry took refuge, doubly terrified by the thunderstorm and by the earl of Leicester.*

During the month of July the barons seem to have drafted their letter of explanation to Pope Alexander IV about the state of affairs in England. They mentioned that they were unable to fulfil the most burdensome papal terms for the Sicilian enterprise, but they wanted to gain papal support against the Poitevins, especially against Aymer, the still unconsecrated bishop of Winchester. Their letter detailed the lawlessness and arrogance of the brothers and beseeched the pope to deprive Aymer of his see.[20] The king also sent off a letter, but though the form was Henry's the sentiments were those of the barons. Alexander wrote back in a conciliatory fashion, but he was not pleased by the turn of events in England. Sicily was in the possession of the triumphant Manfred, and the pope saw his most cherished schemes going up in smoke, without English support. Nor would he agree to sacrifice Aymer. In fact, he later consecrated the despised Poitevin with his own hand and started him back to England. Death solved at least one problem for the barons, for Aymer never reached England.

The rest of 1258 was devoted to putting into working order the new plans of the barons. In keeping with the provisions that aliens should resign their castles, Simon handed over to the king his castles of Odiham and Kenilworth, but he received Winchester. Along with Peter of Savoy, he seems to have shared fully in the work of the baronage. His name is found with the other earls attached to the decisions and deliberations of that fateful year, but his place was not one of unquestioned prominence. The only chronicler who imputes the leadership to him at this time is Walter of Guisborough, who compares him to Simon Macchabeus, rising for the laws and liberties of England.[21] But Walter was writing a half century after the events and may well have been influenced by the indisputable position of leadership which Simon held later. The leadership of 1258 rests rather with one of the other great barons: Roger Bigod, leader of the deputation to the king; Hugh

* See above, page 150.

Bigod, the new and energetic justiciar; or Richard de Clare, richest and most powerful of the barons.

The autumn parliament appointed the earl of Leicester and Roger Bigod, as well as the bishops of Lincoln and Worcester, to serve as their ambassadors at Cambrai. They were deputed by the barons to try and conclude the peace treaty with King Louis, and, especially, to explain plausibly King Henry's absence. Before Simon went, he took advantage of his position to hasten the payment of his debts. On November 6th, by the counsel of the magnates, the king agreed to pay Simon 200 marks of the debts owing him at the Hilary term (January), and the rest at Easter.[22] Once more Simon took advantage of the barons' upper hand to press his own claims against the king. The earl probably stayed on in France after the failure of their mission at Cambrai, for when he reappeared for the Candlemas parliament of 1259, he was described as having been away from England for a long time.[23]

One matter of purely personal importance occupied Simon de Montfort's mind during that midwinter. On New Year's Day, 1259, he dictated his last will and testament to his son Henry. In it he named the Countess Eleanor as his attorney and the guardian of his goods and lands. She was to have the advice and counsel of Richard, bishop of Lincoln, and Brother Adam Marsh. If the countess should predecease him, then his eldest son Henry would fill her place. Above all, the earl requested that the poor men of his lands should be justly provided with their goods, especially in any case where he might seem to have acted unjustly. He hoped to see his earthly debts fully paid – a considerable problem for one whose finances were so extremely complicated.[24] Simon's will shows considerable affection for his wife and a truly pious spirit. But this did not presage any fundamental change in the character of the man, for the year opened by the conciliatory phrases of his will gave few further proofs of a spirit of mildness in the earl.

The baronial scheme of government had been unopposed during the second half of 1258. Hugh Bigod, the justiciar appointed by the barons, had been travelling through the country, hearing cases and trying to provide justice and reform. When the first parliament of 1259 opened in London the week after Candlemas, the barons had a number of solid achievements to their credit. The proposed return of the king's brother, Richard of Cornwall, from Germany had alarmed the reforming party. But after some days of discussion with the barons' envoys and at the request of his brother, Richard agreed to take the oath to the Provisions. One more hurdle had been surmounted. The earl of Leicester also returned in time for the opening of the parliament, accompanied by the dean of Berri, who was a counsellor of the king of France. Undoubtedly, King Louis wanted to know the true state of affairs regarding the peace treaty. His own envoy could report to him whether the English king was really willing to proceed with the negotiations which, after all, had been handled by the barons who were respectfully, but definitely, opposed to Henry.

Two things seem to have dominated that February meeting. There was the continued chore of carrying out in further detail the reforms initiated during the previous summer, and there was the long-drawn-out question of concluding the peace treaty with France, which was Simon's particular task. All did not go smoothly. Parliament was suspended for a time at the beginning of March, possibly over some disputed reforms. A new collection of baronial ordinances were agreed to at the Temple on February 22nd, but were not published until the very end of March. In the Ordinances the king declared that the barons of his council and the twelve representatives of the community had undertaken to observe towards their tenants whatever the king had already promised to observe towards his vassals. This was really a startling step, for it widened enormously the base of the constitutional upheaval. Instead of restricting the reforms of 1258 to the small class of tenants-in-chief, it extended them very widely among the land-owning class.

The fatal cleavage between Simon de Montfort and Richard de Clare began at this time. Perhaps the Ordinances aroused the anger of the earl of Gloucester. Since he was one of the greatest landholders in England, he had a great stake in the matter and may have feared the loss of his own privileges. Whatever the cause, Simon had one of his blazing quarrels with the earl of Gloucester during the suspension of parliament. The earl of Leicester accused

Richard de Clare of wavering in their common enterprise. He lashed out:

> I care not to live or hold converse with men so fickle and false as thee. For we have made a promise and oath to one another in these matters whereof we are treating. And as for thee, my lord earl of Gloucester, the more thou dost excel all men in rank, the more thou art bound by wholesome statutes.[25]

On this note, Simon seems to have left once again for France to carry on the negotiations for the peace treaty. Whatever the immediate cause of the quarrel, its result was a breach between the two most powerful earls. The first angry words were smoothed over, at the instance of Humphrey de Bohun, earl of Hereford, and the earl of Gloucester sent his seneschal through his lands to enforce the new requirements of the Ordinances.[26] But Gloucester was also a member of the embassy to France and the irritation which Simon had kindled in London flared up again in Paris. This time Richard berated Simon for Eleanor's refusal to give up any fragment of the vague claim that she might have inherited to the family lands in France. By epithets and sarcasm, the two erstwhile collaborators were brought almost to blows, to the great amusement of the French.[27]

The exact chronology of affairs is puzzling here and it would be interesting to know the immediate cause of the first explosion. There were several possibilities. Besides the problem of the Ordinances, there was also the drawing up of a new confederation on March 14th between Edward, with a few of his associates, and the earl of Gloucester, the leader of the two Bigods and some of the northern nobles.[28] If the compact with Edward marked a separation of Gloucester from the strongest reforming party, either of these matters might have provoked the quarrel. There seem to have been complications, too, over the new embassy to France which included Peter of Savoy, John Mansel, Robert Walerand, and John de Balliol, as well as the quarrelsome earls.[29] Although the letters of appointment were drawn up on March 10th, Simon certainly remained another week in England, and may not have left for France before the beginning of April. On March 16th, the earl of Leicester withdrew from his agreement to act as surety for the king's debt to some Florentine merchants. The other sureties were the earl of Gloucester, Peter of Savoy, and John Mansel[30] and this withdrawal may have been another example of the earl of Leicester's unwillingness to work with the earl of Gloucester. Whatever the reason for his ill humour, when Gloucester and the other ambassadors returned to England with a formal account of their proceedings, the earl of Leicester remained in France.[31] During the summer of 1259 Simon devoted most of his energies to the negotiations for the treaty and to pressing his wife's claims. Other French matters also claimed his attention. In June he was mentioned as one of the organizers of the match between King Louis's nephew, Robert of Artois, and Amicia de Courtenai.[32]

Henry's favourite feast of St Edward the Confessor (October 13th) had been appointed by the barons as the time for the third of the annual parliaments. It was a natural decision, for this was the time the king was always accustomed to celebrate with all his great nobles around him. On the feast of St Edward in 1259 preparations were far advanced for the publication of the Provisions of Westminster, that detailed culmination of the series of suggested baronial reforms and "the most enduring monument of the baronial revolution".[33] During the celebrations the "community of the bachelory" voiced to Edward, the earl of Gloucester, and others of the council their strong feeling about the conduct of affairs in the kingdom. They said that the reforms demanded by the barons had been made by the king, but the barons themselves had done nothing to the profit of the commonwealth but only to their own good.[34] These bachelors were the substantial undertenants, who would have been present at the October parliament because they were part of the households of the great magnates. The dramatic presentation of their complaints probably added some clauses to the Provisions of Westminster, although it did not materially change the tenor of that document.

It is quite possible that the earl of Leicester did not return to London for the October parliament. The evidence is somewhat confusing. On October 15th, Edward swore to Earl Simon and his heirs aid and counsel, promising to uphold the enterprise of the barons and not to make war on any involved in the coalition. This act was attested by the prince's seal, and by those of his closest associates, John de Warenne, Henry of Almaine, and Roger Leyburne.[35] It is plausible, but not conclusive, that this oath was made in the presence of the earl of Leicester. However, there is another reference to Simon being in France on October 19th for the consecration of the bishop of Evreux.[36] If the earl was in London on October 15th and in Evreux four days later, he must have travelled at very high speed. There is one other small point against his presence in London. It seems likely that if the earl of Leicester had been present when the bachelors came forward with their complaints the chroniclers would have mentioned his name, as they did that of the earl of Gloucester. It is more than likely, too, that the complaints would have then been addressed to him, since he was already considered vitally concerned with the affairs of the lesser men, rather than to Edward, who, although he was the king's son, was not yet twenty-one. Whatever the truth of the matter as to whether or not Simon did appear briefly for the St Edward's day festivities, he had no important share in the work of that parliament. His new understanding, or alliance, with Edward marks another attempt by the king's son to consolidate his own position by being on good terms with the various leaders in the baronial party. The relation with Montfort had particular importance because dissension had arisen between Edward and the earl of Gloucester over their conflicting claims in the west of England.

The end of 1259 found Simon de Montfort in a rather equivocal position. The earl had shared and agreed in the plans and projects for the control of the king. Nevertheless, during the last two years his dominating interest had been in France, not England. After all, most of his time and energies had been devoted to the troubled questions involved in the treaty of Paris. He was not, as yet, committed to wholehearted opposition to the king. Two more years of dissension between Henry and himself, of growing proof of the king's disdain for the sanctity of his oath, finally forced his decision. Not till then did he throw himself into vigorous opposition and refuse to agree to the king's attempts to go back on his solemn word.

Arbitrations and Complaints

The earl of Leicester felt no desire to linger at the French court after the formal publication of the treaty of Paris. He soon went on to Normandy to meet his wife.[1] King Henry, however, gladly tarried in the cordial atmosphere of the French court. King Louis and Queen Marguerite treated him with honour and affection, restoring the self-esteem badly bruised by the barons' continual emphasis on his incapacity and poor government. Henry could enjoy himself celebrating Christmas in Paris, and there was the excuse of family business to settle. Arrangements had been going on for some time for the marriage of his sixteen-year-old daughter Beatrice, to John, the son of the duke of Brittany. The king and the earl of Leicester clashed over the amount of Beatrice's dowry, and the right of the council to be consulted. The earl reminded the king that if he wanted to give lands with his daughter he must remember his oath that he would not give or grant anything of importance without his council's advice. Later, when raking-up old grievances, Henry claimed that Simon had tried to upset the marriage, while the earl insisted that he had only warned the count of Brittany of the king's oath.[2]

All was finally settled peacefully, and the marriage was solemnized in Paris after Christmas. King Henry then started on his journey home, but he had not gone far when the eldest son of King Louis died suddenly. The English king retraced his steps to Paris to be at the funeral of his nephew. It was an impressive procession that accompanied the body of the young and much-loved prince on its last sad journey from Paris to St Denis. As the coffin was carried for burial to the new royal foundation of Royaumont, some twenty miles to the west, many of the principal barons of France and England took turns serving as pall-bearers. Even King Henry himself deigned to put his royal shoulder to the task for the space of half a league.[3]

The earl of Leicester had gone back to England from Normandy, probably around the end of January. He was anxious to be back in time for the February parliament, one of the three which the Provisions of Oxford had ordained should be held annually. Henry felt no urgent desire to keep to the letter of the Provisions on this matter. On January 26th, Henry wrote from France to the Justiciar, Hugh Bigod, explaining that Beatrice's marriage and the funeral of young Louis had delayed him beyond his expectations. He was now travelling at "moderate speed" through the north. Hugh was to send the king the advice of the council on certain matters concerned with arbitrations arising from the recently signed treaty, but Henry specifically stated that the Candlemas parliament was to be postponed until his return.[4]

The members of the council left in England were in an awkward position. Several of the councillors were with the king in France, including the earl of Gloucester, who was of prime importance among the reformers. With him too were such supporters of the king as Peter of Savoy and John Mansel, the brains of the opposition to the barons. Thus, the council which had to reply to the king's letter was incomplete, and signs of the fatal division between the barons began to appear. Gloucester was won over to the king's side during this stay in France. Richard de Clare had already been on bad terms with Simon de Montfort, for their two fiery quarrels had kindled an enmity not easily extinguished. With the aid of this personal animus it was not difficult for the king and his entourage to persuade Gloucester that the barons had gone too far, and deprived the king of his proper rights. Without Gloucester's reinforcement, the members of the council temporized. The Justiciar forbade the Candlemas parliament in the king's name, and the councillors wrote Henry that parliament had been postponed for three weeks.[5]

Meanwhile Simon de Montfort had resumed his place with the council in England. On February 10th, the earl spent a night at

St Albans, making an offering of a precious covering at the martyr's tomb. The next morning he continued his journey.[6] Unfortunately, the chronicler did not add which way the earl was travelling, whether back to London to continue the work of the council, or whether on his way to Kenilworth, annoyed at the king's postponement. At any rate, Simon bent his efforts during February and March towards a word for word fulfilment of the Provisions. Henry later accused him of having held a parliament at Candlemas, but the earl specifically denied this. He admitted that some of the barons had arrived as if for the parliament, for they wished to keep their oath, but the Justiciar had come to them and told them of the king's desire to delay the parliament until his coming.[7] Nevertheless, Simon's activities during these months much alarmed the king, and the echoes of the royal panic are audible in his later complaints. Henry recalled the violent opposition of the earl to the king's projects, the armed arrival for parliament, and the removal of Peter of Savoy – most reasonable of the king's men – from the council. All these things the earl either denied, or claimed had been done with the advice and agreement of the council.[8]

Undoubtedly a deep cleavage was developing in the council. The earl of Leicester was the most ruthless and the most radical of the councillors, and he was attempting to push the others farther than they wished to go. Their reluctance is understandable, for what Simon suggested was unheard of at this time. He proposed to hold parliament without the king in direct opposition to his wishes; he wanted the Justiciar to refuse to send overseas the money the king had requested; and he was willing to provide at least the semblance of armed resistance. It is no wonder that the more conservative heads on the council found these proposals rash and impossible. For the moment, Simon found one unexpected ally in Edward, the king's son, and the two led the opposition against the more cautious Justiciar, Roger Bigod, and Philip Basset. When the king's return was still delayed after Easter (April 4th) – Henry had, as a matter of fact, remained in St Omer for two months – the barons insisted on a parliament in London. Both the earl of Gloucester, who had returned from France before

the king, and the earl of Leicester came armed, and with their
retinues, to this meeting, proposing to lodge within the gates of
the city of London. Edward, at loggerheads with the earl of
Gloucester over their conflicting claims in the west, upheld his
uncle Simon.

The citizens of London feared that the rival parties would
provoke bloodshed and cause the ruin of their city, but they were
saved by the intervention of Richard of Cornwall. Henry had sent
him word of the proposed meeting for, though still safely at
St Omer, the king was avidly collecting the rumours and reports
that came from across the Channel. Since Richard's return to
England in January, 1259, he had been living very quietly on his
estates. Richard showed neither great enthusiasm for the Provisions, nor great antagonism; he took the requisite oath but only so
as to be allowed to return to England. As he bore the proud title of
king of the Romans, he did not want to involve his prestige in a
demeaning struggle with the barons. Richard's instinct was always
to look for the way to compromise. Not being a good fighter, he
felt that bloodshed was wasteful. In this way, his natural instincts
reinforced his shrewdness and his political sense, and made him a
popular arbitrator.

Armed with his brother's warning, he acted with speed and good
sense in this particular commotion. Richard conferred with the
mayor and aldermen of London, as well as the Justiciar and
Philip Basset, representing the moderate element of the council.
They agreed that the armed earls and Edward should be quartered
outside the city. Gloucester chose the palace of the bishop of
Winchester in Southwark, and Edward and Simon occupied the
land between the city and Westminster on the other side of the
river. London provided carefully for its defence in case of necessity.
All citizens over fifteen were to be armed and all the gates were to
be closed at night and guarded by armed men. Even in the
daytime only the three most necessary gates: Ludgate, Aldgate,
and that at London Bridge, were to be open and they, too, were to
be guarded. Richard also arranged that he, Philip Basset and the
Justiciar should lodge within the city with a well-picked neutral
group to be ready, if necessary, to aid in London's defence.[9] These

measures kept peace in the city until the king's return at the end of April.

Meanwhile, in France, Henry was feverishly collecting a body of paid knights to take back to England with him to strengthen his position. His efforts to find mercenaries were made possible by the large sum of money which he was receiving from King Louis by the terms of the treaty of Paris, for Henry was, as usual, in financial difficulties. Although Hugh Bigod, the Justiciar, had finally gathered and sent over the money the king had requested, despite Simon's vigorous opposition, the sum was not sufficient for the royal debts. Henry still faced the worrying problem of getting back his jewels, for they had been deposited in Paris as security for his loans. In England, the king was attempting to rebuild his party. The barons' wish for a parliament coincided with Henry's summons to certain specific magnates, ordering them to come to London on April 25th with the service due by them to the king. The most interesting thing about this letter of summons is the names that were omitted from the list of the magnates. The king passed over most of the clergy and the earls of Leicester and Hereford, as well as the most ardent supporters of Simon and Edward among the barons. The inference is that men like Peter de Montfort and Roger Leyburne were considered openly defiant to the king in their adherence to Simon and Edward.[10]

Party strife dominated the situation in April of 1260. The lines were drawn between the king, Gloucester, and the greater part of the council on one side; Simon de Montfort, Edward, and their immediate followers on the other. Probably Leicester's party had at least the tacit support of most of the clergy. It was a period of great tension which could easily have flared into war. The king brought about three hundred foreign knights home with him, and, though he accused Simon of attempting to find the same kind of support overseas, Henry for once seems to have acted with wisdom and restraint. With the advice and support of his brother Richard, he entered London and lodged at the house of the bishop of London, near St Paul's. He also took the earl of Gloucester into the city with him. Richard of Cornwall withdrew to his house at Westminster; the earl of Leicester and Edward remained outside the wall in the Hospital of St John, and in the open country between the city and Westminster. For a few days both camps trembled on the brink of war, but the earl of Leicester had not yet come to the point where he felt he could oppose the person of the king by force, and the great number of royal mercenaries underlined the futility of such an attempt. Edward sought to see his father, but the king, who had heard many reports of his son's recalcitrance, refused him admission. Henry was afraid that his decision to be firm with his vigorous and arrogant young son and thus bring him back to proper allegiance could not withstand a personal meeting. "Let not my son Edward appear before me, because if I see him, I will not keep myself from kissing him", he exclaimed.[11]

Once more Richard of Cornwall took up the delicate office of mediator, this time between his brother and his nephew. Apparently the king of the Romans appealed successfully to Edward's pride, for he persuaded the young man to submit his case to the two kings, his father and Richard himself. In the assembly of the barons at St Paul's at the beginning of May, Edward announced his submission and gave his reason: since the earls and barons were not the peers of a king's son, they had no right to discuss his conduct.[12] Edward broke with the earl of Leicester and was completely reconciled with his father. Richard served his brother well in bringing Edward back to the royal side. Like Richard himself in 1238, Edward learned his lesson of opposition once and for all, and never again strayed. His quarrel with the earl of Gloucester was settled by the end of June, although Bristol Castle, the main bone of contention, was handed over even earlier to the custody of Philip Basset.[13]

Simon de Montfort had lost a most valuable ally by Edward's defection, and further roused the king's anger against himself. Henry's annoyance was already longstanding. The earl's persistent attempts to force him to financial concessions, the delay in the conclusion of the treaty of Paris because of the earl's intransigeance; these were partly personal quarrels. But there was also the political matter of the earl's share in the baronial scheme of government and, above all, his extreme stand during the last few months. The

May parliament, which saw Edward restored to full agreement with his father, provided the king with what seemed an ideal opportunity to proceed against the earl of Leicester.

In Henry's mind, Simon was mainly responsible for Edward's fling at opposition, and should be called to account. The king's intention was to put the earl on trial before the other magnates and force him to answer, on very brief notice, a series of complaints against him and his actions, both in England and overseas. Earl Simon declared his willingness to answer all questions and to reply to any allegations against himself on the appointed day, though with one slight reservation. For some reason – possibly the earl of Gloucester's fear that the king might turn on him too – the investigation was postponed to the following parliament in July.[14] The meeting broke up and the king withdrew from London to his palace at Westminster. Still concerned over the rebellious tendencies of his barons, Henry found artistic corroboration at Westminster. Four years before he had ordered a special picture for the private wardrobe, where he had his head washed, depicting a king being saved from sedition by his dogs. The painting must have reminded him of his own uneasy situation and underlined his precarious position.[15]

Before the next parliament could convene a new factor was added to the quarrel between Henry and Simon. King Louis of France heard of the English king's proposal to proceed against the earl. Louis's strongly developed sense of justice and absence of personal pique would have made such an attack distinctly abhorrent to him. He was more than willing to sustain his royal kinsman in what he felt were his proper rights, but he did not want to see the restored king use his power to persecute when the times cried out for conciliation and compromise. Besides, Earl Simon was an important man in western Europe – a man of French background and extensive reputation in France – and the French were willing to bolster his position by sending important messengers to deal with the matter. King Louis's choice for this delicate mission fell on Archbishop Odo Rigaud of Rouen, and John Harcourt.[16] Archbishop Odo had been intimately connected with the negotiation of the treaty of Paris, was a personal friend of Simon, and was also one of the French king's most trusted advisors. John Harcourt also came from Normandy, from a noble family whose English lands in Warwickshire had been forfeited after the conquest of Normandy by the French. King Henry had given these lands to the earl of Leicester in happier days, but, as a mark of favour for John's share in the settlement of this affair, the Harcourts were allowed to regain their manor of Ilmington.

Probably the archbishop was instructed by King Louis on the nature of his mission in England during the weeks in June when he was in Paris for *parlement*. Rigaud crossed the Channel on July 4th and arrived in London on the 7th, having stopped in Canterbury to say Mass and pay his respects at the shrine of St Thomas. Very discreetly the prelate, in his diary of his travels, concealed his mission in England under the ambiguous title of "business of the king of France".[17] One annalist was much more outspoken, stating bluntly that the two Frenchmen came to defend Simon de Montfort, accused of *lèse majesté*.[18] The envoys prevailed on the king and Simon to accept a preliminary investigation by a committee of bishops, who were to report to the king as quickly as possible, preferably before July 15th. The king had already drawn up a list of charges against the earl, ready for use. The record of the bishops' investigation still exists, a memorandum in Anglo-French of the proceedings before the council, giving the king's accusations and Simon's answers.[19] It is a fascinating document. Henry had raked up all the charges he could possibly hurl at the earl on a number of matters; his share in the treaty of Paris, the complications over Bigorre, the Provisions of Oxford, and, especially, Simon's part in the resistance to the king in the months just past. In most cases there is almost total contradiction between the accusation and the answer. Many times the earl claimed that the king had misunderstood or had been misled, and then proceded to give his own interpretation of the facts. Sometimes the earl turned aside a just complaint of the king with considerable arrogance, as when:

> The king says that while he was there (France), he ordered his Justiciar in England that no parliament was to be held until his return. The earl says that it may well be that he ordered him.[20]

Certainly, this was not the soft answer that turns away wrath. Nevertheless, Simon had brought forward enough evidence, and had so involved the council in his replies, that the council could not condemn him without, in fact, condemning itself. The matter was dropped and Archbishop Odo was free to return to France, his mission accomplished. During these difficult weeks he showed one further mark of friendship to Earl Simon by appointing his young son, Amaury de Montfort, to a vacant prebend in the cathedral of Rouen. When the archbishop left England on July 22nd, he probably took Amaury with him, for after a rapid trip to St-Germain-des-Prés to report on his mission to King Louis and to be present at the baptism of the newest royal daughter, he returned to Rouen and installed Amaury in his new benefice on August 14th.[21]

Simon was free for the moment from danger of condemnation by the king, but he certainly was not in favour at court. The July parliament had also had to deal with the ever-recurrent Welsh question. The turbulent Welsh had profited by the king's long absence in France to campaign widely in the Marches, and had also attacked the important castle of Builth, west of Worcester, which was in the custody of Roger Mortimer. Mortimer had beaten off this attempt, but, when he was summoned to the July parliament, the Welsh attacked the castle once more, took it, and massacred the garrison. This bad news proved a potent spur to action. The assembly decided to send two armies against the Welsh, and summons were issued for September 1st, when the earl of Gloucester would lead the force from Shrewsbury and Simon himself the one gathering at Chester. It was an ideal opportunity for the king to use the talents of the earl of Leicester, who was universally recognized as one of the strongest fighters of England. It would, at the same time, rid the court of his presence. The chronicler of St Albans voiced the suspicion, quite consonant with Henry's character, that he was given the command with the hope that he might be slain rather than suffer the disgrace of returning defeated.[22]

On the great feast of St Edward (October 13th), when the earl of Leicester was accustomed to render service to the king as

Steward of England, he appointed young Henry of Almain, son of Richard of Cornwall, to serve as his attorney.[23] Some gesture of reconciliation was made on this occasion, for Edward knighted the earl of Leicester's two elder sons, Henry and Simon the younger. This particular St Edward's feast was the occasion of one of the largest creation of knights during Henry III's long reign. The king himself knighted John of Brittany, his daughter Beatrice's husband, and, besides the two Montforts, some twenty-five young men received the belt of knighthood. According to the usual practice, the new knights, with Edward and Henry of Almain, crossed the Channel almost immediately to try their strength and heighten their reputation in various overseas tournaments.[24] Edward was to stay away over a year, much of the time in his Gascon possessions. Undoubtedly the older and calmer heads felt that it would be easier to pacify an unsettled England if the young firebrands were out of the way.

Certainly it was easier for the king to get his own way in the October parliament without the opposition of the earl of Leicester. Changes had to be made in all the great officers of state. Henry of Wingham, the chancellor, had been made bishop of London, and thus must resign his office. John of Crakhall, the treasurer, had died, and Hugh Bigod, the Justiciar and the mainstay of the baronial plan of reform, withdrew from his office. The three men who replaced them were not of the same calibre. A strong baronial supporter, Hugh Dispenser, became Justiciar, but he did not have the independent position or prestige of Hugh Bigod. Two moderate clerics were named chancellor and treasurer. Henry could well be pleased, for this set of officials were far easier for him to circumvent than the previous three. The danger of civil war subsided a little, for the barons had been divided, and an important group of them now sustained the king instead of blocking him. Even the earl of Leicester had temporarily withdrawn from active opposition. Perhaps soon the king could attempt to disband the hated council, which fettered his acts, and rule in proper state.

Although conditions had improved a little, there were still many outstanding problems for the king to settle at the beginning of 1261. One of the most important was to arrange with his sister and

Simon the settlement of their personal claims, according to the terms of the agreement preceding the treaty of Paris. Two years had been the time limit for the settlement, and a year was already past. Henry took the initiative in the beginning of January and submitted all the matter to the arbitration of King Louis, or if the king could not act himself, then to Queen Marguerite and Peter le Chambellan. However, this was only to stand if Simon and Eleanor could be persuaded to do the same.[25]

So many disputes are mentioned as being submitted to arbitration that it is important to find out what the thirteenth century meant by the term, and what powers it implied. It was a very popular means of settlement for all kinds of quarrels. Anyone without natural or legal handicaps could act as an arbiter, if they were chosen by the mutual consent of both parties, and both sides agreed to accept the arbitration. It was easy enough to escape from an arbitration any time before the arbitral sentence was given – almost any excuse would do – but there was supposed to be no appeal once the award was made. As Beaumanoir, the great French lawyer of the period, said: "An arbiter is a kind of judge who has no jurisdiction, except such as the parties give him by virtue of compromise."[26] The procedure varied from country to country and was, in many cases, very loose. As the influence and knowledge of Roman civil law became more widespread, it gradually hardened. The documents of the time are cluttered by all kinds of legitimate excuses for the lack of success of so many arbitrations. The most frequent were the refusal of one of the named arbiters to act; withdrawal of one of the interested parties; or change in the agreed dates. In so many cases, despite all the formal preliminaries, no decision was ever reached. This dispute with Simon and Eleanor was one of the inconclusive arbitrations which dragged on and on with nothing achieved.

By March, King Henry had succeeded in getting the earl to submit to the award of King Louis. Henry's motive for being willing to do so was transparently clear. He had to keep on good terms with the French king, and his letter underlines that fact.

To the French king. Whereas various contentions and complaints have long been between the king and the said Simon and Eleanor, as he knows, and Louis at another time, as the king remembers, made an earnest request to him on their behalf, the king, because he reputes the prayers of Louis as a command and wished that he understand the truth of his action in this matter, submits himself in all the premises to his award, as the earl does likewise.[27]

Before the earl and countess of Leicester returned to England in March, they had been busy in France pursuing still another legal claim, this time against Eleanor's Lusignan relatives over lands and moneys in Angoulême. Like all the countess's legal affairs, it had complicated roots and involved a long-drawn-out struggle. The whole affair underlines one very common characteristic of the century, exemplified vividly by the earl and the countess, the general tenacity of the people in their pursuit of their right, however faint and remote. An extraordinary volume of legal process was required to settle such quarrels peacefully.

This particular claim went back a long way, to the inheritance Eleanor might have been presumed to expect from her mother, Queen Isabella, who was the heiress of Angoulême. The county of Angoulême had been disputed between Isabella's husband, King John, and the count of La Marche, but the settlement of 1214 provided for the surrender of the count's claim to Angoulême, as well as the marriage of the royal infant Joanna to the count's son. After King John's death, when Isabella came back to Poitou and suddenly married the fiancé of her young daughter, she kept hold of her lands in Angoulême. In order to buttress her claim, she urged Henry, during the disastrous campaign in Poitou of 1242–3, to renounce to her and her second husband all the rights and claims that he might have on the county of Angoulême and the castles of Cognac, Jarnac, and Merpins. Henry weakly consented, and also promised that he would have Richard of Cornwall and Eleanor make the same renunciation "if at any time they were in our power".[28] Here was the hub of the problem. Eleanor was not in Henry's power in 1242 – she had remarried in 1238 – and she had not come again into this power. Nonetheless, Isabella and Count Hugh proceeded to divide the lands of Angoulême among their numerous children in blissful disregard of any claims which might arise from the children of her first marriage.[29]

By the autumn of 1260, Eleanor had commenced the legal fight against her Lusignan relatives which was to continue for ten years. It was settled finally by the judgment of the *parlement* of Paris, reinforced by the command of King Louis himself. The real reason for the original claim is unknown. There are several plausible possibilities. Simon may have wanted to use these claims of his wife as still another stick with which to belabour the hated Poitevins. Both husband and wife may have felt that it was the part of wisdom to increase their holdings and revenues in France. King Louis seemed to be more favourable to their claims than Eleanor's brother had ever been, especially now when Simon was under such a cloud of suspicion at the English court. Perhaps there was no deeper motive than the desire to exploit their legal claims to the last fraction, and to wring out the last possible penny to aid their continually confused finances.

In November, 1260, Count Burchard of Vendôme constituted himself surety for Guy and Geoffrey de Lusignan and William de Valence for the large sum of 1,500 marks of silver to be paid to Eleanor as compensation, if the brothers did not observe a compromise made between them and the countess.[30] Both sides appointed proctors to represent them, and two knights were chosen as arbiters. Eleanor first presented her complaints at Poitiers in January, 1261, at what was probably a preliminary formal hearing. In February, the arbiters set the Tuesday to Saturday of the fortnight after Shrove Tuesday (March 22–26) for hearing and settling the award at the abbey of La Couronne, Angoulême. There is a record of the defences made by the Lusignans to Eleanor's claims, but we do not know if the knights who had been chosen to act as arbiters ever gave any award. If they did, it could not have proved satisfactory to the countess for, by the end of 1262, she had taken her case to Paris. She dropped the case against William de Valence, probably because he returned to England permanently in the spring of 1261. With Guy de Lusignan she came to a special arrangement, which allowed for further arbitration. It is an illuminating commentary on the frequent inability of arbiters to conclude their task that, in this case, one of the arbiters admitted six years later that he was resigning because he was going away, and even then the affair had not been concluded. In 1262 Eleanor pleaded her case against Geoffrey de Lusignan and Hugh XII before the central court of *parlement*. No judgment seems to have been given at this time, but in November both the earl and countess were busy in Paris on the affair. From there they wrote to King Louis's brother, Alphonse of Poitiers, about it. As count of Poitou, he was overlord of La Marche and the Lusignan lands, and thus had a special interest in the matter.[31] This long-drawn-out law case is still another ingredient in the extraordinary mixture of private and public business, in France as well as in England, occupying the earl and countess during these years. Relatively unimportant in itself, it attracts attention because it proves how widely the interests and resources of such a couple might range.

While the king was trying, more or less wholeheartedly, to conclude his private quarrel with his sister and Simon, he was doing everything in his power to end his humiliating submission to the baronial council and his enforced oath to the Provisions. The gradual slackening of the baronial might during 1260 encouraged the king to strike out in an attempt to destroy the Provisions completely. He disregarded the council and relied, as before, on a close-knit circle of advisers drawn from his relations and clerks. Calling the magnates together at the end of February, 1261, he denounced the rule by the council as the rule of a small clique, who sought not the advantage of the king and kingdom, but their own private gain.[32] Thereupon, Henry went to London and established himself in the Tower – the strongest and most invulnerable of all his castles – and proceeded to enact changes in his own name. He appointed new keepers of castles, called in all the moneys he could raise, and once again acted like a monarch in complete control of the administration. Secretly the king had sent off a special messenger to the pope, seeking absolution from his oath to the Provisions. His envoy in this case was Master John Mansel, nephew of the great John Mansel who was the master-mind of the king's strategy. Since Master John had personal business at the Roman curia which had been pending for some time and had already received licence to go, he could leave England with his main errand unsuspected by the barons.[33]

During the interval of secret, anxious waiting for the papal pronouncement, Henry agreed to an arbitration with the barons and put forward a series of complaints. There is little doubt that the king was not in earnest about submitting to arbitration in these matters. During March Henry was striving to procure further delay in any action by the barons, so that he could gain time for the safe arrival of the papal bull which he was confident would release him from his obligations to the hated Provisions. The royal complaints were an odd mixture of the basic and the trivial. They ranged from the important claim that the council had debased the royal dignity and stripped the king of his inherent royal rights by refusing him the use of his seal and the right to appoint his own officials, to the plaintive statement that his baggage had been attacked by robbers at Alton (on the road to Winchester). Henry was angry too that the royal castles and houses had been allowed to fall apart, for such a lack of concern for buildings particularly offended the king's artistic and architectural good taste.

All the time Henry was on the attack. He turned on the council and attacked their own administration claiming that they had failed in reform, failed to do justice within the kingdom, and had hindered the proper conduct of the king in regard to France, Wales, and Sicily.[34] It was a long bill of indictment, and the council answered with considerable moderation. But no real compromise could be arrived at, even if there had been real good will on both sides. The king argued from his preconceived notion of kingship. Although he had been forced to put it into abeyance by the Provisions of Oxford, it was still his guiding force. He was the king, and it was essential to the office of king that he have the right to pick his own officials and control his own government. On the other hand, the council expressed very clearly the revolutionary nature of the Provisions, for they envisaged the subordination of the king to the advice of the council, and even its ability to act against the king's will. In the phrase added to Bracton, they would bridle the king. Between two such diametrically opposed conceptions no fundamental compromise would really be possible. One or the other must prevail.

The earl and countess of Leicester were back in England by the middle of March, when they put their seals to the agreement to submit their quarrels with Henry to the arbitration of Louis or his queen. Probably Simon had a share in drawing up the replies of the council to Henry's complaints, although the tone of their answers was milder than when the irascible earl answered such complaints on his own behalf. While this inconclusive arbitration was proceeding, Master John Mansel succeeded, on April 13th, in obtaining from Pope Alexander a bull revoking the Provisions, and returned speedily to England. The difficulty was to ensure that he would be unmolested on entering the realm, for at Dover the baggage of those returning was often searched. If the papal bull was found by anyone not in sympathy with the intrigues of the king, it would be confiscated before it could be published and given practical force. Henry acted with uncharacteristic speed. The castle of Dover – the front door and key of England – was in the custody of Hugh Bigod, as were the rest of the Cinque Ports, and Hugh was still a baronial supporter, although he was no longer Justiciar.

At the end of April, King Henry sallied forth from London, marched hastily to Dover, and dismissed Bigod, replacing him by Robert Walerand, the most trusted and capable of the royal secular staff. Within the next two weeks, Henry secured new oaths of fealty from the men of the Cinque Ports and the seacoast counties of Kent, Sussex, and Hampshire. In this same swing he also made sure of Rochester castle, with its commanding position on the river Medway, halfway up the main route to London. By the middle of May, the king was safely back in the Tower. Bolstered by the success of his moves, Henry went to Winchester to spend the two weeks till the feast of Pentecost on June 12th. There, in the much-loved surroundings of his birthplace, he published the papal bulls of absolution which had been safely smuggled into the country. Freed from the hampering effects of his oath, the king immediately asserted his regained power, and deprived of their offices the baronial appointees for Justiciar and chancellor. The presence of paid French troops, imported to strengthen his hand, fortified Henry in his boldness. When the alarmed magnates heard of the king's actions they planned to meet him armed, to try and protect their reforms. But Mansel warned the king of their intention, and Henry slipped back to London and the safety of the Tower before the disorganized opposition could regroup.[35]

Throughout July the king was at the Tower, and the attempt to settle the personal quarrel continued. On July 5th, the king and the earl and countess of Leicester again agreed on arbitration for all the quarrels lying between them. Philip Basset, the new royal appointee as Justiciar, and the ever-present John Mansel were the king's representatives and Walter, bishop of Worcester, and Peter de Montfort, those of Simon and Eleanor. To help them come to an award before All Saints, two Frenchmen, the Duke of Burgundy and Peter le Chambellan, were to serve as mediators and try to settle the affair in England.[36] No sooner had this further effort been made to terminate the long-standing quarrel of the earl of Leicester with the king than Henry exercised his royal prerogative to the limit. The king high-handedly removed the sheriffs and custodians of the castles who had been selected by the terms of the Provisions of Oxford, and substituted his own nominees, all strong royalists.[37] This at last roused the barons to the realization of the king's plans to reverse completely the accomplishments of the last three years.

This threat reunited the nobles, even the earl of Gloucester and the earl of Warenne. From a meeting-place near London, on July 18th, they joined in begging King Louis to take on the arbitration of their differences with their king. The letter's phrases show their feeling of urgency and almost despair:

> Being aware of the desolation, destruction, and irreparable loss which threaten the whole land, so that it cannot be avoided in any way by any other, after God, except you alone, may it please you to take up this burden.[38]

This arbitration on the public complaints and demands of the barons became inextricably entangled with the arbitration over the specific demands of Simon and Eleanor. The duke of Burgundy and Peter le Chambellan refused to act, and the dispute was handed over to Queen Marguerite of France. King Louis's position in the background emerges very clearly. The French king wanted to see justice done to the earl of Leicester and his wife, and he was anxious, as well, that the king should remain in discussion with his barons so that the truth of Henry's cause might "be declared to all, lest reason should seem to be subordinate to the king's will".[39]

But among the lesser citizens of the realm, as among the great nobles, the happenings of the summer had roused distrust. In August Henry issued a manifesto to the shires to try to counteract the general discontent, which, like the baronial agitation, centred on this important question of the sheriffs.[40] Apparently Simon de Montfort made a hurried trip to France at the height of the confusion, for Henry wrote to Louis in considerable trepidation over the activities of the unpredictable earl. Anything which might jeopardize Louis's essential support would naturally terrify Henry.[41]

During August and September the issue was joined over the question of the sheriffs. The change made by the Provisions in the method of their selection was the most popular, as well as the most intelligible, of the whole series of reforms. For the lesser folk, the sheriff was the immediate personification of the royal authority. On his competence and willingness to do justice rested their whole relation to the king. The rival parties struggled in the shires, and Henry's appointees had difficulty in maintaining their hold over some counties. In many places, the barons appointed "custodians" of the counties who were, in fact, the baronial nominees for sheriff.

The blatant refusal of the barons to fall in with the king's changes was emphasized by the leaders of the magnates. The bishop of Worcester and the earls of Leicester and Gloucester issued a summons in their own name for three knights from each county to come to St Albans on September 21st to treat on the common needs of the realm. Here was revolution indeed, and the calling of a whole new class into the general discussion of the affairs of state which had always been restricted to the great lords. But whether this gesture was inspired by a desperate need for greater support, or by conscious political theory, it came to nothing. Henry got wind of the barons' summons, and bade his own sheriffs order the knights to come to Windsor, instead of to St Albans on the day appointed: "so that they may see and understand that we propose to do nothing except what we know to be fitting with the honour and common utility of our realm".[42] Uncertain which order to obey, the knights probably stayed at home, for no meeting at all seems to have been held, either at Windsor or St Albans.

Both sides organized their forces and prepared for conflict. The king summoned all in England whom he thought even vaguely trustworthy for military service. Once again the build-up of foreign mercenaries began, and arrangements were made for their admittance and payment. Meanwhile the barons met in London and its outlying districts with their bands of armed followers. Both sides appeared determined to persevere. Then by another of those sudden and inexplicable changes, frequent in the history of the time but perpetually baffling, the whole picture shifted completely. Again the earl of Gloucester withdrew his strength and support from the barons, and came to an understanding with the king. Furious at this betrayal, Simon de Montfort left England, declaring that "he preferred to die without a country, than as a perjurer to desert the truth".[43] With the two great earls gone, the other barons felt leaderless. After some discussion, they went to Kingston to treat of peace with the king, and there, at the end of November, terms were arranged. The terms show the regained power of the king. The troublesome problem of the sheriffs was left in abeyance for that year. The method of appointment after that was to be submitted to arbiters, but the ultimate decision rested with Richard of Cornwall, who was naturally bound to uphold the king's prerogative. All but a fragment of the baronage agreed to these terms.[44] By the end of 1261, a completely triumphant king had regained all that he had lost since 1258. With Leicester in voluntary exile in France, and the king, aided by Richard of Cornwall, in undisputed power, the winter of 1261–2 seemed to mark the final passing of the baronial scheme of government.

During 1262 Simon de Montfort remained in France, observing the situation in England as an onlooker. For the first six months King Henry seemed to move from strength to strength, and the impatient earl must have felt that there was no one left in England who maintained the sworn confederacy, or took account of the solemn oath to uphold the Provisions. The papal censure was repeated. Since Pope Alexander had died a month after he granted the first bull of absolution, Henry sent proctors to the new Pope, Urban IV, urging a re-issue. Others seem to have taken advantage of the change of popes to make representations also, for the king's proctors reported that there were others at the papal court nominally working for the king, but actually in sympathy with the barons.[45] But, by the end of February, Pope Urban acceded to Henry's demand, and again absolved Henry from his oath to the Provisions.[46] In May the question of the sheriffs was settled by the formal award of Richard of Cornwall, stating that the king must be free to choose whomsoever he wished.[47] Before Richard returned to Germany he warned the king, who seemed to be contemplating another attempt at arbitration over the quarrels with the earl of Leicester, that once the award was given it would be better for everyone if he kept it faithfully.[48] Richard knew his brother's failing only too well. He was thoroughly aware of the part played by his own prestige and discretion in rescuing Henry from his difficult position and restoring him to the plenitude of power. Now Henry was once more on his own and personally responsible for the next steps.

The unfinished business with the earl of Leicester preyed on the English king's mind. Henry's attempt to have Simon declared a traitor in the trial of July, 1260, had failed, owing to the friendly intervention of King Louis's messengers and the opposition of the magnates. But the events of the last two years had not made Henry any fonder of his determined and rebellious brother-in-law. The disputes between them, though submitted to arbitration so often, never came to any real conclusion. Also the earl was the most prominent of the tiny group of nobles who stood out against the settlement on the matter of the sheriffs. It must have rankled in Henry's mind that this interloper, who continued to oppose him, should still be welcome in France, and be treated with courtesy by King Louis. Now was the time to discredit the earl, finally and completely, in an open trial in the French court. Perhaps that would alienate his French supporters, for Henry hoped and believed he had dispersed the English rebels.

In the middle of July, King Henry left for France, and by August he was settled near Louis's palace of Vincennes. Henry hoped to collect further material for his charges against the earl by summoning some of the leading men of Gascony to meet him in Paris. Perhaps the violent animosities aroused by Simon's Gascon administration could provide fresh ammunition for the king's case.

August must have been devoted to the hearing, and fortunately the report remains.[49] The charge and counter-charge give a very clear picture of the opposing natures of the two men, and their total and permanent inability to understand each other's point of view. One defect must be marked against Simon de Montfort. He was very reluctant to accord due weight to King Henry's generosity. It was a cardinal fact that without the earldom of Leicester, to which his claim was at the best shadowy, and the gift of the king's sister in marriage, he would have had neither position nor wealth in England. Obviously, the king's weakness and indecisiveness at crucial moments irritated his high-tempered brother-in-law beyond bearing. At the same time, the earl had little of the genuine affection for the king which Henry had once showed to Simon, although the royal friendship had now soured into deadly rancour. This hearing also came to no conclusion. At the beginning of September, the English king and most of his company fell desperately ill. For some weeks Henry's life was in danger, and the dispute with the earl had to be put aside.

Meanwhile, in advance of the hearing before King Louis, Simon, too, had taken a radical step. Perhaps impelled by his anger and disgust with King Henry's manoeuvrings, he sent Raymond Bodin, his proctor for Bigorre, to swear homage for Bigorre in his name to the church of Le Puy. The homage of Bigorre was a hotly disputed subject, but the English king had bought the claims of the church of Le Puy some years before. It may be that the explanation for Simon's curious decision to repudiate Henry's position, and incidentally assert his own title in Bigorre, lies in his anger with Henry's decision to arraign him before the French king.

During the autumn Henry stayed on in France, gradually

recovering his strength, and Simon apparently made another of his lightning journeys. On October 8th, Henry wrote to Philip Basset and Walter de Merton, who were in charge of the government in England, that all hopes of a settlement with the earl of Leicester had vanished completely, and that the earl was hastening to England to sow new discord. The Justiciar and the Chancellor were to take counsel with the leading men of the royal party on how best to parry this attack.[50] Before the warning could have arrived, Simon seems to have appeared in London for the great feast of St Edward, which always brought the barons together. The earl claimed to have a papal letter enjoining the observance of the Provisions of Oxford, and declaring that Pope Urban had discovered that he had been misled by Henry's proctors, and revoked the absolution of the previous February. Over the protests of Philip Basset, Simon read this supposed missive to the assembly, then disappeared again, and returned to France.[51] There is the question, of course, whether this story is really credible. Despite the melodramatic flourishes, it is quite possible that Simon had obtained a letter drafted by a baronial supporter in the papal curia, but never agreed to by the pope. The report of the king's own proctors the previous autumn underlined the fact that there were members of the opposition at work in the curia. But support of the barons' cause was never part of papal policy, though even a suggestion of it might have encouraged the badly disheartened baronial opposition.

In the middle of November, Simon was back in Paris, pursuing Eleanor's claim to rights and lands in Angoulême. Perhaps he discussed his English affairs with the French king. At any rate, King Louis, who was more than ever anxious to see an end to this long-drawn-out quarrel between Henry and the earl and countess, spoke to Henry about it once more when they were together at Compiegne at the beginning of December. Once more arbitration before Louis was agreed upon. After Henry returned to England at the end of December, he appointed John of Chishull archdeacon of London, and the knight Imbert de Montferrand, as his proctors, and sent them off to France at the end of January, 1263. The phrases of Henry's letter to Louis reveal the pressure that the

French king was exerting, and the rancour that Henry harboured towards the earl:

> And although both the law of kindred and the argument of lordship and the manifold kindnesses of the king of France should dispose the king to confide in him above all mortals, the king requests of him, out of regard for the king's honour and indemnity that this business shall not suffer a relapse, especially as the earl has disturbed the king and his realm to such an extent that the realm has long suffered and still suffers no slight loss.[52]

These proctors sent home a very full and illuminating report of their mission. They had delivered the king's treasure to Paris and found Edward there safe and well. From Paris they went to call on Queen Marguerite at the palace of St-Germain-en-Laye, some twelve miles west of the city. Since they had been ordered to discuss the matter with her first, they explained it all. Much interested, she suggested that they should wait to present their petition until she herself was present at court, and could add her counsel and advice. But even with the most earnest efforts of the French king and queen, and a private discussion between King Louis and the earl of Leicester, the matter progressed no further. Simon was suspicious of the genuineness of the offer and the sincerity of Henry's counsellors.

> The earl had well said that you wanted nothing but good, but that some of your advisers did not much care for peace or would promise it without compulsion. Wherefore . . . it did not seem to the earl, on account of certain things which we will explain to you verbally when we come to England that he could now make peace in accordance with his honour.[53]

With the failure of this attempt, even the indefatigable French king gave up, for a time, the hopeless struggle for a settlement. Public matter of great moment stood between the king and the earl, and their debates on principle were made more acrimonious by the bitter residue of unsettled personal quarrels.

At the end of March, Henry's proctors were back in England and, in formal recognition of the futility of their task, they were asked to surrender the documents they had carried with them. These included the charter of the French king about the 15,000 marks security for the settlements of the demands of the earl and countess, a charter of the earl's about restitution of manors, and various other items pertaining to the same business.[54] It was more than three years now since the formal publication of the treaty of Paris, and the final settlement it called for between the king and the earl and countess of Leicester was even more remote than ever. Both sides had made vague gestures of compromise, but neither would really retreat from their main position. Trickery on the king's side, and intransigeance on the part of Simon, made a satisfactory legal compromise unattainable. Now ended the era of legal battles, of complaints and arbitrations. The smouldering dispute was soon to break out into open war.

The King's Opponent

Many changes had transformed the baronial party before Simon de Montfort was called to lead it in the spring of 1263. Defection and death had wrought havoc on the original group which had supported the Provisions of Oxford. The Bigods had gone over to the king. The death, in July 1262, of Richard de Clare, earl of Gloucester, rich, powerful, and of great prestige, left an enormous gap. Even before his death, when Gloucester's devotion to the reforms envisaged at Oxford and Westminster slackened, and he inclined to the king's side, his weakness dealt a dangerous blow to the solidarity of the barons. The quarrels which had raged between Simon de Montfort and Richard de Clare were significant because they revealed the cleavage in the party, both over Richard's distrust of the Ordinances, extending the reforms to the lower tenants, and over Simon's insistence on the satisfaction of his wife's claims in the treaty of Paris. The schism was based less on high political reason than on insistence on continued privilege, but it effectively split the reformers. Richard died relatively young – he was only forty – and this, added to his narrow escape from posioning in 1258, may have led to the contemporary rumours that he was poisoned at the table of Peter of Savoy. Young Gilbert, his heir, personifies the new character of the baronial party. Besides Simon and his devoted supporters, it was made up of young, vehement men who were inspired less by idealistic passion than an emphasis on their own rights. They sought Simon de Montfort as their leader because of his prestige and ability, but these grasping youths did not share his principles, and would easily fall away when they had satisfied their own desires.

Gilbert de Clare was under twenty-one, so that the king did not have to give him seisin of the Clare lands and honours immediately. While Henry was in France Gilbert crossed the Channel to try and persuade the king that he should be given his lands at once, notwithstanding his age. Henry apparently thought more highly of the letter of his rights and the possibilities of rich gain for the royal treasury, than of the wisdom of placating a high-tempered young man who could easily become a dangerous enemy. The Gloucester lands and castles in Wales and the Marches were given to Humphrey de Bohun, and the honours of Clare and Gloucester were also handed over to royal custodians.[1] This was strictly within the king's rights, but it infuriated young Gilbert, particularly as the king made no effort to mollify him. The immediate result was to alienate the young heir of Gloucester so that he turned again to the baronial party which his father had forsaken, ready to co-operate in opposition with the earl of Leicester.

While Henry lingered in France, going on pilgrimage and trying to shake off the aftermath of his serious illness, the Welsh again broke into open revolt in the Marches. Llywelyn, prince of the Welsh, had done more than any national leader before him to unite his people as a coherent body against the English, and especially against the Marcher lords, who were the visible holders of power in the disputed areas. The conflict between the Welsh and the Marchers was endemic, and tended to flare into greater violence whenever troubles in England improved the Welsh chances of success. At this time, Edward, whose interest in the Marches was great because he was the earl of Chester, was out of the realm, and most of the other Marchers seemed unwilling or unable to fight.

Henry returned to England at the end of December, 1262, unsustained by the mood of high confidence in which he had set off for France in July. Even nature conspired against him. It was a bitterly cold winter of ice and snow, so cold that the Thames froze solid, and for three weeks men rode and walked from one bank to the other. When the king came back to London, his favourite palace of Westminster burned down almost completely.[2] Naturally, there were the usual pessimists who interpreted this as an omen of evil fortune.[3] Henry needed no discouraging omens. He was still weak from his illness, and faced almost insoluble problems.

The Welsh danger was immediate and pressing and, though the baronage were not united against the king, they showed little enthusiasm for supporting him. In what seems to have been a vain effort to rally popular support, the king reissued a series of "constitutions", which were, in fact, the Provisions of Westminster with a few additional clauses. He mentioned specifically that this was done: "of the unforced and free will of the king, in his full and free power, and by the counsel of his faithful lieges".[4] It is baffling to speculate why Henry should have done this. He had spent the last four years trying to escape from the bonds of the Provisions of Oxford and Westminster. He had sought and gained papal absolution on the grounds that his oath was invalid because it had aeen extracted by force. Now the king went ahead and swore – under no apparent pressure – to the hated Provisions. The motives behind this unexpected act are cloaked in mystery. Perhaps it was one last desperate attempt to gain popular favour and persuade the people that further reforms were to be discussed by Roger and Hugh Bigod, Philip Basset, and the earl of Leicester. This is what the London chronicler suggested.[5] Perhaps Henry wanted to impress both King Louis and Simon with the genuineness of his efforts to pacify the realm, while his proctors were busy trying to come to terms with the earl at the French court. Whatever the reasons for the reissue, it seems to have made little if any difference to Henry's later conduct or to his ultimate desire to be released from the Provisions.

In February Richard of Cornwall returned from Germany and Edward from France. They provided badly needed strength and advice for Henry from the members of his own family. The Welsh erupted into violence again, and Edward personally led an expedition against them as soon as he returned. But he had little support from the Marcher lords and gained small advantage. There was trouble in Kent as well as in the west. Roger Leyburne, once Edward's close friend and follower, turned to revolt and plunder of the royal manors, and there was even rumour of an assault on Dover. The disturbed situation of the country meant a precarious balance of forces. The king tried to ensure the loyalty of his subjects by ordering the counties to swear fidelity to himself, and to Edward as his heir. He then required the same oath to Edward from every citizen of London over the age of 12.[6] It was a last desperate effort to enforce loyalty among the lukewarm and openly rebellious. Rumblings of imminent revolt were growling in the shires, and the disaffected barons looked to France and de Montfort.

The negotiations between Henry and Simon, despite the most patient efforts of King Louis, had ended in stalemate. Simon had left England a year and a half before because he felt that the barons did not want to keep their solemn oath to the Provisions. At this desperate juncture a number of the magnates sent for him, begging him to come back and lead them. The earl's acceptance is typical of the devoted, but high-handed, nature of the man:

> Conquered again by their prayers he came to England, saying that he was signed with the Cross and was as gladly willing to die fighting among bad Christians, for the freedom of the land and Holy Church, as among pagans.[7]

Arriving in England at the end of April, the earl of Leicester seems to have gone to a secret meeting of the magnates at Oxford. There he joined Gilbert de Clare, the earl of Warenne, and others of the barons and they decided that all who went against the Provisions of Oxford should be regarded as capital enemies.[8] Henry of Almain, eldest son of Richard of Cornwall, had returned from overseas at the beginning of March with the earl of Warenne and Henry de Montfort, and had become a new and enthusiastic convert to the baronial cause.

The sequence of events here is very confused. Some of the barons sent a letter to the king under the seal of Roger Clifford, one of the young Marcher nobles, which seems to spring directly from the meeting at Oxford. They begged the king to keep the Provisions and renounced fealty to all those who wished to go against them, saving only the king and his immediate family.[9] After this, some of the Marchers moved directly to attack their enemies in the west. According to Wykes, there was a parliament in London at the very end of May and the earl of Leicester led the barons in opposition.

They complained about the foreign-born, and murmured against the king and queen and Edward for their "perjury" in not observing the Provisions of Oxford.[10] The complaints may have been idealistic, hinging on the king's disregard for that whole nexus of administrative reforms which was implied in the popular use of the term "Provisions of Oxford", but the subsequent action was lawless. They devoted themselves to plunder and pillage, especially of the lands and goods of the foreigners and adherents of the king.

The first attack of the baronial supporters, in early June, was on the hated bishop of Hereford, Peter of Aigueblanche. Bishop Peter was one of the most offensive examples of the coterie of aliens who had gained preferment in England. He had come in the first invasion of Savoyards, as a clerk in the train of William, bishop-elect of Valence. Four years later, in 1240, he had received the bishopric of Hereford, and from then on was busy with many royal commissions. The general hatred of him was caused particularly by his prominent share in the Sicilian affair, when he had used fair means and foul to raise money for the pope. The bishop was conscious of his unpopularity and had once hoped to remedy it by begging the Franciscans, then gathered in general chapter, to restore his good name in their sermons. The friars held out against such a misapplication of their preaching, and added, rather insultingly, that they did not wish to lie![11] Spurred on by their pent-up hatred, the barons attacked the bishop in his own church, and imprisoned him in the castle of Eardisley, confiscating all his goods and dividing them up among themselves. Then they marched south-east to Gloucester, where the castle was in the custody of another of the royal favourites, the alien Matthew de Bezil. There seems to have been some local pride involved here, for Matthew had been disputing the office of sheriff with a baronial nominee and had been able to eject him. After four days of siege the castle was broken into and, despite Matthew's attempt to hold out in the most strongly fortified tower, the barons captured him and sent him to join the bishop of Hereford in captivity.[12]

By this time, the earl of Leicester had taken charge of the army, and from Gloucester they marched north to besiege Bridgnorth. The townspeople at first defended themselves vigorously against the baronial force. Then, simultaneously attacked by the Welsh from the west, they admitted the barons, as surrender to the earl of Leicester seemed the lesser of the two evils.

During June there was general confusion throughout the realm. Bands of baronial supporters fomented trouble in many of the counties. Foreign clergy were dispossessed from their churches and manors, merely because they were foreign. Also the lands and belongings of those who were – or were only suspected of being – unfavourable to the Provisions were pillaged and plundered. Unfortunately, this was the pattern of much of the fighting of 1263, for plunder and loot were felt to be the reward for removing the foreigners. The contagion spread throughout the realm and brought hardship and bad feeling. In such confusion, even if all the barons had acted with the highest ideals, many innocent were likely to suffer with the guilty. But for many of the irresponsible among the baronial force, ideals were merely a shield to cover their settlement of private scores and the increase of their own wealth.

While the barons' army stayed in the west under the control of the earl of Leicester and the king's position grew steadily more precarious, Henry had spent Whitsuntide at Westminster. Despite the troubles with the barons he was busy revolving in his mind what he could do to beautify his rebuilt palace there. His recent visit to France reminded him of the great cycle of Old Testament windows in King Louis's Ste-Chapelle, and he resolved to have similar paintings on the walls of his private chamber. In all this dispute about the proper position of a king, a great picture of the coronation of St Edward the Confessor gleaming over his bed would help to reassure him of the sacred character of his kingship. It was far more satisfactory to issue orders to his craftsmen and painters to provide a work of beauty than to take up the uncongenial task of dealing with the irrepressible barons.[13]

But the problem nevertheless had to be faced. London was doubtful in its loyalty, but Henry could be safe there behind the strong walls and impregnable defences of the Tower. This was purely defensive, some offensive action should be taken to cut off the baronial advance. Henry had to make sure of Dover, and his communications with the continent. He sent Edward off to exact another oath of fealty from the men of the port, and provided supplies for the strengthening of the garrison. This was achieved, but it left Henry penniless in the Tower. He must have money, for the lifeline to France was of little use unless he could scrape together enough money to pay foreign knights to bolster his weakened forces. The rich merchants of London should have been willing to help him, but they would not give the royal party even a half-penny on credit.[14]

The earl of Leicester was equally anxious to discover whether the Londoners were baronial supporters. The question was asked straightforwardly in a letter from the barons, under Simon's seal, which arrived around June 24th. Did the citizens of London wish "to observe the ordinances and statutes made to the honour of God, to the fealty of the lord king, and the utility of the whole realm, or would they rather adhere to those who wished to infringe upon them?"[15] The citizens went to the Tower to interview the king and his inner circle; the queen, Edward, Richard of Cornwall, and Robert Walerand. They told him that the "community" of the city wished to observe the Provisions, and then sent a message to the barons' army in Kent to the same effect. Though the "community" of London swore to keep their oath, they were not really united. The great magnates found themselves being pushed aside by the "ribaldi", or lower classes, who were enthusiastic supporters of the barons. As in the rest of the realm, disorder and rioting were cloaked under the pretence of driving out the foreign-born. Such upheaval harmed trade and commerce and further alienated the greater men, who stood aside and often looked for chances to aid the royalists secretly.[16]

The last week of June, 1263, saw events moving rapidly to a climax in both camps. On the 26th, Edward, probably encouraged by his father's desperate need for money, obtained entrance to the New Temple. Like so many other of the Templars' establishments, their house in London was frequently used as a kind of bank and safe-deposit vault. The king's son said that he wanted to see his mother's jewels, but instead, with the assistance of his confederates and some iron hammers they had smuggled in with them, he smashed open caskets in which money was stored. In this desperate raid Edward took away £1,000 of sterling from the treasure of the magnates and merchants of the land.[17] Armed with this wealth and pursued by the furious distrust of the Londoners, the king's son withdrew to Windsor with the Frenchmen from his own household. Later many of the foreigners who were ejected from London went to form part of his garrison there. John Mansel, the king's most trusted adviser and the richest clerk in England, fled secretly overseas from his refuge in the Tower, taking with him some of the foreign ladies. The king's younger son, Edmund, accompanied them as far as Dover, and then remained at the castle there, which he hoped to hold for his father. The news of John Mansel's flight infuriated Henry of Almain, a zealous convert to the baronial cause. Pursuing the escaping clerk to Boulogne, Henry himself was captured by a French knight and held overseas.

Meanwhile, Simon de Montfort, at the head of the small baronial army, was on his way towards London, fresh from his successes in the west. He was intercepted by the messengers of Richard of Cornwall, on his way up the Thames valley to his castle of Wallingford. Richard wanted to arrange a parley, but Simon refused the offer. Such a discussion would have clarified his position at a time when he preferred to have it remain cloudy. Despite his army, he had made no open moves against the king and was not, legally speaking, in revolt. At the same time, speed was essential if the earl was to try and cut the royal line of communication with the continent, and put himself in a commanding position. Instead of pausing to parley with the king of the Romans, he avoided London altogether, and swung his army south-east, through Guildford and Reigate, and then on to the coast. At the same time he sent a committee of bishops to King Henry in London to discuss the basis for peace. While the king and the prelates argued in London, Earl Simon went on to Romney where he was greeted enthusiastically by the Kentish knights and the men of the Cinque Ports. Notwithstanding their oath to Edward less than a month before, they hastened to swear allegiance to the demands of the barons. By July 12th, Simon was in Canterbury to receive the three bishops' report of their parleys with the king.

Henry had little choice but to accept. The Londoners were enthusiastic in their acceptance of the barons' cause, and Simon's manoeuvre controlling the ports barred the king from help abroad. Henry was forced to give in with as good grace as possible.

Essentially the demands of the barons were the same as before: the recognition of the Provisions, the custody of castles by baronial keepers, the governing by Englishmen, and the expulsion of the aliens, and although Henry was willing to submit, Queen Eleanor was not. The queen had her full share of the haughty Provençal temper, and she would not give in tamely to a pack of rebels. She determined that she would leave the safe refuge of the Tower and make her way up the river to Windsor. There she would join Edward and brace her son, at least, to combat against these detestable barons. But when the queen's boat came to London Bridge the Londoners recognized her, and showed their dislike for her. From the houses on the bridge they taunted her with names and epithets, and even threw mud and stones upon her company. Only the arrival of the mayor of London saved her from real harm, but her voyage to Windsor was impossible. The mayor lodged her at St Paul's in the house of the bishop of London, for the king was afraid to admit her to the Tower.[18] This insult to the person of the queen had unfortunate results. It roused in Eleanor undying hatred for all concerned, so that her personal influence was continuously exerted against any compromise between king and barons. Also it encouraged her to greater efforts with her sister and brother-in-law in France to gain their help in overthrowing the rebels.

Simon de Montfort returned from Kent to London, having made sure of Dover Castle. At his father's command, young Edmund surrendered it to the bishop of London, who held it temporarily for the barons. The king and the earl agreed on peace and the arrangement was published. By its terms, Philip Basset, the royal appointee as Justiciar, was dismissed, and Hugh Dispenser replaced in the position from which he had been removed two years before.[19] The Kentish chronicler mentions that the earl of Leicester was made steward of England. Certainly Simon had held that title and exercised its functions before. Perhaps the position was reemphasized because of the earl's rather broad interpretation of the steward's duties and rights. This same chronicler was rather cynical in his comment on the third of the baronial appointments, that of Roger Leyburne as steward of the king's household. Naturally a Kentish man would look sourly on Roger, who had been the instigator of much of the revolt in this year, and had burned and plundered in Kent with little regard for the rights of others. So, complained the chronicler, he who was lately the chief enemy of the king, a persecutor of the churches of God and especially of the archbishopric of Canterbury, was made the steward of his court "and thus from Saul was made Paul, and from the wolf a lamb."[20]

Edward's activities were a disturbing element in the effort for general pacification. During this summer, the earl of Leicester and the barons had their first experience of Edward's tendency towards trickery. As the author of the *Song of Lewes* was to say later, "he was a lion for pride and ferocity, but a pard for inconstancy and changeableness, not keeping his word or promise, but excusing himself with fair words".[21] While Simon de Montfort was occupied in Kent trying to arrange the release of Henry of Almain in France, Edward slipped away to Bristol to try and improve his situation in the west. Unfortunately, while he was there, trouble broke out between his paid soldiers and the townspeople. The citizens denounced their homage and prepared to besiege Edward, with full confidence in their success. In this awkward situation, the prince sent for Walter de Cantilupe, bishop of Worcester, leading cleric in the west and a mainstay of the baronial party. Edward promised the good bishop, that if he was rescued, he would make peace with the barons and go directly to court to swear his agreement to the peace. But, once delivered from Bristol, the king's son repudiated his promise and instead hastened to take refuge in Windsor, from where he harassed the surrounding countryside. The barons could not allow this to continue and stood ready with their army to besiege Windsor. Edward came out to treat with his opponents, but, after his last ruse, his good faith was suspected by Bishop Walter and Earl Simon. They kept the prince from re-entering the castle, and thus guaranteed its surrender. The alien garrison was escorted to the coast on their way back overseas.[22]

The summer of 1263 was one of general upheaval in England. In London, the lower classes, aided by a mayor who was one of the popular party, seized power and displaced the old oligarchy. Much the same process was also noticeable in the counties. The unrest probably accounts for one of the few new steps taken by the baronial government at this time. The barons appointed a new official for the counties called the "guardian of the peace". These knights did not replace the appointed sheriffs, who were generally left undisturbed, but they seem to have superseded them on all important matters. By the terms of their appointment, they exercised all the powers, except financial, which normally belonged to the sheriff. Especially they were meant to see that justice was done to the despoiled, and that would-be plunderers were restrained.[23]

These new measures showed the extent of the rapid baronial victory, which appeared so conclusive. The era of the Provisions seemed to have returned again. But many things had changed in England in the years between 1258 and 1263, among them the character of the baronial party. The fight for the Provisions was no longer a joint effort, concurred in by all the great barons. In 1263, Simon de Montfort led a faction, and Wykes's contemptuous remark that those who followed the earl were "boys . . . malleable as liquid wax"[24] had a strong element of truth. The party also included Simon's devoted old friends and followers; most of the influential prelates and such nobles as Peter de Montfort and Hugh Dispenser. But most of the older and wiser heads among the great barons stood aside, not completely committed to the cause.

Meanwhile in France, King Louis watched with anxious eyes the disappearance once more of the royal authority and the unsettled condition of England. He seems to have been in touch with Henry during the summer, and decided that the best way of dealing with the situation was to summon Henry to the French court in his capacity as a peer of France, and to require the attendance of the barons also. Henry's letter of August 16th certainly suggests that there had been previous correspondence between him and Louis, for he says that he and the queen and his sons are coming to see Louis "to have his counsel and aid for the amelioration of the king's estate and to talk about other things as with his lord".[25] However, although the barons were willing for Henry to go to France, they wanted to be sure that he would return in reasonable time. They remembered that the French air in 1260 had caused Henry to be very casual about his commitments to the barons.

Parliament was called in London on September 8th to arrange for delegates from the barons' side to represent them at Boulogne. Certain other matters were discussed briefly. Since it was the first meeting since the settlement of peace between the king and Earl Simon, the Provisions of Oxford were once more publicly promulgated and ordered to be completely observed throughout the realm.[26] The truce made by the earl and the bishop of Worcester with Llywelyn and the Welsh was ratified until the end of November.[27] Some of the first baronial captives were freed, among them the bishop of Hereford and Matthew Bezil. The choice of delegates to support the earl of Leicester fell upon two ecclesiastics, the bishop of Glasgow and the archdeacon of Oxford. John de Cheyham, the bishop of Glasgow, had been archdeacon of Bath, and a papal chaplain, until the pope appointed him to his bishopric. As a papal man, the barons may have felt that he would be regarded as a relatively impartial envoy. Richard of Mepham was much more of a baronial supporter. He was a great friend of Thomas de Cantilupe, himself the nephew of the bishop of Worcester, and both showed strong sympathy for Simon's position. In a letter from Westminster just before the close of parliament the king reminded the earl to be sure to be present at Boulogne on the Sunday (September 23) before Michaelmas to treat with the kings of England and France on "certain arduous business . . . as you love our honour and yours".[28]

Both parties converged on Boulogne armed with accusations and counter-accusations. The court of the king of France included many of the French magnates, and most of the Provençal relations. The already inflamed temper of Queen Marguerite, furious at the insult offered her sister by the London rabble, was made more irascible by the complaints of the foreigners who had been exiled from England – or had prudently exiled themselves. These court refugees spent their time bewailing their lot and begging vehemently to be allowed to return to England and their former possessions.[29] It was indeed a distinguished, and partisan, gathering with which the earl of Leicester and his two supporting ecclesiastics had to deal. The English king and queen laid grave complaints against the earl, citing injuries, imprisonments, occupation of the royal castles, and depredations of churches.[30]

The chroniclers differ notably in their description of the barons' defence. One said that their proctors argued that the barons of England ought not to answer for their actions in the court of the king of France, but should be judged by their peers in the court of the English king.[31] Another claimed that the earl of Leicester answered the chapter and verse of Henry's accusations and satisfied the king of France with his answers.[32] At any rate, no final decision was made at this time, and both Henry and the barons returned to England for the feast of St Edward and the October parliament which had been decided on before they went away. The king left Queen Eleanor in France at the hospitable refuge of King Louis's court. She was surrounded by several of her relatives, including prominent English exiles like the archbishop of Canterbury and his brother Peter of Savoy, as well as such ardent, and hated, royalists as the bishop of Hereford and John Mansel. But exile did not mean any relaxation in the queen's efforts to raise funds and forces for the king and Edward, and she tried every possible approach. She even attempted to get assistance from King Louis's brother, Alphonse of Poitiers, but that shrewd man refused to be entangled in matters which he felt were not matters of immediate personal concern. In other directions, the queen's efforts met with success, and the men and money she raised in the two years of active warfare had a practical effect.

The October parliament saw, once more, the spectre of division in the barons' ranks. The earl of Leicester had agreed the previous summer that there should be arbitration on the disputed sections of the Provisions of Oxford. The problem of how they were to be amended had to be considered at this meeting. The king claimed that he should be allowed to choose the officers of his own household and put them in their positions. This, superficially, was a most reasonable demand. It was a right which was enjoyed by even the least of the barons. But, if it was permitted to the king, it would open the door for a distinct and opposing administration, free from the control of the council and accountable only to the king. The barons were on the horns of a dilemma. Their decision was made no easier by the equally reasonable demand of the royal party that those who had been unjustly despoiled in the course of the upheaval should have justice shown to them.[33] This was refused, either because many of the barons had no intention of disgorging their loot, or because they believed that it was impossible in the unsettled state of the country to distinguish between just and unjust. There was general discontent, of which Edward took full advantage. Working behind the scenes with promises of lands and rents, he began to entice away many of the young hot-heads who had been following Simon. On the excuse of seeing his young wife at Windsor, Edward entered that castle, seized control of it, and made it a focus for the opposition to the barons. Soon King Henry went to join his son there. For a few weeks the balance quivered between the two parties and then the scales tipped decisively to the side of the king.

The baronial party began to disintegrate. Such important young magnates as the earl of Warenne and Henry of Almain turned their back on the earl of Leicester. Young Henry's defection particularly hurt Simon. When that young man came to the earl and said that he could no longer fight against his father, the king of Germany, his uncle, the king of England, and all his other kinsmen, he asked Simon's permission to depart and swore that he would never bear arms against him. The earl turned on him with contempt: "Lord Henry, I had accepted your person most cordially, not because of your arms, but because I was hoping for special constancy from you. Go and return home with your arms; I do not fear them."[34]

Another tie was broken, and the seeds of a lasting hatred planted between the young Montforts and their cousin Henry which was to bring them all to a bloody end. The defection of the great barons gave the signal to the younger men, who had only joined the party for hope of gain. Roger Clifford, Roger Leyburne, and others of

their type were reconciled to the king, encouraged by the induce-
ments offered by Edward, their original patron. The two young
earls, Gloucester and Derby, remained as did Earl Simon's own
old supporters, and a fair number of the lesser nobles. It was
merely a fragment, but the earl of Leicester was bolstered by his
own confidence in the essential rightness of his cause.

> Even if everyone falls away from me, I with my four sons will
> stand by fearless for the just cause which I have already sworn to
> uphold, to the honour of the church and the utility of the realm,
> nor will I fear to undergo war.[35]

This unwavering sense of his own righteousness and unwillingness
to break his oath, this lack of any of the statesman's ability to
compromise, made him despise the changeableness he saw in
others. He said with disgust to his intimates that he had been in
many places, among pagans and Christians, but had never seen
such infidelity and deception as he had experienced in England.[36]

By the beginning of November, the collapse of the baronial
party was almost complete and, as one chronicler put it, "the
power of the king began to breathe a little".[37] Before Simon's
strength had waned too greatly, the preliminary steps for a truce
between the barons and the king had been put into motion. By the
usual intermediary of a committee of bishops, the two parties
agreed to compromise on King Louis as an arbitrator again, and
submit to his decisions.[38] During November there was practical
truce, with the king at Windsor gathering once more into his own
hands the threads of the administration which he had been forced
to relinquish. Henry sent abroad anxious letters to the exiles,
begging them to assist in explaining his cause to the French king
and also in filling his ever-empty coffers. Simon withdrew from
London to his stronghold at Kenilworth.

Meanwhile propaganda of all sorts filled the air. The king had
been using the shire-courts for the publication of letters and
proclamations giving his side of the argument. The barons seem to
have profited greatly from the favourable preaching of the friars
and the satirical popular songs. Sometimes the methods were quite
subtle. The Tewkesbury chronicle includes a long letter by "a
certain faithful Englishman" – a distant relative of all anonymous

"friends" – who warned the barons of trouble ahead and subtly decried the position of Earl Simon. The earl of Leicester grew old, the letter said, and the barons might need another leader. Besides, rumour had it that he expelled some aliens and protected others. He had given the extensive lands of John Mansel to his own son, which was wrong, and cast doubt on whether Simon truly laboured for the common cause.[39] This letter was probably the work of some enthusiast for the earl of Gloucester, who wanted to see that young man the leader. The writer had cleverly picked on the weakest spot of the earl of Leicester's character. Simon always used his periods of ascendancy to enrich himself and his family. In this case, the July peace had hardly been settled when the earl persuaded the king to present Simon the younger with all of John Mansel's lands in England, though the clerk had only fled to France a few weeks before.[40] This gift made the young Simon extremely wealthy, and undoubtedly roused jealousy. This flaw of the earl's had caused trouble before and was to cause more again. While both sides paused and gathered strength, rumour and counter-rumour circulated throughout the kingdom.

King Henry was the first to break the truce. He seems to have summoned his supporters to Reading, and then, at the beginning of December, gone on to try and seize the castle of Dover, which was still held by the baronial custodian, Richard de Grey. Dover was essential to Henry's plans, for possession of its castle meant virtual control of the entrance to England. In the absence of Richard de Grey with Earl Simon, the castle was held by a group of knights of whom John de la Haye, a strong baronial supporter, was the best known. When the king with his magnates, in military array, sought entrance to the castle, the garrison refused, saying that they could not surrender the castle without the consent of its proper custodian who had received it according to the form laid down by the Provisions. Henry tried unsuccessfully to gain entrance peacefully, as he was not yet willing to attempt a siege. His earlier optimistic conviction of his success had led him to send for the queen and her two uncles, the archbishop of Canterbury and Peter of Savoy, but at this repulse he had to countermand the order. He then withdrew hurriedly from Dover, possibly because he heard rumours of the imminent arrival of Earl Simon.[41]

When the news of King Henry's precipitate departure for Dover had come to the earl at Kenilworth, Simon immediately started across country to London by way of Northampton and Dunstable, gathering his followers as he went. Till he received further information, he camped with his followers at Southwark, across the river and outside the walls of London. As the royal army marched back from Dover, some of the citizens of London sent letters to the king secretly. They proposed to lock the gates of the city and take the keys to the king, so that, when the royal army attacked, the Londoners who favoured Simon could not reinforce him, nor could the earl fall back on the safety of the city. It was a clever ruse, for the king's army far outnumbered that of the earl, and, caught as Simon was in the bend of the Thames, there was no chance for retreat if the city was barred. The earl prepared his little army for the attack, but at the last moment the citizens of London discovered the trick plotted by their wealthier members. They rushed to the gate and broke the chains which held it so that the earl and his force could enter safely. The king and Edward desisted from following them into the city and another truce was patched up, while the earl and his followers rested safely in London.[42]

During these troubled weeks negotiations had been continuing on the intended arbitration by King Louis on all these contentions. Just after the king's attempt to trap the earl of Leicester, a French knight landed at Dover with the letters about the arbitration. According to the formal letters of agreement given by the leading barons on December 13th, it was to be completed before the coming Pentecost.[43] A few days later King Henry also gave his formal adherence to the arbitration before Louis in "all things high and low" between himself and the barons.[44] For the last time the French king would endeavour to make peace between Henry and Simon, as he had tried vainly to do so often before. Now the issue between them was more fundamental and more sweeping than in the previous disputes. There was more at stake than certain specific acts of omission or commission. What Louis was really asked to pronounce on at Amiens was the whole basis of royal power, and the rightful share of the barons in the exercise of that power, for that was the essential meaning of the Provisions of Oxford.

When the last arrangements had been made for the trip to France right after Christmas, Henry withdrew to Windsor and Earl Simon left London for Kenilworth. There he heard that Roger de Mortimer had been given three of his manors in the Marches, manors that he and Eleanor had received from the king in the summer of 1259 when the negotiations for the treaty of Paris were in process. Roger had devastated the manors, and taken the earl's bailiff a prisoner until a sizeable ransom was paid.[45] Here was still another item to be added to the earl's score against the king, but he was destined not to present it in person. Henry, with Edward, Hugh Bigod, and some others, arrived in France by December 27th after a stormy and uncomfortable crossing. When the earl left Kenilworth for France, his horse fell at Catesby – a hamlet some twenty miles to the east – and Simon's leg was broken. He was forced to return to Kenilworth to let the bone knit, so he sent orders to his supporters in London as to who should be appointed as proctors for the baronial cause at the court of France. The group included young Humphrey de Bohun, the son of the earl of Hereford; Simon's eldest son, Henry de Montfort; the reliable Peter de Montfort; and a few lesser magnates. The clerks, who would carry the weight of the technical pleading, were headed by Master Thomas de Cantilupe,[46] the saintly and learned chancellor of Oxford. Thomas was a good choice as a pleader in the French court, as well as a prominent supporter of the barons. King Louis himself had come to visit him and his brother while they were young students at the University of Paris. After attending the council of Lyons in 1245 and being named papal chaplain, Thomas continued his studies, taking civil law at Orleans and a further course of study at Paris in canon law. When he returned to England, he went to Oxford to teach canon law and, in 1262, was named chancellor of the university. The prestige and learning of such a man insured that all the resources that technical knowledge could provide would be devoted to the barons' case.

Recently the complaints of both the king and the barons on this occasion have been discovered and published.[47] They suggest that the procedure followed at the French court was the new civil procedure in arbitration which would have put both parties on an even footing. Since the case was submitted to a foreign court, it was not equitable to use the laws of any particular country, and this developing form of arbitration served as a kind of international convention. In the documents there is no matter of great novelty, but a firmer and fuller statement of the disputes that lay between the king and his barons. The king, in his complaints, emphasized the points which struck him as most telling. The barons refused the king the right to choose his own officials, the servants of his own household, and the men who should hold his castles. Then – and this point infuriated Henry above all – the barons claimed: "that all who opposed their constitutions should be held as capital enemies by all of the realm".[48] The king primarily took his stand on his right to appoint his own officials, and on the fact that, by his coronation oath, he could not concede or do what the Provisions required.

The barons' complaint covered far more ground. They emphasized Henry's financial exactions, his misuse of wardships and escheats, his denial or sale of justice, the unfair favour given to the foreign-born, the unreasonable exactions from merchants, the drain of the foreigners on the treasury, and the misuse of crusading funds for Sicily. These abuses, except for the ones touching the foreigners and the Sicilian affair, are mentioned in the baronial case as having been remedied at one time by the charters, but those provisions were not observed. From these specific points, the barons went on to give their version of the events following 1258 and to explain what they were trying to do. Their defence was the king's oath, both in 1258 and 1263, to observe the Provisions.[49] The other two documents which form part of the barons' brief, so to speak, were less general in scope. The second consists of direct answers to Henry's list of complaints. The third seems to be, not an integral part of their case, but a kind of memorandum on some of the specific complaints they themselves had against the king. It is interesting, and typical, that of its six items two deal with injuries to the property of the earl of Leicester. On the first occasion the king ejected the keepers Simon had placed in the castle of Winchester, which had been handed over to him by the council. The second complaint deals with Roger de Mortimer's devastation of the earl's Herefordshire manors of Dylwyn, Lugwardin, and Marden, and his seizure of the earl's bailiff from Dylwyn, who was thrown into prison until he could pay 200 marks ransom.[50] This incident underlines and explains the personal bad feeling between the earl of Leicester and Roger Mortimer, which continued through raid and counter-raid to the awful vengeance of Evesham.

Such was the case prepared by both sides, but King Louis was influenced in his arbitration by more than these documents. The pope had appointed a legate for this affair, Guy, cardinal of Sabina. Guy Foucod, or the Fat, had a distinguished past and a more eminent future. Trained in the law, he had served the king of France until the death of his wife. Then he turned to the priesthood, where he rose rapidly in the papal service. While he was still busy on his work as legate, he was elected pope as Clement IV. There was no question from the very beginning of his appointment that his sympathies were on the side of King Henry. This is not surprising. Henry had received absolution from two popes for his oath to the same Provisions to which the barons now wished to hold him. No pope could be strongly in favour of a government which impeded any English help in the Sicilian affair, railed against all foreigners, and tried to expel foreign ecclesiastics from benefices they had been given even by the pope himself. The pope heard the version of the case given by the exiles and by the French king, whose information came mainly from the royalists, and armed his legate with the fullest powers to compel all to obey him.[51] But Louis was a man noted for strict justice and resistance to pressure, and Queen Marguerite had tried to influence him before and failed.

When the moment came for King Louis to give his decision at Amiens on January 24, 1264, the French king swept away the Provisions, declaring them null and void. He went back to the details of Henry's complaint, and specifically mentioned that the king had the right to appoint all the officials of his realm and of his household. He threw out completely the barons' argument about the foreigners, saying that the king might call and use aliens as seemed fit to him. Louis underlined the basic point again: the king was to have full power and unrestricted rule in his kingdom. With such a sweeping vindication of the king's rights and powers, he added just one note of caution; that he did not intend by that ordinance to derogate from any royal privileges, charters, liberties, and praiseworthy customs of the kingdom of England which had existed before the time of the Provisions.[52]

Now it is possible to see here an echo of the barons' complaints in which they claimed that many of the king's actions were against the ancient charters. It provided a tiny loophole in Louis's sentence of condemnation, and it was by this loophole that the earl of Leicester sought to escape from this award which he could not accept. His most vigorous admirer among the chroniclers says that it was this exception which impelled the earl of Leicester, and others who had more trained intelligence, to hold firmly to their proposal to conserve the Provisions of Oxford, because they were founded on that charter.[53]

Much criticism has been voiced of King Louis for the uncompromising nature of his award. The work of a peace-loving king, it brought England not peace, but civil war. However it is difficult to see how Louis could have decided differently in the framework of his time. In medieval terms, the king must have the right to govern his realm. He must be recognized as the superior of his subjects, with unrestricted power within his own sphere. The barons' claim to appoint the king's officials encroached on that sphere, and Louis could not conscientiously agree to a derogation from the essence of the royal power as he knew it. What Louis did not, and could not, determine, was exactly where the sphere of the king's power ended and how an unjust or unwise king could be kept from overstepping the boundaries in his turn. The problem had not been solved by arbitration. If Leicester's party would not recognize the award and finally give up the Provisions and the scheme of limitation they implied, the country must turn inevitably to civil war. But the earl would not, could not, forswear his oath. He was ready to fight the king himself in upholding his ideal of royal government.

13

The Rise to Royal State

The Mise of Amiens put an end to any hope of the barons that they might gain the assistance, or even the grudging non-interference, of King Louis, in their efforts to control the king. Although both sides had agreed, in the most solemn terms, to accept the decision of the king of France, the mise was immediately rejected by the barons. Some, like the earl of Leicester, took their stand on its recognition of the charters of ancient liberties. Others merely disregarded it. The people of London and the lesser barons argued that they had never made themselves party to the arbitration, and therefore were not bound by its terms.

Almost immediately war blazed again. Before the Mise of Amiens Roger Mortimer had caused trouble in the Marches by burning and devastating Simon de Montfort's properties there. After the unsuccessful settlement, violence flared once more in the west. The earl of Leicester had already made a treaty of friendship with Llywelyn, the prince of Wales, which improved Simon's tactical position against the Marchers. Early in 1264 he sent his two eldest sons, Henry and Simon the younger, at the head of a large army to attack the Mortimer lands and castles, and thus revenge their father. They seized the castle of Radnor and devastated the surrounding lands. When Edward returned from France, he followed the young Montforts to the west, but, instead of confronting them, he contented himself with seizing the castles of young Humphrey de Bohun, a prominent baronial supporter, and handing them to Mortimer for custody. Yet a third army was operating in the west at this time, the private force of Robert de Ferrers, the young earl of Derby. Robert violently attacked

225

Worcester and, despite the resistance of its citizens, found an unexpected entrance into the old castle and destroyed the city.[1]

Gloucester was the first meeting between the opposing forces. The army headed by the young Montforts, on its way back from Wales, entered the town of Gloucester by trickery. John Giffard, a strong baronial man whose castle of Brimpsfield was not far away, and Roger Clifford, now the royal custodian of Gloucester, had been carrying on a private feud for some time. Each searched for an opportunity to outdo the other, but Giffard seems to have had the more fertile imagination. He and another knight disguised themselves as wool-merchants, and loaded their horses with wool-packs. Disguised in their Welsh mantles, they led their horses over the bridge to Gloucester's gates, and sought permission from the gate-keepers to enter and trade. As soon as the gates were undone, the pseudo-merchants threw off their mantles and showed themselves armed from head to foot. Terrified, the poor gate-keepers threw them the keys, and the baronial army streamed across the bridge in the wake of the false traders to take possession of the town.[2]

They had more difficulty with the castle, which contained the wives of some of the leading Marcher lords. The Montforts initiated a siege of the royalists in the stronghold, only to have Edward and his army approach from their rear. The king's son had mended one of the valuable bridges over the Severn and succeeded in entering the castle with his force. When Edward saw that the barons' army was so small, he proposed to attack them the following day. But the de Montforts gained reinforcement from the earl of Derby and the balance of strength again tipped in their favour. Edward recognized that attack was futile and turned to parley instead. In the presence of the bishop of Worcester, the king's son and Henry of Almain parleyed with their cousin, Henry de Montfort. They sought a truce till March 13th, and Edward promised that he would have his father the king observe the will of the barons in all things. In view of Edward's trickery when faced with a similar situation the year before, Henry de Montfort was extremely gullible to accept this offer. But he was blind to the danger, perhaps relying on cousinly love and friendship, and immediately agreed to these terms. Henry de Montfort called off his army and led it back to the family stronghold at Kenilworth. The barons had no sooner departed than Edward broke his word and the terms of the truce. He imprisoned the burgesses of Gloucester, who had favoured the baronial army, seized their goods, and fined them heavily. Then he marched back to Oxford to join his father.[3]

While these opposing armies struggled in the west, King Henry had been busy in the eastern half of the realm. Two weeks after the French king had published his mise at Amiens, Henry travelled to the French Channel port of Wissant and sent messengers over to Dover. The king demanded the surrender of the castle to his men, but the castle guard refused. Despite this setback, the king returned to England on February 15th, bolstered by the encouragement of Hugh Bigod and Roger Leyburne. From his resting-place at Dover Priory he made one more effort to effect the handing-over of the castle by peaceful means, but that, too, failed, so the king went on to Canterbury after he had had the Mise of Amiens recited to his supporters.[4] Safely back in England, the king had to deal with a troubled realm. Henry was morally aided by Louis's strong maintenance of his claims to royal power, but the Mise of Amiens had not pacified the realm. This was a task which required all of Henry's limited capabilities for swift action.

The king decided to hold parliament at the beginning of Lent, but London, the usual meeting-place, was much disturbed. In any case, the weight of opinion in the city was strongly in favour of the barons. The king picked Oxford instead for his headquarters, and went there by way of Rochester and Windsor so as to avoid London altogether. Reinforced by Richard of Cornwall, who joined him at Windsor, the king moved on to Oxford. It seemed wise for the king to order the scholars to leave the town during the time that he was there. The royal order claimed that the presence of a large number of soldiers in the town would make it no place for studious clerks.[5] As a matter of fact, the "studious clerks" had been indulging in one of their periodic conflicts with the burgesses of the town, which had started as a student prank and ended as a pitched battle.[6] The king was justifiably suspicious of the trouble that might follow when he added to this explosive mixture the royal supporters whom he summoned to join him there to perform their military service.[7]

At the same time, perhaps on the more sober advice of Richard of Cornwall, Henry tried again to make peace with the barons. The king appointed two eminent clerics as his proctors to seek out Simon de Montfort and investigate the possibilities for peace.[8] The king of France, still concerned about the situation, had sent over another of his envoys to try and pacify both sides. His messenger this time was John de Valenciennes, an eminent knight from the Holy Land, who had already taken part in the discussions with the earl of Leicester in the beginning of 1263. On March 18th, a truce was arranged till the end of the month to give the barons time to send their representatives to Brackley, a favourite place for tournaments and political discussions, to treat before John de Valenciennes. The king's proctors had been to Kenilworth to discuss the matter with Simon de Montfort, and he had promised to have baronial representatives at Brackley.[9] Henry seems to have had little confidence in the success of these negotiations, since he sent out his military summons at the same time.

Both sides were poised on the edge of open warfare. Kenilworth was the barons' headquarters, for the earl of Leicester had remained there since his accident, resting his broken leg. Simon was infuriated and ashamed at his son's over-easy acceptance of Edward's terms at Gloucester, and the consequent damage to the baronial cause in the west. At Oxford, William de Valence despoiled the surrounding countryside, while the king awaited the turn of events.[10] The most notable riots were in London, where the citizens were carried away by the general spirit of lawlessness. Hugh Dispenser was the baronial custodian of the Tower, but he was incapable, and perhaps unwilling, to halt the aroused Londoners. The citizens did not restrict their attacks to the lands within the city; they streamed out to Isleworth, the manor of Richard of Cornwall, and burnt and devastated it. They even spoiled his carefully constructed fishpond, letting out both the water and the fish. At Westminster, they burned down his house.[11] These unprovoked acts of aggression against his property infuriated the king of the Romans. Until this time Richard had been the unemotional arbitrator, but this destruction of his wealth inflamed a tender spot. From this time on Richard would be among the foremost in urging his brother the king to put down the rebels with all the strength in his power.

Open conflict moved a step nearer, as both parties gathered their resources. The king collected his army, reinforced by a number of paid foreigners, and a large contingent of Scots, and prepared to put down the barons. Simon, apparently recovered from his accident, went to London, the centre of the baronial strength, and was joined by Gilbert de Clare. The king's army made the first move. Marching on Northampton, they flew the great Dragon standard – the banner of red samite on which the dragon's fiery tongue appeared in constant movement and the beast had eyes of sapphire[12] – which Henry had designed so lovingly twenty years before. There a good-sized baronial force was gathered, led by Peter de Montfort and Simon the younger. At first the king was refused admittance, but his army finally gained entrance through a break in the wall near the priory of St Andrew, which the prior was believed to have weakened himself. Simon the younger rode so vigorously in his efforts to repel the attackers that he charged directly into their midst, and was captured when his horse fell backwards. The town was taken on April 15th. Some of the baronial defenders fled to the church, and others retreated to the castle, but all were seized and held. Young Simon was sent to Windsor for safekeeping, and the king's men despoiled the citizens of the town "to their last half-penny".[13]

When the earl of Leicester heard of the attack on Northampton, he moved north to lend assistance. He had only reached St Albans, about twenty miles from London, when he was pursued by news of a rebellion planned by the Jews of London. This was even more urgent, so he immediately retraced his steps. According to one chronicler, he uncovered a plot to fire the city the following week. The Jews were supposed to have had skeleton keys made for all the gates, and there were rumours of underground passages.[14] Whether or not the story was true, it may well have served as an excuse for the ensuing cruelties, for some four hundred Jews were slaughtered by the baronial supporters. Wykes, who usually looked for the worst possible motive to impute to the barons, but who also knew a great deal about London, claimed that the massacre was due to the fact that the baronial party had run out of funds. They killed the Jews so that they might seize their riches, and Wykes accuses Simon de Montfort of taking a share of the plunder.[15]

During these wretched weeks before Easter (April 20), the opposing armies afflicted the land. Edward went with a force to the north to take vengeance on the lands of Robert de Ferrers, and burned and devastated the lands of Derbyshire and Staffordshire. John Giffard, entrusted with the custody of the castle of Kenilworth for the earl of Leicester, took the neighbouring castle of Warwick, for the earl of Warwick was suspected of being a royal sympathizer. Giffard imprisoned the earl and his wife, and totally destroyed the castle, for its nearness to the great baronial stronghold of Kenilworth made it a dangerous centre to have in the hands of the royalists. The main army of the king took Leicester and Nottingham, and the sad statement of the chroniclers echoed the troubled conditions:

> There was no peace in the realm; all things were wiped out with slaughter, burnings, rapine, and plunder; everywhere there was wild crying and lamentation and horror.[16]

While the king lingered in the Midlands, the earls of Gloucester and Leicester worried about protecting the line to the coast and the valuable port of Dover. Gloucester had been in Canterbury, treating the Jews there as harshly as they had been treated in London. He used his castle of Tonbridge as a base for operations, for the disturbance in the west affected his large holdings there. The king had sent Roger de Leyburne and John de Warenne, among others, to fortify and guard the castle and town of Rochester. The castle there was one of the great strongholds of Kent, massively built and further protected by its position in a bend of the river Medway. Strategically, it guarded the main road between London and Dover. The barons could not look with equanimity on the presence of a strong royal garrison there, and so, in Holy Week, they besieged the place. One baronial army, led by Gilbert de Clare, approached from Tonbridge, while Simon de Montfort brought down a great force from London.

On Good Friday (April 18th), the earl of Leicester forced an entrance to the beleaguered city by sending a lighted fireboat, filled with pitch, coals, sulphur, and fatty pork, against the bridge, and the fortifications built on it. When these were destroyed, the baronial army broke in and pillaged the city, giving little heed to either the sacredness of place or time. On Good Friday evening, they broke into the church of St Andrew, stole the gold and silver, and profaned the church, "for the holy places were made the stables of horses and filled with the uncleannesses of animals and the filth of corpses".[17] The following day the barons' forces took the outer bailey, or courtyard, of the castle, but the defenders held out manfully in the great tower. Both sides refrained from fighting on Easter Sunday, to mark the feast with proper respect, but set to again on Easter Monday. All week the siege continued unsuccessfully. On Saturday the news came to the barons of the imminent arrival of the king's army, and also of the danger that the city of London might be betrayed to Edward by certain traitors. Fearing the loss of London, Simon immediately sent back to the city as guard those Londoners who formed part of his army. Richard de Grey, the baronial custodian of Dover Castle, who had come up to assist in the siege of Rochester, withdrew to the port again, taking young Richard de Montfort with him. Leaving merely a skeleton force attacking the castle, the earls of Leicester and Gloucester also returned to London.[18] Since London was the centre of their strength, they wanted to find out the true state of affairs in the city, and it was a good place from which to observe the king's manoeuvres.

The king had not wasted time. His army marched with all speed from Nottingham to Rochester, taking only five days to cover the one hundred and fifty miles. He raised the siege of the castle, which had been practically abandoned when at the point of success, and then took the offensive to strengthen the royal position in Kent. First, Henry, with Edward and Richard of Cornwall, took the earl of Gloucester's castle at Tonbridge and left a royal guard there to prevent its use by the earl of Gloucester. From Tonbridge, the king marched east to Winchelsea, one of the Cinque Ports, and swore the men of the Ports to his peace. This achieved, he turned westward again, and travelling by way of Battle and Robertsbridge, he came to rest at Lewes on May 11th. There the king and his retinue were received in the Priory, and Edward and his men lodged in the earl of Warenne's castle.[19]

Ever since Henry set out from Oxford at the beginning of April, the king had acted with uncharacteristic decisiveness and speed. Probably the presence of both Edward and Richard of Cornwall encouraged him in planned and coherent action. One of Henry's great weaknesses had always been his inability to stick to the main point at issue. This time, however, he seemed to have a better realization of the requirements of the moment. He knew that his position was far better than it had been. At the same time, he did not control London or Dover, and if he was to profit from the frantic attempts of his queen to raise money and men for him, he must be sure of the coast and his communications with France. His party seemed in the ascendant, but his cause needed the assurance of a resounding victory.

Simon de Montfort could not afford another defeat, if the baronial movement was to be regarded as anything more than disorganized revolt. After watching the king's manoeuvres in the. south-east, the earl moved his army, reinforced by a rabble of Londoners, to the little village of Fletchling, a few miles north of Lewes.[20] It lay protected within the forest, and the baronial army was aided by the archers of the Weald, that wooded country between the north and south downs. These bowmen served as valuable auxiliaries and guerrilla fighters, emerging unexpectedly from their woods to harass the king's baggage trains and pick off stragglers.

In hopes of avoiding the final break, the barons were willing to parley. First they sent the saintly bishop of Chichester, with a letter bearing the seals of the earls of Leicester and Gloucester, repeating their continued claim that they only hoped to overthrow those who were truly the enemies of the king and the kingdom. They still considered themselves Henry's faithful subjects. Perhaps this peace mission was purely formal, but the barons seem to have been willing to reinforce their suggestions with an offer of some £30,000 to make peace and pay damages. Rishanger, the strongest baronial partisan among the contemporary chroniclers, suggests that this offer might have succeeded except for the refusal of Richard of Cornwall and his incitement of Edward. Richard's pride was hurt at a group of upstart barons daring to dictate to two kings, and besides he yearned for revenge for the damage done to his properties. Another embassy, led by Bishop Walter of Worcester and the bishop of London, had no greater success. Henry, in a formal letter, denounced the barons and defied them as enemies. There was a letter of defiance from Richard and Edward, too, but it was not merely formal, like the king's. It breathed a fiery spirit of rancour and revenge, calling the barons "perfidious traitors". The barons also withdrew from their oath of homage to the king. The final decision had been made. The war, so long waged in fact but never formally recognized, came at last to the point of direct conflict between the leaders of the opposing parties.

King Henry had grounds for confidence in the outcome. He had the larger army – how much larger it is difficult to say, for the contemporary estimates of the number of men involved on both sides vary enormously and are often astronomically inflated. His position at Lewes, however, was not ideal strategically. In the thirteenth century, the valley of the river Ouse was tidal up as far as Lewes, and much of the lowland near the town was marshy. The priory of St Pancras, where King Henry was entertained, was in Southover, outside the main part of town, and the downs stretched to its very walls. Also, from Lewes Castle, farther to the north, Edward and his retinue would emerge almost immediately into open country. Just north-west of the town, the slope of the downs rises steeply to a height of four hundred feet, and it was this hill which gave scope to Simon de Montfort's military ability in ranging his troops and making geography counter the advantage of superior force.

On Tuesday night, hidden within the forest, the baronial army prepared themselves for the battle of the morrow. The earl of Leicester created new knights, for many of the young men who fought in his army, including the young earl of Gloucester, had not yet been knighted. Prudently, Simon arranged for his forces to wear white crosses on their fronts and backs, over their armour, for in the anonymity of mail it was hard to know friend from foe. Fortified by the benediction and the absolution of the bishop of Worcester, the army was ready to try its strength. The knights and the foot soldiers moved quietly through the forest on the path to Lewes, hoping to surprise the king's forces. Henry had placed soldiers at the top of the hill to the north of Lewes to watch for the barons during the days of negotiation. After two nights on guard, they were tired from their watch and returned to the town. Only one guard was left and he, lonely and exhausted, fell asleep under a thorn bush. In the early hours of Wednesday, May 14th, the baronial army fell upon the luckless man in their march, and quietened him before he could give warning of their approach.

The earl of Leicester paused on the brow of the hill, in sight of the bell tower of Lewes priory, divided his forces and planned his strategy. Two of the earl's sons, Henry and Guy, commanded the right wing, and were to descend the hill to the west of the priory. The earl of Gloucester had command of the centre, the most honourable position, and on the left wing were the Londoners, mostly foot soldiers, led by Henry of Hastings and Nicholas de Segrave. Simon himself, with the remaining force, planned to hold back from the action until the conduct of the battle demonstrated where his reserve could be used most profitably. The earl also knew that many of the royalist army thought that he was still unable to sit his horse because of the accident to his leg, and so he placed at the top of the hill the special cart he had been using. Next to it he planted his own banner, hoping to mislead the royalists into a wasteful attack upon it. To add flavour to the trick, he had imprisoned a couple of the London burgesses who had opposed the baronial party in the cart, expecting that they would be attacked by their own friends.

His plans complete, the earl was ready to move. Some of the early foragers for hay and straw saw the baronial troops approaching down the hill, and hurriedly urged the king to rise and take arms. On the right flank of the royalist army, Edward, with William de Valence and John de Warenne, the lord of Lewes Castle, emerged to fight the descending Londoners. The king in the centre, distinguished by the great Dragon standard, approached the barons from the downs outside the priory walls. On his left, the king of Germany and Henry of Almain attacked the wing led by the young Montforts. At the first shock, the lightly armed and unmounted Londoners opposing Edward broke and fled. Edward's charge was given vehemence by his hatred for the Londoners who had insulted his mother. He and his supporters chased the fleeing men up the hill, down through the brooks, where many died, drowned or inexorably entrapped in the marsh. The poor fugitives were pursued for some four miles, before Edward turned his men back towards the battle. But the insistence of the king's son on his private vengeance on the Londoners was disastrous for the rest of the royal army. With Edward's company withdrawn, and the balance of forces less uneven, the barons fell with all their reserves on the king's centre line. Having killed the royal charger, they made Henry captive. King Henry had done his best. He was not warlike by inclination or ability, but he had fought bravely, if unsuccessfully. Meanwhile, Richard of Cornwall had not been covering himself with glory. When it became obvious that the barons were winning the victory, he retired hastily to a nearby windmill and barred himself in, while the mocking barons jeered at the haughty king of the Romans turned ignominious miller. He was finally forced to surrender, and joined the other baronial prisoners in the priory. When at last Edward returned from his chase of the Londoners and a ferocious attack on the poor burgesses imprisoned in the earl's cart, he found the field deserted, his father captured, and many of the leading royalists fled to safety at Pevensey castle, some seventeen miles to the east. Edward burned to continue the battle with the assistance of the royalists still in control of the castle, but at nightfall the barons were in command of the field and darkness put an end to the fighting.

The victory at Lewes meant a great change for the earl of Leicester. For the next fifteen months, although the forms of government remained substantially the same, the hand at the controls was that of the earl, not the king. The decisiveness of the battle completely changed the pattern of English politics. But, though the military ability of the earl had won him a valuable victory it had not solved his difficulties, but rather added to them. Almost all the chroniclers emphasize the miraculous nature of Simon's victory. One author, in fact, even had Archbishop Thomas Becket and St George joining the battle on the side of the barons to show the divine commendation for their cause.[21] Unfortunately, no miracle solved the massive problems which remained. There was the urgent need to pacify England, which had suffered so sorely from the unrest and civil war. There was the less immediate, but more difficult, problem of regulating the position of the king, and the share of the barons in the government of the realm. These complications, and others, had to be unravelled, but the first move was to provide for a firm peace.

On this immediate problem, the friars, both Franciscan and Dominican, seemed to have served as messengers. Thursday was occupied by negotiations as the friars scurried back and forth between the forces of the barons in the priory, who held the king as captive, and the troops of Edward in the castle. On Friday, May 16th, Edward and Henry of Almain gave themselves up as hostages in the place of their fathers. They were to be kept as captives until some decision was made on the Provisions, which ones ought to be maintained and which ones could be reasonably rejected.[22] By Saturday, the wheels of government had already begun to turn for the new conquerors. A letter went out in the king's name notifying his castellans that peace had been made, and ordering them to refrain from fighting around their castles. A special command was sent to Drogo de Barentin, the stalwart king's sergeant who had custody of Windsor, that he should release the prisoners of Northampton held there, particularly Simon the younger and Peter de Montfort.[23]

The immediate pacification begun, there remained the more difficult problem of settling the form of government. The earl of Leicester still stood by the Provisions, despite their double condemnation by the pope and King Louis, although he agreed to accept a few necessary changes which did not affect their principle. Despite the previous failure, he apparently saw no way to make the Provisions legal and binding except by French arbitration once more. It is hard to understand what Simon felt this recourse to

French judgment would achieve. Perhaps he believed that his resounding success in battle would convince Louis of the justice of his cause. Perhaps he thought that the exception made by the French king in the Mise of Amiens of the rightful liberties granted by the charters could be expanded to take in the whole system of government. In any case, whether the earl's move was one of desperation or of hope, the Mise of Lewes arranged for arbitration by French bishops and nobles, together with some practical clauses about the release of prisoners and the apportioning of ransoms. Letters were sent to France on May 26th to get King Louis's assent, but there was no answer.[24]

At the end of June, a new provisional form of government was set up, which revised the original barons' Committee of Fifteen. It called for three electors to appoint nine councillors by whose advice the king should reign. The underlying idea seems to have been that there would always be some of these sworn councillors in the king's company. The Three retained the basic power, for they could advise the king to remove any of the Nine and substitute others. The personnel of the group shows the earl of Leicester's predominance. He was one of the three, with the earl of Gloucester, and the bishop of Chichester, who was a strong Montfort partisan. The Nine elected included Peter de Montfort, the bishop of London, and young Humphrey de Bohun, all known partisans of the earl of Leicester. The Nine were subordinate to the Three, whose decision did not need to be unanimous. In this way, the earl could easily gain his way, and there is considerable justice in the remark that: "The whole scheme is nothing more than a veil to cover Simon's autocracy."[25] What in fact happened was that the young earl of Gloucester was excluded from the business of the government and kept away from the king, a situation which drove him first to complaint and then to rebellion.

Simon's immediate problem was the support of his hardly won success. The most important castles had been committed speedily after the battle to proved baronial supporters. Simon relied heavily on his own family. He had given Dover and Cinque Ports to Henry his eldest son by the end of May and followed that up in July with the grant of Corfe, the almost impregnable fortress in Dorset.[26] It took the barons some time to dislodge Drogo de Barentin and his garrison from the control of Windsor. Numerous letters were sent to him, in the king's name, commanding him to come to London, and by the end of June the sturdy sergeant at last had to comply. In the barons' concern over this fortress, they refused to allow even the non-combatant relatives of the royalists to remain. Edward's wife, Eleanor of Castile, was to take her household to Westminster. Joan, the wife of William de Valence, had been keeping the princess company, but since Joan was awaiting the birth of a child, she was told to take refuge in some nearby religious house until after her delivery.[27] Apart from these personal upheavals, the series of orders in the patent rolls mark the wholesale change-over of the castles and counties from royalist to baronial custodians.

There was much royalist activity in France. Many of the fugitives from the battle of Lewes had fled from their first refuge of Pevensey to France, where the exiles were watching the struggle with avid concern. The fleeing lords brought the news of the crushing defeat to the English queen and her knot of supporters, and stayed with her for a while "mourning happier times".[28] But Queen Eleanor was not the kind of woman to waste much time on fruitless grief. She had already been busy trying to raise money and troops, and ships to convey them. Her correspondence with King Louis's brother, Alphonse de Poitiers, shows her vigour and insistence. Just before Lewes, she had written to him, begging him to put an embargo on the English ships in his ports of Poitou, and turn them over to her. She planned to use them as a fleet whose task would be to make a diversion against the English coasts, as well as to transport an army of volunteers who had been recruited on the continent. Alphonse tactfully refused this suggestion – it was a violation of the law and a source of perils. But, despite his caution, the matter did not end there. Eleanor still tried to get boats from the citizens of Poitou, this time on a voluntary basis, and Queen Marguerite also influenced her brother-in-law to arrest some of the baronial supporters as they crossed Poitou. King Louis, who was just even when his relatives were involved, intervened himself to order his brother to release the men.[29] But, even without Alphonse's co-operation, Eleanor, aided by her uncle, the archbishop of Canterbury, and by the tacit good will of the French king and queen, was busy raising an invading force.

A menacing army collected at the Flemish ports of Bruges and Damme, sustained by Queen Eleanor's energy and by her desperate use of every expedient to raise money. In August she even sold to King Louis, for £20,000 (*tournois*), all the rights which the treaty of Paris had given Henry in Limoges, Cahors, and Perigord. This desperate expedient was forced on her by her lack of funds, for she had exhausted in June the £58,000 which were the residue of the amount promised for the upkeep of 500 knights in that same treaty.[30]

During July, the danger of this invasion from the continent was the greatest threat to England. On July 8th, the earl, in the king's name, sent a general summons throughout the country for armed men, foot soldiers as well as mounted sergeants, to come together to save the country from the expected invasion of the aliens. This was more than the usual feudal levy; this was, in fact, the host of the old days, with representatives from every village, town, city, and castle of the realm.[31] Of course, not all the men demanded by the proclamation honoured the summons. Many from the north and west, where the country was still in the hands of royal sympathizers, never appeared. A large army gathered in the east, watching the waters of the Thames and the Medway, scanning the reaches of the Channel, but no invading navy crossed the horizon and finally the amateur soldiers could return home.

Meanwhile, the papal legate, the cardinal bishop of Sabina, worked busily in France with the royal exiles. He was wholeheartedly in favour of the king, and used all the fulminating power of the church to discourage the barons; he attempted to win away the clerics who formed such an important part of their support. The official attitude of the pope and curia was opposed to the general attitude of the clergy of England. Practically all the English prelates and the great mass of lesser clergy, of monks and friars, supported the barons' cause with enthusiasm. Their encouragement meant popular propaganda for the earl – a fact

borne out by the remaining records which display their partisanship.

The legate attempted to gain entrance to England, but that was
refused him. Balked in this, he stayed in Boulogne and cited the
English bishops to appear before him there. The bishops took
refuge in the reasonable excuse, which caused the legate to
reproach them, that the barons would not let them leave the
realm. Finally, after considerable discussion, the bishop of
Winchester, Master John of Exeter, and the bishop of London,
Henry of Sandwich, were sent over to interview the angry legate.
The cardinal demanded action, and sent back by these two
prelates a letter of interdict, commanding them to publish it when
they returned to England. It called for the excommunication by
name of the earl of Leicester, his sons, and his followers, and
placed under an interdict the city of London, all the lands of the
earl of Gloucester, and all the towns of the Cinque Ports. In the
legate's opinion, these were the people and places which had
showed themselves most recalcitrant to his mission. But when the
bishops returned to Dover, their luggage was searched before they
were allowed to land, and the legate's interdicts were torn in little
pieces and thrown into the sea. The searchers threatened the
bishops with death if they dared to publish the injunctions as the
legate had commanded. Wykes added suspiciously that he himself
was not sure whether this search was spontaneous, or was invited
secretly by the bishops as an easy way to escape from their
dilemma of obedience to both the legate and the barons.[32]

From the middle of August until the beginning of October, the
king was in Canterbury, as the baronial government tried to arrive
at some form of arbitration which would be acceptable to the
French and the papal legate. Letters went back and forth to the
French court at Boulogne and Henry of Almain, one of the
hostages for the conclusion of the peace, was freed from custody for
a short term to serve as messenger. The barons hoped that his
personal appearance at Boulogne would give further force to their
contentions that the form of peace after Lewes had been agreed to
willingly by the king. But, despite the inclusion of Simon's great
friend, the archbishop of Rouen, on the list of arbiters, no final

pacification ever came. The legate was unremittingly hostile to any of the barons' claims. The barons, in their turn, refused to remit any of their insistence on their basic demand that the councillors of the king must be Englishmen and denizens with a crucial role in the government of the realm. It was the duty of councillors to advise the king upon the appointment of officials, and see that he observed the ancient charters of liberties. Nor would they allow him to incur immoderate expenses or exercise extravagant liberalities.[33] It was obvious that there was no common ground for compromise. The legate, further annoyed by the barons' destruction of his letters, prepared to excommunicate the baronial supporters from outside the realm, and, on October 21st, the sentences were duly published in France.

In England there were still military problems to solve. A small group of royalists had remained at Pevensey, and, despite the recurrent efforts of Simon the younger, they stayed entrenched there. Much more dangerous, however, was the continued resistance of the lords of the March. In July, the earls of Leicester and Gloucester had had to lead a quick excursion to enforce peace upon them. They had some success. Roger de Mortimer and James of Audley came to them in Montgomery during August and gave hostages for their good behaviour.[34] But that peace seems to have been most illusory, for the Marchers refused to surrender the captives which they still held from Northampton, nor would they turn over their castles and towns to new keepers.[35]

Some of the Marchers decided on a desperate stroke to try and free Edward, who was imprisoned in the castle of Wallingford. A group of reckless young knights, led by Warin of Bassingbourn, rushed across England and stormed the castle. The force of their surprise attack carried them into the first court, but then the castle's garrison managed to repel them with the assistance of some of the engines of war with which Richard of Cornwall had strengthened the castle in quieter days. The story goes that the garrison threatened to deliver Edward to them – but in a mangonel! Apparently, the king's son himself begged his would-be rescuers to desist, but, in any case, the attempt failed.[36]

The earl of Leicester was worried by this further evidence of the strength and boldness of the Marcher lords, and took his valuable hostages to Kenilworth for safer keeping. The great castle had been reinforced by the earl with all kinds of the most up-to-date military equipment, and the earl seems to have retained a consulting engineer. In his wife's accounts for 1265, there are numerous payments to Master William, the engineer, for his work at Kenilworth. William seems to have remained in the earl's employ until there was no longer cause for his services. He was paid off after the earl's death.[37] Not all the prisoners were guarded as closely as Edward. Richard of Cornwall and his younger son, Edmund, remained at Kenilworth until after Evesham, treated with honour and consideration by the countess of Leicester. After all, Richard was her brother, and her household accounts show that she gave considerable care and attention during the year of their detention to seeing that they had an adequate supply of luxuries and fine clothing.[38] Once his important prisoners were safely tucked away in the great keep, behind the spreading water-works, Simon applied his mind once more to the acute problems of the disturbed realm.

The whole kingdom "trembled with the horrors of war".[39] The chroniclers agree that it was a time of devastation and despair. The custodians of castles laid waste the fields and carried off the cattle in the neighbourhood of their fortifications. Neither high nor low observed the king's peace. Highwaymen attacked clerics and merchants, robbing them of their goods and frequently killing them as well. Many of the men of the Cinque Ports turned to piracy, seizing ships and goods from natives and foreigners impartially. Even the poor peasants lost all they had, down to the very straw of their beds. Naturally prices for foodstuffs soared, and caused still more suffering. All normal trade was very much lessened, and a weak attempt was made at economic self-sufficiency. The more ardent of the earl's supporters wore garments of natural-colour cloth, proving that they had been too patriotic to send it out of the country for the usual processes of dyeing and finishing.[40] In the midst of all this economic unrest, which gnawed at the well-being of the realm, the earl also had to worry about recurring rebellion.

There was still no peace in the west, and another punitive expedition had to be sent out to compel the Marchers to submit, for they refused to answer the summons to the November parliament at Oxford. The rebels had taken precautions to protect themselves from baronial reprisals by breaking all the bridges over the Severn, even the particularly strong one at Worcester. But Llywelyn's Welsh troops harassed them from the west and they were forced to sue for peace. The terms were hard, and concentrated much power in the earl of Leicester. Simon held the town of Bristol, in Edward's place, and also the great honour of Chester with its castle and county, one of the proudest holdings of the king's son. The castle of Gloucester was temporarily committed to Simon the younger.[41] The rebels themselves were to abjure the realm for over a year. When peace was finally made, steps would be taken to free Edward from his humiliating position as hostage.

The earl of Leicester was at this juncture the greatest man in England. He added to his acquisitions in the west the wardship of the lands of John de Balliol, one of the great northern lords, and the castle of Porchester, controlling the harbour of Portsmouth.[42] The contrast between this overwhelming might and the pitiable position of the king raised doubts and forebodings in England which were echoed by the chronicler of St Albans. He contrasted the king's rather meagre Christmas at Woodstock with the brilliant celebration at Kenilworth, where Simon presided over a vast throng of his own household, swelled by one hundred and forty knights and many supporters.

> All things were ordered by him, the monk says dubiously, all the castles of the king were committed to his control. Now even the king himself, who was already in the fiftieth year of his reign, had nothing but the shadow of a name.[43]

The earl could enjoy his Christmas feasting, but the seeds of disunion lay hid behind the gorgeous display. The sardonic goddess of Fortune prepared to spin her wheel once more.

The Spin of Fortune's Wheel

Before the earl returned home for the Christmas festivities, he had made the king send out summons for a great parliament at London on January 20th. The make-up of this assembly is very interesting, because the claim of Simon de Montfort to be the "father of the House of Commons" is based mainly on it. The parliament depended very heavily on the lesser people. Only five of the earls and about twenty of the tenants-in-chief were summoned, probably an accurate estimate of the relative weakness of de Montfort's party among the great mass of the baronage. But the religious magnates were strongly represented and representatives from some of the boroughs and the knights of the shire were included. It seems reasonable to believe that the only deep principle behind this choice of men summoned to the assembly was that of expediency. The choice was made on the basis of their strength and usefulness to the barons' party, not as a matter of conscious innovation. But this parliament, as well as the years of the civil war, extended the interest and concern of a far wider group than ever before in the affairs of the realm. When peace returned, under the strong rule of Edward I, the precedent at least remained, and Edward's parliaments show considerable experimentation in their make-up, calling, at various times, members of various classes.

This winter parliament of 1265 was a long-drawn-out affair, lasting from January to March. Its major achievement was the formal settlement of peace. On February 14th, in the chapter-house at Westminster, the king bound himself to the re-issue of the charter of liberties and that of forests, as well as to the arrangements made after the battle of Lewes. The earls of Leicester and Gloucester, and the citizens of London, were given security that the king would not proceed against them. The Marchers were to be banished to Ireland and were not to return for three years without the common consent of the realm. The threat was added that if they did not observe all these terms, it would be lawful to rise against them. With the settlement of these outstanding problems, Edward and Henry of Almain were freed from their position as hostages.[1] Edward's freedom from confinement was more apparent than real, for he was closely surveyed by constant companions of the earl of Leicester's choosing. In the middle of March, Edward solemnly renewed his gift of Chester to the earl, and also included the northern castles of Newcastle-under-Lyme (Staffordshire) and the Peak (Derby).[2] The king and his son seemed to have fully accepted the dictates of the earl, who ruled apparently unchallenged. But, at the moment of Simon's greatest baronial power, another quarrel split the baronial party as effectively and more disastrously than in 1259.

While parliament was meeting, the earl of Leicester's sons had called a tournament at Dunstable for the middle of February to which the earl of Gloucester prepared to go. But Simon de Montfort was much concerned over the planned meeting. Tournaments were always dangerous, for sham warfare only too often turned into pitched battles, and the troubled state of the realm could not withstand many more shocks. Earl Simon prevailed on the king to forbid the tournament and threatened his unruly sons himself, "that unless they obeyed his order, he would put them in such a place that they would not enjoy the benefit of either sun or moon".[3] The young Montforts unwillingly obeyed, but the prohibition of the meeting infuriated the earl of Gloucester and many of the other knights who had gone to considerable expense to equip themselves for the affair. General grumbling was heard, and the baronial support for Earl Simon began to melt like the spring snow.

Although Gilbert de Clare was disgruntled by the cancellation of the tournament, there were more serious matters at issue between the young earl and the overmastering Simon de Montfort.

Gilbert accused Simon of keeping foreign knights in the land, and in his own retinue, a practice expressly forbidden by the Provisions and all the settlements after Lewes. Then there was the extremely touchy subject of the captives taken at Lewes. The earl of Gloucester felt that he was being denied both recompense and prestige for the prisoners he had taken at the battle. This could be an important matter, for captives belonged to the person who took them, and had to buy themselves free by the payment of a ransom, which made them quite a financial asset. When Gilbert sent to Simon demanding the banners of his captives, the earl of Leicester brushed his request aside with a short and arrogant retort.[4] This abrupt dismissal of a reasonable request lent force to the general and growing fear that the earl of Leicester was usurping the whole power of government. The supporters of the earl of Gloucester, and the other disaffected barons, began to grumble that the earl of Leicester took all the royal castles into his own hand, "arranging the whole kingdom by his own desire".[5]

Simon's treatment of another great earl also raised the forebodings of the earl of Gloucester. Robert de Ferrers, the young earl of Derby, had been one of the barons active in the west in the months before Lewes. Although Robert was officially part of the baronial party, he seems to have used the turmoil in the land as an excuse for robbery and devastation. He did not form part of the barons' contingent at Lewes and, in the ensuing months, the earl of Leicester had been vainly trying to parley with him on his many offences, and the damages he had caused. Finally, the earl of Derby was captured and imprisoned in the Tower of London under strong guard. This angered and worried the earl of Gloucester, who feared that the same fate might be in store for him. After all, if the earl of Derby, who was married to the king's niece, could be put away as a common criminal, no one in the realm was safe.

A quarrel broke out between the two earls, Leicester and Gloucester, which rivalled in intensity the one that Simon had had with Gilbert's father. Powerful motives encouraged the break-up; arrogance, injured pride, and greed. In addition there was suspicion and distrust on both sides. Gilbert de Clare bitterly

resented the pride and the spoils of the earl's four sons "so that
secretly or openly he did not cease to detract from their glory".[6]
Then, too, in an era when the watchword was "Down with
aliens", the cry could justifiably be raised against the earl of
Leicester. He was an alien, too, and yet he presumed to subjugate
to himself the lordship of the whole kingdom. For his part, Simon
de Montfort doubted Gilbert de Clare's wholehearted adherence
to the cause, because the earl of Gloucester had allowed the
Marcher lords to shelter in his lands after they had promised to
abjure the realm. With so many unresolved problems between
them, the fatal cleavage was almost inevitable. Gloucester withdrew from the parliament without leave and headed for his lands
in the west, taking a fair number of knights with him. Prominent
among his company was John Giffard, who was also in trouble
with the earl of Leicester because of his occupation by force of
lands belonging to other magnates, against the terms of the Mise
of Lewes. Arrogance, self-interest, and lack of discipline opened
widening chasms between the various factions of the barons.

The uneasiness of the earl of Gloucester over the concentration
of power exercised by Simon de Montfort is quite understandable.
The earl of Leicester had many of the greatest castles of the realm
in his own hand, most notably Chester, as well as his personal
stronghold of Kenilworth. Other important castles had been given
to his sons. Henry had Dover castle, the Cinque Ports and Corfe.
Simon the younger was put in charge of Porchester. Probably this
was not all due to family feeling. Much of it arose from the earl's
uneasy belief that there was no one else he could really trust. After
all, he had expressed himself bitterly more than once on the
subject of these perfidious and changeable Englishmen.

But besides this acquisition of power which could, perhaps, be
satisfactorily explained, there was the undoubted and obvious fact
that the Montfort sons in particular had used their position of
influence to feather their own nests. The eldest son, Henry, was
popularly nicknamed the "wool-merchant", for his seizure to his
own uses of wool brought to the ports.[7] Simon the younger, from
his appearances in the records, seems to have been a fiery, but
unreliable young man. His besetting weakness was to be more

interested in plunder than control of his army. During much of this period between Lewes and Evesham, young Simon apparently devoted to a vigorous pursuit of the young widow, Isabella de Fortibus, twice a countess and quite the richest matrimonial prize in England. Isabella later complained that he had "pursued her from place to place with horse and arms desiring to capture and seditiously abduct her", until at last she found refuge in Wales.[8] His attempts to capture Pevensey ended in dismal failure and he exercised the perquisites of his office as constable of Porchester by seizing ships of the Gascon merchants. In one case, his father ordered him firmly to hand over the ship of a merchant from Bayonne without delay, complete with all its goods and merchandise, and added in annoyance, "so that it may not be necessary for us to urge you further on this".[9] Amaury de Montfort, the young clerk of the family, was named treasurer of York, in place of John Mansel, who had recently died overseas.[10] Even Guy and Richard de Montfort had some little share in the family fortune – they were given deer for stocking their parks.[11] All this largesse of the earl of Leicester to his own was only too obvious, and bitterly resented by the other barons.

The family ties were emphasized at the last great family gathering of the Montforts at their castle of Odiham after the end of parliament in London. Edward, no longer a hostage but still closely controlled, spent at least two days with the countess of Leicester there. He was travelling in the company of his two cousins, Henry de Montfort and Henry of Almain and a fairly large retinue, for they had some eighty horses with them.[12] The earl himself arrived on March 19th to spend two weeks with his wife.[13] It would appear that Guy and Amaury were also present.[14] There was a great deal to discuss in this encounter and the earl was travelling in almost regal state, for he had over three hundred horses in his train. So many problems beset them that there could have been little time for the usual feasting, especially as the Lenten restrictions bore heavily on their diet. The countess had to hear of all that had passed in London, and there was much news to share, particularly the break with the earl of Gloucester. At that time the situation did not seem impossible. There was still the hope that the quarrel could be smoothed over, as other quarrels had been before, But the more basic and inescapable problem of the nature of the earl's government lay athwart their path, tarnishing the glamour of their present state with the grey fog of uncertainty and defeat. The earl had no legal justification for his deeds, except his victory in battle, and his subsequent possession of the king's person and the king's seal. But he carried on the government in the king's name, although it fought against the very essence of the principles for which the king himself stood. Perhaps the earl's title as Steward of England could be stretched to provide him with some further legal sanction. He must make the king write to the aged countess of Leicester, still active as a recluse at Hackington, and demand her explanation of what the office of steward had been in the time of her husband, fifty years before.

Before he left Odiham, the countess must have known the line her husband would take. Even if he could get no further confirmation of his powers, even if he lost the support of the other barons, he would continue. The momentum of power hurried him on, for he had gone so far that he could not turn back. There were only two possibilities if he remained in England – total victory or death. The coward's way of flight was unthinkable. The family party broke up on April 2nd when the earl rode away to join the king and go to Northampton. Husband and wife parted for the last time, the earl to continue the struggle in the west as the situation continually deteriorated, while Eleanor bent her efforts to rallying support in the east, finally settling herself in Dover castle.

The earl's immediate interest at Northampton was a tournament, called by his sons for April 20th.[15] The disappearance of winter was always a cause for festivity in the Middle Ages and Thomas Wykes cheerfully, and rather incongruously, underlines the varied delights of April: "With the coming of springtime, when kings are accustomed to go to war, when the woods grow green, and the birds for joy sing the most cheerful songs."[16] Simon de Montfort waited to see if the earl of Gloucester would reappear for this tourney, but Gilbert was suspicious, and refused to move from his western lands. It was necessary to face Gilbert in person and try to heal the breach, so the earl of Leicester took the king and Edward with him and headed for the west.

Apart from the quarrel with the earl of Gloucester, there was further cause for concern. The Marchers, despite the many treaties and settlements which had been arranged with them since the battle of Lewes, had never really accepted any terms. Simon de Montfort would find no satisfactory way to force the obedience of these rebellious lords, for the country was too unsettled, and they sheltered behind the convenient protection of the earl of Gloucester. The earl of Leicester's strongest ally in the west was Llywelyn, the prince of Wales. But any treaty the earl made with Llywelyn was, in fact, a two-edged sword. Since any advance made by the Welsh was made at the expense of the Marcher lords, they naturally regarded the prince with fear and loathing. The Marchers were almost independent chieftains. They balanced their dislike of the growth of the royal power in their lands against the danger of invasion by the Welsh. As the earl of Leicester drove the baronial party into closer alliance with the Welsh, he inevitably alienated the Marchers. The earl of Gloucester's lands were on the fringe of the March and he shared in the Marchers' concern. Besides, Gilbert became seriously worried over his own power when he saw his dreaded rival adding to his other holdings the great earldom of Chester, for this brought him uncomfortably close to the lands of Gloucester's earldom.

Suspicion was the keynote of the encounter between the two earls in the west. When Leicester, with the king in his train, came to the town of Gloucester, he fortified the city and castle, fearing an attack. Meanwhile the earl of Gloucester and his supporters lay hidden outside the city in the Forest of Dean, while messengers ran back and forth between the two camps, seeking some form of peace. There seems to have been a brief reconciliation and an agreement on arbiters, including the stalwart bishop of Worcester, but nothing really came of it, and the breach widened. The earl of Leicester, still trailing the king and Edward with him for greater safety, moved on across the river Severn to Hereford, escaping an attack from Gilbert de Clare's forces.[17] The revolt in the west was encouraged by the news of the landing of two of the most important of the exiles. At the beginning of May, William de Valence and John de Warenne, two staunch royalists, came ashore in William's lands at Pembroke, at the south-western tip of Wales, and brought with them one hundred and twenty armed men.[18] The party of opposition began to grow and attract recruits. In fact, as one monastic annalist puts it, "to speak in poetic language, lady Fortune spread her wings and more generously carried the earl of Gloucester on her shoulders than the earl of Leicester, and so the army of the earl of Gloucester grew from day to day in number and strength, while the other's decreased".[19]

Meanwhile, Gloucester took the final step to separate himself from Earl Simon. Gilbert de Clare arranged to meet Roger Mortimer, always a bitter enemy of de Montfort's, and, after some initial hesitation, they joined forces to oppose the earl of Leicester and liberate the king. Their first move was to attempt to free Edward from the surveillance which checked him so closely and irked him so much. A plan was hatched for Edward's escape, aided by Gilbert's brother, Thomas de Clare, who still pretended loyalty to the earl of Leicester's party. In fact, Thomas was not only Edward's room-mate, but his close and trusted friend. The king's son obtained permission from Earl Simon to go outside the walls of the city of Hereford regularly for exercise. His confederates sent him a magnificent horse and, on the appointed day (May 28th), Edward tried out the various horses of the members of his guard, commenting on their abilities. When he had tired them all, he leaped to the back of his special charger, held in reserve for this moment, and galloped away. He easily outdistanced the winded horses of his jailers, and bidding them a contemptuous farewell, he reached the safety of Mortimer's castle at Wigmore, some twenty miles away, before the discomfited company could catch up with him.[20]

A few days later at Ludlow, Edward and the earl of Gloucester agreed on the terms for their confederation. It all sounds so familiar. The same cry of reform is heard, this time from Gloucester, the same desire to see the native-born as counsellors. Gloucester urged, as the price of his aid, that if:

he (Edward) was able to obtain victory, the old good and approved laws to be observed, the evil customs which had grown in the realm to be abrogated, and that he should induce the king that he should remove the foreign-born from his kingdom and his council, nor permit them to have the guard of castles, or any kind of administration in the realm, and that it should be ruled by the counsel of the faithful native-born.[21]

The echoes of the Provisions of Oxford sound behind these terms of 1265 and, ironically, they speak with a different voice. Montfort, the idealistic leader of the early years, had become the harassed administrator, constantly denying freedom in his effort to maintain it. The king's son was to reap the grain from the harvest of his father's mistakes, as well as those of his revolutionary uncle. The lords turned to Edward's leadership with enthusiasm, for he seemed to promise the reform they still held vital, and which the old king had never honestly executed. But, at the same time, the prince had a legitimate title and acted within the framework of rights and responsibilities which sustained the medieval idea of kingship.

In Hereford, Edward's escape demonstrated to Earl Simon the acute danger of his own position. This realization appears even in the sober language of the entries on the patent rolls, for a series of desperate messages went out to his sons and supporters in the south as well as a general summons for knight-service.[22] From Hereford, Simon went on into Wales. The earl had no other choice but to extend his treaty with Llywelyn, so as to receive further aid from him, no matter how expensive the terms were. Edward's generalship isolated Leicester's army west of the Severn, for all the bridges had been broken at Edward's command, even the strong one at Worcester. All along the river precautions had been taken to make the crossing difficult, if not impossible, for the earl's army. The little boats which normally rested at the water's edge were all dragged up on land, and wherever there had been passable fords, ditches were dug. Held back at the Severn, Simon led his army and the captive king from Hereford south to Monmouth, hoping to find ships to transport his forces across the Bristol Channel and safely into Bristol itself, for Earl Simon still held the town.

Hearing of the earl of Leicester's desperate attempts to find boats, the earl of Gloucester sent out some of his own ships. They sunk or captured eleven of the transports dispatched by Bristol, and forced the others to return empty. Simon was forced to return the eighteen miles to Hereford, for his army was hungry for bread, which the Welsh soldiers lacked. East of the Severn, Edward, with a constantly growing force of nobles, forced the surrender of Worcester, and then successfully besieged Gloucester.[23] On both sides of the Severn, the armies pillaged, burned and devastated the countryside. But the earl of Leicester was in the most dangerous position. He had to get his men back across the river and safely to London or Kenilworth. In either place, he could regroup and find reinforcements. By the beginning of July, organized government had ceased, and even the forms of administration had broken down. There were no entries on the patent and close rolls. All the kingdom rang with rumours and alarms, as men waited, fearfully or hopefully, for the final, inevitable encounter between the opposing forces.

During the long June days, the Countess Eleanor moved her household from Odiham to Porchester, through Bramber and Winchelsea to the vital fortress of Dover. Simon the younger had been carrying on a rather desultory siege of Pevensey on the Sussex coast, when he received his father's orders to abandon this attempt and bring an army to the aid of his father in the west. Young Simon did not comprehend the urgency of the situation, or was incredibly over-confident, for he went first to Winchester, which he sacked and pillaged, killing the Jews there. Slowed and sated by their loot, he and his followers went on to Oxford, and lingered there for another three days. Finally he arrived at Kenilworth on July 31st with a large army which he had collected throughout the southern and midland counties. The army was tired after its march and celebrated its arrival at the baronial stronghold by a feast and the relaxation of any guard. After all, they thought, Edward was safely in the west and there was no imminent danger, the barons could spend the night comfortably in their beds outside the confines of the castle.

But Edward was a far craftier and abler general than his brash young cousin. The prince had heard through his scouts – one of whom seems to have been a woman in man's clothing – of the whereabouts of the barons' force. By a hard night march from Worcester, some thirty miles away, Edward's army came to Kenilworth at dawn. The surprise was complete. The royalist force quietly waylaid the barons' forage carts which had been sent out very early to find food. Although the horses that pulled the carts were not particularly good ones, they were fresh and could replace some of the exhausted mounts of Edward's men. Then, with no alarm given, they fell on the sleeping baronial army. One chronicler suggests that many of the barons were recovering from the effects of too much wine at the previous night's feast. Whether this was true or not, Edward and his men captured the most important knights of the relief army before they even had a chance to arm. Young Simon only saved himself by fleeing naked from his bed and seizing a small boat which fortunately lay near at hand. In this he crossed the wide lake to the safety of the castle. Having taken many valuable prisoners, Edward returned to Worcester to keep watch on the Severn and the main army of the earl of Leicester.[24]

The earl had brought his army from Hereford, and the day after his son's fiasco, he managed to ford the Severn at Kempsey, a few miles downstream from Worcester. This manor belonged to Simon's good friend, the bishop of Worcester, and was a safe place to spend the night. The earl of Leicester knew of Edward's base at Worcester, only three miles away from Kempsey, and planned his march to Evesham during the night. During the heat of August the darkness was cooler, as well as more concealing. At Evesham, two roads and two possibilities faced the earl. He could head for Kenilworth, where he confidently expected the reinforcements gathered by his son, or he could take the longer main road to London, hoping to enter the city and find further support before Edward and the other lords could catch him. But the decision would have to be postponed for a little. King Henry was tired, and all the army needed food. They paused at the abbey of Evesham to hear Mass and refresh themselves after the fifteen-mile march. And, for Earl Simon, there was to be no way out from Evesham.

Edward knew of the arrival of the barons' army, and, unlike Simon, he also knew that there would be no reinforcements. This time the geographical advantage favoured the king's son. Evesham lies in a fertile valley, in a deep bend of the river Avon. To the north, the main road runs up the steep side of Greenhill. There were only two ways out for the barons' forces, over a narrow bridge across the river, or up Greenhill. Edward paused, out of sight of the abbey, and divided his forces. He sent a wing under Roger Mortimer's command to circle the town and to cut off any retreat by the barons over the bridge. His own troops and those of the earl of Gloucester descended the hill in front. The story goes that Edward added trickery to good generalship. Perhaps he remembered that deceptive cart of the earl of Leicester at the battle of Lewes. Having captured several baronial banners in the skirmish at Kenilworth, the advancing royal troops hoisted them first. They hoped that the earl's outposts might be deceived into thinking that the oncoming army was really the longed-for reinforcements from his son. The ruse was successful. Simon's barber had gone up to the top of the abbey bell tower to view the advance when he saw the false banners exchanged for the rightful standards of Edward and his supporters. Horrified, he called to the earl: "We are all dead men, for it is not thy son who comes as you believed, but the king's son from one part, the earl of Gloucester from another, and Roger Mortimer from the third."[25]

At long last the final encounter had come. Edward had learned his lesson well in the hard school of battle. When the earl of Leicester emerged from the town, armed and prepared for battle, he looked at the disposition of his enemy's forces and turned to his men with his favourite oath: "By the arm of St James, they approach wisely; nor have they learned this manner from themselves but from me."[26] Upheld by the conviction that he died for God and justice, he refused to flee from the field, as some of his supporters urged. The situation was desperate, but there was no honourable way out: "Let us commend our souls to God, because our bodies are theirs."[27]

The hard-pressed baronial army was ready for the unequal struggle. Even King Henry was armed, and in the anonymity of the charge, was wounded on the shoulder. Pitifully he cried out to save himself: "I am Henry of Winchester, your king. Do not harm me." For, as the same chronicler adds, "he was a simple man, peaceful, not warlike".[28] Fortunately King Henry was safely disengaged from the fray, for this was a battle where personal passion ensured that there would be no token struggle, but a fight to the death. Earl Simon fought on as one inspired, with his little group of companions and ardent supporters. When his charger was killed under him, he continued the fight on foot. Gradually the infuriated nobles closed in, like a pack of hounds, on one whom they had once revered and now detested. Their blood lust was heightened by the frenzy of combat and even the earl's strength and ability could not withstand the sheer weight of numbers. Young Henry de Montfort was killed, Hugh Dispenser the Justiciar, the earl's old friend Peter de Montfort, and many others. Finally the earl himself went down under the relentless attack. His head was cut off and his lifeless body shamefully mutilated. Drunk with victory and the satisfaction of personal hate, the Marchers stuck the earl's head on a lance and sent the bloody sign of their conquest to Roger Mortimer's wife at Wigmore. Simon the younger bringing aid, too late, came in view of the victorious troops with their grisly trophy, and returned to Kenilworth to mourn. One cannot help hoping that remorse for the desperate consequences of his own foolishness lent bitterness to his sorrow.

"Such was the murder of Evesham, for battle it was none."[29]

The shocked chroniclers describe this August day as one of portents and miracles. The extreme blackness of a violent summer thunderstorm and great bolts of lightning reminded the pious of the blackness of the day of the Crucifixion.[30] Robert of Gloucester, whose personal knowledge brightened his chronicle of these doings in the west, recalled the day vividly, that it was dark and overcast with a few large drops of rain. "This saw Robert . . . and was very sore afraid."[31] The figure of the great earl of Leicester had so dominated the realm of England that his death seemed a catastrophe which even nature recognized.

At Evesham itself, steps had to be taken to clear away the results of the battle. Edward ordered the monks of the abbey to bury the dead decently. The mutilated remains of the great earl were carried off the field by the monks on a rickety old ladder, covered with a ragged cloth, and his body, with those of the other nobles, was buried in the abbey church. Edward himself came to the funeral of Henry de Montfort and wept, for they had been brought up together, and shared a bond of affection from their boyhood days. Henry de Montfort has been King Henry's godson, as well as namesake.[32] But the passions of the more vengeful royalists had not been glutted, even by the earl's death and dismemberment. They muttered that it was unfitting for his body to have Christian burial, for Simon had died while under sentence of excommunication and was infected with the leprosy of treason. Finally they prevailed, and the earl's body was exhumed and thrown aside in a secret place.[33] The complaints of the royalists were doubtless encouraged by the veneration shown to the earl of Leicester's grave by the common folk, and the general talk of miracles done there. They hoped, vainly, that by destroying the place, the legends that encircled it might die as well.

Final reparation seems to have been made. Amaury de Montfort, the clerk of the family, was the only one who had managed to retain any favour in the sight of Pope Clement IV, who as legate had found the earl of Leicester "the pestilent man".[34] Amaury went to seek the pope at Viterbo, and complained of the slight to his father's memory. In May, 1267, Clement wrote to the legate Ottobuono in England to enquire about the truth of Amaury's assertions that although his father had asked for and obtained absolution before the battle of Evesham, and had given signs of repentance before his death, his body still did not have church burial.[35] The matter must have been gone into thoroughly, for the following year the legate duly declared at a general council of prelates in London that the Pope had absolved the earl of Leicester and all who were killed with him, adding that the Roman curia had been deceived in the sentence.[36] Perhaps it was after this ecclesiastical removal of any stigma upon the dead man that the final interment, of which the annals of Waverley speak, took place. According to this account, the king gave permission for the bodies of the earl and his son, as well as that of Hugh Dispenser, to lie at the lower step before the high altar of the abbey church at Evesham.[37] The passions roused by the great struggle had died down and the king's position was assured. King Henry could afford to be magnanimous and let the body of his great opponent rest in peace at last.

15

⁑ Full Circle

Under the great shock of the battle of Evesham, the Montfort fortunes crumbled and broke. The earl and his eldest son were dead. Guy was picked up on the field, a mass of wounds, and for some weeks hovered near death. But all opposition did not die with the Montforts. London was still in the hands of the barons' party. Dover castle was in the possession of the countess of Leicester herself and, in pockets throughout the realm, the desperate men of the opposition dug themselves in for resistance to the death. Impregnable Kenilworth withstood a long siege and was finally conquered by hunger in December, 1266. The disinherited in the fen country of the east held out for another year. But the issue itself was never again in doubt, despite the islands of resistance. The royal power, free and unfettered, once more ruled the land.

Much of the ensuing unrest and continued opposition was due to King Henry's malicious and vengeful treatment of the vanquished. The terms originally forced upon them were so hard that there was no advantage in giving up the fight. The immediate result of the royal victory was unchecked jubilation and looting among the king's followers. Almost immediately the king gave them licence to reward themselves at the expense of the lands and possessions of the rebels. Henry withdrew his assent from all the acts he had been forced to pass while under the earl's control and did not have custody of the great seal. As always, cruelty and greed stained the record of the victors. In the midst of so much hatred and the forcible seizure of the lands of others, one pleasant note of consideration for the sufferings of the lesser people marked the king's behaviour. Almost immediately after Evesham Henry settled pensions on the widows of two of the officers of his household – one his cook – who had perished at the battle of Lewes.[1] But his generosity was reserved for those who had been faithful to him. There was no mercy nor forgiveness for any of the Montforts, or for those who had opposed the king.

Two widows held the strongest castles of the kingdom – Dover and the Tower of London – for the baronial party. Hugh Dispenser's wife had been left in charge of the Tower, which her husband held as Justiciar, when he went to fight and die with the baronial army. After the disaster of Evesham, his widow freed all the political captives and only retained in custody those, like the earl of Derby, who had been accused of crimes. She surrendered the Tower to the royalists, and found a safe place of refuge with her father in her mourning.[2] He was Philip Basset, one of the strongest royalist supporters and a close counsellor of the king, who was well able to secure clemency for her. The matter was not so simple at Dover. When the tragic news was brought to the countess of Leicester, she succumbed for a time to her natural grief for her husband and her first-born. But mourning was a luxury she could not afford. Plans had to be made. Eleanor's first move seems to have been to arrange for the prior of the House of God at Dover to carry her messages to the king as soon as she heard of the outcome of the battle.[3] After all, she was still Henry's sister, and she may well have hoped that his family feelings would be too strong for him to want to wreak ultimate vengeance on her and her children. But – with the stubborn petulance of the weak and self-willed – the king would have nothing to do with his sister. From the time of the battle of Evesham, Eleanor is always given her formal title only in any communications to or about her. Only once, almost by mistake, is she called the king's sister. Her first attempt repulsed, the countess stayed in her stronghold, returned to her widow's dress of russet, and waited to see how she could salvage her fortunes and those of her children.

The king called a parliament at Winchester for September 8th, and there the victors, still drunk with their own success, insured the continuance of the struggle by imposing the stiffest terms on the

vanquished. The supporters of the baronial party were declared
disinherited and their lands forfeit. The Londoners were deprived
of all their special privileges and their ancient liberties, and the
chiefs of the faction opposed to the king were held in prison.[4] The
Countess Eleanor had sent several messengers to plead her cause
at this parliament,[5] and perhaps they had also instructions to see
which way the wind was blowing. She had already taken one
further step. Her brother, Richard of Cornwall, had been the
virtual prisoner of the Montforts at Kenilworth. After Evesham,
he could be released and used as a pawn for improving their
situation. This possibility seems to have been clearly thought out
by Eleanor. She sent off two of her most reliable servants to
Kenilworth with messages, for Richard himself as well as for
young Simon.[6] The king of the Romans was duly freed, but before
he left the great fortress he promised, in a cordial letter, to try and
act as a loyal friend to his sister, and her children, and their
people, so that they might be able to obtain their rights in England.[7]
The letter was undoubtedly a condition of his release, but Richard
also had real cause for gratitude. His nephew, young Simon, had
protected him from the fury of the garrison when the news came
of the earl of Leicester's death and shameful mutilation. The furious
knights would have gladly killed their captives in retribution for
the vengeance taken on their own leader.[8]

Once Eleanor had heard of the temper of the September
parliament, she realized that it was essential that her younger sons,
who had not been involved in the actual fighting, should be sent
away from England before it was too late. The plan was made for
young Richard – the almost unknown member of the family – to
go to Bigorre, and by September 25th his passage to Gravelines
had been paid for, and his clothes and companions arranged.[9]
Some rumour of his escape must have reached the king, for Henry
wrote to the barons of Dover and the other ports at the end of
September, commanding them not to allow the countess, or any
of her family, or, in fact, any one at all, to cross the Channel
without the king's licence or special mandate.[10]

There was more than outraged pride at stake here. Eleanor still
had the remnants of the money collected for the war by the barons.

It was a sizeable sum, some 11,000 marks, and Henry was extremely anxious to lay his hands on it. But the countess's ability to get her sons away, even with such precious freight, was greater than the king's ability to control the ports. By October 10th, Henry was writing to King Louis that he had heard that Amaury and Richard de Montfort had gone to France with the money. Henry wanted it applied to the account for damages suffered by the French merchants during the troubled times, and felt that Eleanor and her son should be forced to cede it to this purpose.[11]

The king was carried on a wave of vindictiveness. When the great feast of St Edward was celebrated in London on October 13th, Henry pronounced the solemn disinheriting of all those who had borne arms against him or Edward, of those who still adhered to Simon the younger, and of all those who remained with the baronial party after the battle of Evesham. This sweeping condemnation unfortunately promoted bitterness and continued revolt. Under such conditions, a rebel had little to lose by continuing to fight. The king gave away all their lands to his own supporters, and one of the scandals of the time was the fortunes made by the more avaricious and ambitious royalist supporters.[12] Some of the older and wiser heads held aloof from this arrogant use of the king's newly regained personal power. Richard of Cornwall, Roger Bigod, and Philip Basset led the magnates who did not give their assent to this disinheriting, but their disapproval was marked by withdrawal rather than active opposition.[13] The spectre of civil war was too horrifying to conjure up again.

Spurred by the king's boldness, the nobles who had been held in custody in Dover castle by the countess of Leicester and its keepers, John de la Haye, bribed some of their guards and struggled to take possession of the castle. When Edward heard of their attempt, he brought an army to Dover and besieged the castle from without.[14] The countess realized that further resistance was futile, and bent her efforts to making the best possible settlement with her nephew. Edward was more generous than his father, for he received to his grace and favour the members of the countess's household who wished to remain in England, and agreed to restore their lands.[15] There seems to have been a lack of the personal vindictiveness in Edward's feelings, which so disfigured his father's for when the prince wrote to the chancellor, insisting on this settlement, he spoke of his "most dear aunt, the lady countess of Leicester".[16] But though Eleanor did her best for those who had served her faithfully, she and her family had to go into banishment. At the end of October, the countess and her young daughter Eleanor sailed out from Dover harbour to exile in France. The twist of fortune provided that their lonely and sorrowful departure should almost coincide with the triumphant return of Henry's queen from her two years of exile, accompanied by the new legate Ottobuono.[17] France was to be a haven to the countess as it had been to the queen, but the countess of Leicester, unlike her sister-in-law, never looked on England again.

Eleanor's family were scattered. Amaury and Richard were already in France. Guy, still recovering from his wounds, was a prisoner at Windsor. Simon the younger was wandering in the north, in the Isle of Axholm, with some of his desperate followers. They could not hold out for long against the military might of Edward, who had taken an army north to attack them. Terms were arrived at in January, 1266, at Northampton. Simon the younger was to leave England and to receive a small pension of 500 marks a year, in place of his inheritance. At the same time, he was to keep his oath to do nothing to the detriment of the king or the realm.[18] The terms were hard, although not unbearably so, but there was little choice, even with the intercession of Richard of Cornwall who tried nobly to live up to his share of the bargain with his sister. Simon agreed to the arrangement, and went to London under supervision. There he slipped away, repudiating his promise, and found safety for a time in Winchelsea, which was still in the hands of the rebels. From there he made his way to France where he hoped to find aid to bring back to the help of the rebels, who still held out in the castle of Kenilworth. Rumours of his efforts reached England, encouraging the besieged and worrying the king, but nothing came of them. Simon's future in England was, in fact, finished. Guy, too, managed to escape to France in the spring of 1266, by bribing some of his jailers. From this vantage-point of security, the Montforts looked for ways to improve their fortunes.

It must be remembered that, although Eleanor and her family had suffered very heavily by the defeat of the barons' cause, everything was not lost. For the moment it looked as if all their great possessions in England were swept away in the flood of hate, but there were other possibilities in France. The countess of Leicester retired to the Dominican convent of Montargis to live the rest of her life, but it was a purely physical retreat. She remained as interested and as active in pursuing her interests and interminable legal battles as she had been before. King Louis was kind to her, and used his good offices in her favour more than once. There was the matter of her suit against the count of La Marche over the recognition of her rights in Angoulême. The *parlement* judged in her favour in 1267, but the count was very slow in carrying out the court's award.

Another decision was given in 1269 requiring the count of La Marche to give her a revenue of £400 a year in land, and £800 arrears for his two years non-compliance.[19] King Louis himself sent an order to his seneschal in the district to enforce the order before the expiration of the time-limit.[20] This was really quite a sizeable award, for it was equal to the amount she had been receiving in England for her Irish dower rights. Probably Eleanor owed her success in her case in *parlement* more to the desire of the French king and his officials to exercise their newly won jurisdiction over the lords of Poitou and ensure that the great vassals of those parts realised that they were subject to the laws and courts of the French king, than to the essential merits of her case.

King Louis never ceased to play his role as upholder of justice and settler of quarrels. He always maintained his interest and concern in the problem of peace in England. Pope Clement IV was none too pleased by Louis's objectivity, for Clement himself never forgot or forgave the conduct of the barons and their vigorous rejection of his embassy, when he was legate. There is a personal hatred for the earl of Leicester easily discernible in the tone of his letters on the subject. Soon after the news of King Henry's victory had reached the pope at Viterbo, Clement wrote to Louis exhorting him not to aid the countess of Leicester or her son to recover property in England, which the earl had most justly lost.[21] Despite the pope's rancour, the French king continued his efforts as peacemaker. In September, 1266, King Henry once more agreed to submit to Louis's award all the quarrels that lay between Henry and the Montfort family.[22] But the English king reminded his brother monarch that he had listened to the French messengers on the subject because of Louis's reputation and previous assistance. He hoped that the French king would not forget the many damages and injuries that the Montforts had caused to the realm.[23] As usual, the arrival at a settlement was delayed, but Louis showed – as he had at the time of Simon's trial in 1260 – his willingness to use the most important men of his realm to bring peace between the Montforts and the English king.

In May, 1267, King Louis sent to England a group of envoys headed by his butler, John of Acre. John of Acre was one of the most important nobles of the French court. His position as butler was a highly honourable one, for he was the son of John of Brienne, who had once been king of Jerusalem and emperor of Constantinople. The importance which King Louis attached to these negotiations can be judged by the eminence of his emissaries. The French envoys and the most intimate private counsellors of the English king, "the secretaries", settled down together to hammer out an agreement. Owing no doubt to the French influence, the terms agreed upon were generous to the defeated Montforts. Simon the younger was to receive his father's lands, although he must sell them to the king or his sons, Edward and Edmund, if they so demanded, at a price set by the king of France. The countess of Leicester was to have £500 a year for her dower lands in England, or, if she was unsatisfied with that arrangement, she could plead for justice in the king's court by her proctor, and the king would see that justice was done to her.[24] But although this settlement was arrived at, it does not seem to have been carried out. Perhaps the more vindictive nobles felt it was too generous to the family of the arch-rebel. Perhaps Simon the younger did not really trust the pious promises of his royal uncle. In any case, Simon the younger did not take up his inheritance in England.

As the first violent passions of the civil war receded a little, the good judgment of the legate, Ottobuono, and the mediating efforts of King Louis worked to some purpose. At the end of 1266, when the French negotiations had only begun, the long siege of Kenilworth was won by famine. Before the starved and tattered remnant of its garrison agreed to lay down its arms, the king issued the edict which was to bring peace and justice at last to the war-torn land. In the royal camp outside Kenilworth, on October 31st, Henry published the Dictum de Kenilworth. The Dictum reversed the first angry policy of vengeance and disinheritance, and extended to all the rebels the right to buy back their lands. The rates were set at various levels, ranging from twice their annual value for those very lightly involved, to seven times their value, for the most hardened rebels. Since ten times the annual value was considered the normal purchase price, these rates were fairly stringent, but not confiscatory. At the same time as this effort was made to reabsorb the rebels into the corporate body of the kingdom, the king reaffirmed unflinchingly his unfettered royal power and right to govern, saving, as always, his fidelity to the charters. But though the barons' cause had gone down to defeat, Simon de Montfort himself retained his hold on English imaginations and consciences from beyond the grave. This is manifested by the article of the Dictum which begged the legate, by ecclesiastical censure, and the king, by corporal punishment, to prevent Simon de Montfort from being regarded as a saint or just man, since he died excommunicate. The uneasy king claimed that vain and foolish miracles were being published abroad as having been done by Simon.[25] But legal prohibitions had no effect on the popular memory. They could not prevent an informal canonization enshrining the memory of the great earl whom many considered a martyr for England. Collections were made of his supposed miracles; reference was frequently made to him as a saint; and even a whole office was composed in his honour, probably by some of his most enthusiastic partisans among the friars.[26]

With the rebels brought to terms and the final pockets of resistance gradually conquered by Edward, England returned to relative peace and stability. The Statute of Marlborough in

November, 1267, gave concrete expression and permanent shape to some of the reforms which the barons had sought. It embodied most of the legal clauses of the Provisions of Westminster in this final and amplified reissue. The Statute reaffirmed the validity of the charter and especially emphasized the fact that the kingdom was again under the rule of law. This emphasis on law and the king's justice in this famous statute made it an excellent preamble to the reign of Edward, for it was in these very fields that he was to make his greatest reputation as king. But both the Dictum and the Statute of Marlborough bear the impress of the activity of the legate who was, perhaps, more responsible than any one for the successful pacification of the realm. Nevertheless, the legate had another commission in England as well, and that was to preach the crusade. Edward himself embarked on the great expedition to the Holy Land which Louis of France desired so ardently. With King Louis's second crusade, a long era came to an end in both England and France. The saintly French king died in 1270 at Tunis, before he even reached the Holy Land. Both Henry III and Richard of Cornwall died in 1272, before Edward returned. Henry had ruled for fifty-six years and, despite the upheaval of the barons' war, the realm had won through at last to peace and order.

After 1267, the Montfort family had little further interest in England, except to extract the last iota of their legal rights. The countess of Leicester had taken her case to the Roman curia, where King Louis interceded with Clement for a favourable hearing for her. In January, 1268, the pope assured the French king that he would show justice to the countess and her sons. A few weeks later Clement had to deal with Henry III's grievance, for the English king was annoyed that the pope would even listen to the countess of Leicester pleading against him. The pope remarked rather tartly that, without meddling with the king's rights, he wanted his own to be preserved, and that it was up to the king to show cause, if possible, for declining to appear in answer to the countess's petition.[27] The countess was tenacious of her legal rights, hoping, no doubt, to improve the position of her sons, but they had turned to other lands to make their fortunes.

Guy de Montfort and Simon had both gone to Italy in 1268.[28]

There they turned to the good offices of their cousin Philip de Montfort. Philip came from another branch of the Montfort family which had important possessions in the crusaders' lands in the east, as well as a seigneury in southern France. Through this family connection, both Guy and Simon found possibilities of advancement in Italy. Guy acquitted himself outstandingly at the great battle of Alba, in the summer of 1268, and the road to fame and fortune looked promising. Simon joined him at the end of the year, and shared in the distribution of some important Neapolitan fiefs. After being entrusted by Charles of Anjou with increasing responsibilities, Guy was named vicar of Florence and Tuscany, an important office. He buttressed his position by marrying Margherita Aldobrandesca, daughter and heir of the Red Count, the most important man in southern Tuscany. But the rising Montfort fortunes were checked again, this time by their own vengefulness. In March, 1271, the two brothers perpetrated one of the most famous crimes of their time, and made the name of Montfort synonymous with traitor. The story belongs to this account, for the act sprang directly from the tragedy at Evesham.

Many of the notables of the European world were in the town of Viterbo in the middle of March, 1271. The cardinals were in session, still bickering over the election of a pope to replace Clement IV, who had died at the end of 1268. Louis's son, Philip, had paused in his sad journey back to France bearing his father's body for burial at St Denis. Charles of Anjou, who was now king of Sicily, had come up from the south, and many of the other notables of St Louis's last crusade had paused in the Italian town on their way home. Edward, still on crusade, had sent his cousin, Henry of Almain, to Italy on a mission of reconciliation with the young Montforts. But, when Guy and Simon heard of their cousin's presence in Viterbo, their anger overwhelmed them. They remembered Henry's traitorous withdrawal from his confederation with their father, and the subsequent loss of baronial support. Above all, they remembered the murder of Evesham, and the shocking indignities inflicted on their father's corpse. Losing all restraint, the brothers, and some of their knights, came on Henry as he was hearing Mass in the church of San Silvestro on

Friday, March 13th, and immediately attacked him. After the first wild assault, Henry's body was dragged out into the square and there maltreated. The brothers had taken their revenge.

The consequences of their momentary madness ruined the futures of both the Montforts. Spiritual and temporal maledictions were heaped upon them. They were excommunicated and their lands were confiscated. Simon seems to have died, hiding in some obscure refuge, in the same year as the murder. Guy was partially protected by the strength of the family into which he had married, and he managed to outlive papal censure and regain his position with the forces of Charles of Anjou. But ill-fortune still dogged him, for, in 1287, when he led an expedition against the Aragonese who had taken Sicily from the French, he was captured and imprisoned in a Sicilian fortress, and died there four years later. Guy left two daughters, but no sons.

The fate of the rest of the family was less striking, but no less unfortunate. Richard de Montfort disappears completely from the records early in 1266. Amaury, the clerk, never gave up his claim to the title of treasurer of York, a post which his father had forced the king to give him. But it was an empty claim, for King Henry had immediately denounced the appointment after the battle of Evesham, and given the post instead to Edmund Mortimer, the son of Simon's great enemy. Amaury, however, was aided by the old family friend and benefactor, Archbishop Odo Rigaud, who gave him permission to take the subdiaconate and major orders from any bishop on the Continent.[29] The young clerk went to Padua to continue his studies and apparently went in for medicine, as in 1272 he finally returned to the abbot of Monte Cassino three medical treatises he had borrowed.[30] Although a bout of illness at Padua saved him from condemnation as an accomplice in his brother's crime, Edward was never really convinced of his innocence and regarded him with considerable suspicion. But Amaury had been busy at the papal court, and was regarded with favour. He was named a papal chaplain, and gained the pope's assistance in his efforts to retain his title as treasurer of York. It was Amaury, too, who persuaded the pope to withdraw the sentence of excommunication that had been passed on his father.

Though the Montfort sons were regarded with hatred and contempt by their royal cousin, he was always more than just to his aunt. When Edward, now king, returned from the crusade, after his father's death, he passed through France on his way home. From Melun, outside Paris, where he had stopped to see King Philip in August 1273, he wrote to his chancellor:

> We . . . have remitted to Eleanor, countess of Leicester, all indignation and rancour of our mind which we had conceived against her on account of the disturbance lately had in our realm, and we have admitted her to grace and our firm peace.[31]

Eleanor was to be allowed to plead against the king, or any others of the realm for her rights. Considering Edward's fury at the younger Montforts for the brutal murder of Henry of Almain, this was a noble concession, even if the king of France had requested it. But Edward on this occasion seems to have gone beyond the bare demands of justice. During this stay in Paris, he loaned his aunt £200, for she was, as always, financially embarrassed.[32] But she was more careful than in her youth, for the loan was rapidly repaid.

The whole matter of Eleanor's dower was again re-opened. In October, Philip wrote to Edward that Eleanor still complained about it, although the 15,000 marks which was supposed to have been left in the Temple at Paris until the matter was settled, had been removed after the battle of Evesham. Philip was anxious that Edward should rectify this as soon as possible.[33] Edward acted swiftly. At the end of the month he ordered the heirs of the earl Marshal to answer at the Exchequer to the countess of Leicester for the debts they owed her.[34] The royal settlement of £400 a year for Eleanor's dower lands in Ireland had ceased to be paid after the battle of Evesham,[35] and, in any case, many of the Marshal heirs were also behind in their payments to the Exchequer. Although it is very hard to disentangle the holders of the lands which should have been Eleanor's in these disturbed years after the civil war, Edward apparently saw to it that his aunt also regained at least some of her English dower lands. The Dunstable annals assert that he gave them all back, and that she held them for a year before her death.[36] In the Close Rolls, two months after Eleanor's death, the king ordered his sheriffs to see to it that the corn already sowed, and the other goods of the countess of Leicester in the manors of Wexcumb and Bedewynd, Luton, Crendon, and Weston were handed over to the executors of her will.[37] These lands, at least, returned to the countess's control.

From her retreat in France, the countess of Leicester enjoyed briefly the improvement in her finances brought about by Edward's justice and generosity. But her troubled career was almost at an end. On the eve of Easter (April 13th), 1275,[38] Eleanor died in the convent of Montargis. She had spent her retirement there, in a house which had been founded by her husband's sister and which had many connections with the Montfort family. In her loneliness and exile she had been most kindly treated, especially by the French royal family. Even Queen Marguerite, who had been so vehement in her hatred for the English rebels, seems to have served as her good friend, and to have been with her at the end.

As a last request, Eleanor had begged the French queen to intercede with Edward to show pity to Amaury and allow the carrying out of her will.[39] But, in death as in life, the countess's debts remained to plague the king. Nine years after her death, a debt of £160 (Tours) owing to the French king was finally paid off. Two years later, in 1286, the executors of Eleanor's will wrote to Edward that Eleanor owed the abbess and Cistercian convent of Saint-Antoine near Paris £220 16s. They had assigned the money to the religious from the debt owed by Edward to the countess on the question of dower.[40] With the king's payment, and the discharge of the Marshal heirs of their debt at the Exchequer,[41] the curtain was at last rung down on the countess's great law case. For fifty-five years it had trailed through the courts of England and France, and through all the ups and downs of fortune, the proud and passionate countess had single-mindedly maintained her rights.

Amaury de Montfort was his mother's heir, and with Guy in hiding in Italy, it fell to the clerk to take care of his sister Eleanor. Years before, Earl Simon had arranged for her alliance to

Llywelyn of Wales. The marriage was performed by proxy in France, just before the countess's death when the Welsh messengers came to complete the contract with Simon's widow and her daughter, now about twenty-three. Towards the end of 1275 Eleanor and Amaury set sail for Wales, fearing to travel by way of England. But King Edward was not anxious to see the daughter of the great rebel married to the always rebellious Welsh prince. By chance, the little expedition was caught by four ships from Bristol, and the Montforts were taken prisoner and handed over to the king. Edward treated Eleanor kindly, and kept her under honourable surveillance at court, but he had no sympathy or mercy for Amaury. He was imprisoned in that grim fortress, Corfe castle, where other royal prisoners had languished before.[42] When peace had been settled between England and Wales, Eleanor was finally allowed to marry her prince, and King Edward himself provided the feast on the celebration of the marriage at Worcester on the feast of his patron saint, 1278.

Eleanor retained the affection of her royal cousin and seems to have had some influence upon him. She interceded with him for the carrying out of her mother's will in England, and reinforced "with joined hands, bent knees, and tearful sobs" the request made by the pope for Amaury's release from captivity.[43] Only two months before her own death in childbirth, she had the joy of knowing that the king had at last acceded to the requests of the pope and the bishops of England, and freed Amaury from his prison. Though liberated, Amaury never regained the favour of the king, and was never reinstated in his English lands or offices. Unfortunately, the countess of Leicester's youngest son seems to have inherited more from his mother than just her estates. He had the same persistent litigiousness and sharp tongue, and he exercised both against his cousin the king. Although Amaury achieved nothing notable, his claims and pretensions were enormous for, in his will dated at Montargis, 1289, he described himself as "earl of Leicester by hereditary right, and palatine of Chester, and steward of England".[44] His later history is not clear. After a time in France, he apparently went to Italy and served briefly as tutor for Guy's daughters. There is a curious story that he put off his clerical state and turned knight before his death, but that is merely one chronicler's speculation.[45] At any rate, before 1300 he was dead.

Thus, by the end of the thirteenth century, Simon de Montfort's immediate family had disappeared from history. There were no male heirs. After young Eleanor's death in childbirth in 1282, her little daughter was taken to England and brought up by the Gilbertine nuns at Sempringham, where she died in kindly obscurity in 1337. The Montfort line in England died with her, and only Guy's daughters remained to carry the proud and tragic memories of their inheritance to the noble houses of Italy. From the quiet castle of Montfort-l'Amaury the turn of Fortune's wheel had carried the Montfort family to its peak of fame in the troubled, exciting years of Earl Simon's power. Then the wheel had spun again to plunge them into the darkness of death and exile and the virtual disappearances of their family.

16

Conclusion

Simon of the mountain strong,
  Flower of knightly chivalry,
Thou who death and deadly wrong
  Barest, making England free

Not the holy ones of yore,
They on earth who travailed sore,
  Came to such despite and scorn;

Feet and hands dissevered,
Pierced corse and wounded head,
  Flesh and harness stript and torn.

So with God our champion be
As our whole defence in thee
  Dying, leaves the world forlorn.

HYMN FOR SIMON DE MONTFORT[1]

The earl and countess of Leicester were a vivid pair, and their lives can still compel interest across the gulf of centuries. Since their career was packed with incident, it is possible to trace their share in the great events of their own time. We can arrive at a partial estimate of the contribution made by the earl to the constitutional development of England and to the rise of parliament, although the scholars still disagree among themselves. But it is exceedingly difficult to form a just judgment on the personal character of Eleanor and Simon. The distorting lens of whole-hearted enthusiasm or unremitting enmity colours the multiplicity of the records and blurs our focus on the character of the man. It is even harder to try and recreate his wife, for, like so many medieval women, she is described by the contemporary chroniclers in the conventional stereotypes which provide no key to her complexities. It is obvious that the earl and countess of Leicester were a loyal and devoted couple who worked hard to advance each other's interests. But, despite their hasty marriage, no ember of passion glows through the scanty personal documents, though Eleanor's grief on hearing of the loss of both husband and son at Evesham was deep and unfeigned. Devout, but proud and high-tempered; faithful, but litigious and obstinate; Simon and Eleanor stand apart, isolated above their followers. No talented contemporary pierces the screen that time and distance have created to block our understanding.

The earl of Leicester had reached the peak of his achievement before his death. He had upheld the sanctity of his oath to the bitter end, though in maintaining faith to the Provisions, he had broken his faith to the king. His provisional government, between Lewes and Evesham, turned away from the main road of medieval political evolution. This kind of limited monarchy was a dead end for the Middle Ages. But in his unceasing and unsuccessful efforts to combine control of the king with recognized legal forms, Simon made some valuable experiments which became fruitful precedents for later development. Edward, as heir to the throne, learned more from his turbulent uncle than the military skill he displayed at Evesham. The prince had seen the boundaries of the royal power tested, and he discovered by sad, practical experience where the king must recognize and admit the rights of the community of the realm. But, until the earl's death, there could be no peace or stability in England. The necessary return to order and the rule of law could only be achieved when the towering figure of Earl Simon no longer rallied the desperate and the devoted to what he was convinced was a holy cause.

The character sketches of the earl given by the contemporary chroniclers are weakened by the pious platitudes of contemporary hagiography – the nightwatches and prayers, the hair shirt and mortifications, as well as the high-flown comparisons with Christ and Simon Peter.[2] It is hard to judge whether they really described the man, or whether they merely felt that this should have been the appropriate behaviour of one who was hailed as a martyr. Although Simon was a man of strong faith and was particularly interested in the thought of the religious leaders of his day, he gave no great indications of sanctity. His career was stained by excessive harshness and pride, as well as by the taint of greed in his pursuit of land and riches. The paradoxes and contradictions of his character perplexed his contemporaries, as they have confused later generations of students. But behind all the varied judgments lies proof of a vivid and compelling personality, towering above his contemporaries, able to influence and even revolutionize his times.

By the manner of his death, Simon de Montfort ensured his passage into legend. The stories of miracles, the popular songs, and the hymns that gathered around his memory and his burial place were the contributions of the lesser folk of England. The earl's faults alienated him from his equals, who were repelled by his arrogance and by his unfailing emphasis on the last farthing of his rights. The history of his relations with the weak, but generous, King Henry and with the fiery earls of Gloucester, Richard and Gilbert de Clare, show the most unpleasant side of his character. From his inferiors, and from the clerics, both great and small, he won steadfast devotion and undying support. The paradox of a French adventurer gaining popular canonization as a martyr for the freedom of England brilliantly illuminates the peculiar closeness of Anglo-French relations during this century, and the inextricably emmeshed private and political interests of the great barons of France and England.

Earl Simon's eulogistic contemporaries compared him with another great fighter for the rights of England, the "blisful martyr", Archbishop Thomas Becket.[3] For the enthusiasts, both these men were equally fighters for justice:

> Earl Simon sought Thomas, Simon waged the cause of Thomas, and with Thomas he wore away false laws by martyrdom.
> Thomas sun of the east, Simon star of the west, each man of pious mind fought for justice.[4]

The comparison is enlightening, for there actually were many likenesses in the personalities of the two men.[5] Both shared many of the Norman traits of the stock from which they sprung. In each there was a hard directness which was impatient with any fuzziness of mind. Both, too, had a kind of militant efficiency which could easily degenerate into brutality. But Archbishop Thomas and Earl Simon shared more than a common heritage. Despite the century which divided them, they were the same type of man, as was Simon's greatest clerical contemporary, Robert Grosseteste. They made an enormous mark on their times, and helped to develop a whole new pattern of government, but they had no ease of self-expression, no pervasive charm of personality which could explain to other generations their feelings and beliefs. Arrogant and immovable when convinced of the right, they were men to inspire admiration, but not love. Archbishop Thomas set the boundaries of the medieval king's right of interference in the affairs of the church. Earl Simon underlined the lengths to which the community of the realm would go to ensure the recognition of their stake in good and just government. Ironically, the peace of England and the solution of the problems these men raised were best served by their tragic ends, for, despite the opposition they had encountered, the manner of their deaths ensured that their lives were not spent in vain.

T

Appendix

LANDS HELD BY EARL AND COUNTESS OF LEICESTER

Lands of the earl of Leicester
From the earldom of Leicester

LEICESTERSHIRE

borough of Leicester	Begworth
Hinckley	Thornton
Earl Shilton	Desford

HAMPSHIRE

Chawton

WILTSHIRE

Compton

DORSET

From the "lands of the Normans" granted Simon by the king
lands of Richard de Harcourt in
Northampton and Warwickshire (Ilmington)

SUFFOLK

Sproughton

BERKSHIRE

Ilsley

CAMBRIDGESHIRE

Barton   Girton

LEICESTERSHIRE

Chorley

Lands of the countess of Leicester

From dower and maritagium by right of her marriage to William Marshal, earl of Pembroke

BEDFORDSHIRE

Luton

Spenhamlond and Woodspeen

Toddington

BERKSHIRE

Newbury

Shrivenham

Wantage

GLOUCESTERSHIRE

Begworth

HAMPSHIRE

Norton

KENT

Brayburn

Kemsing

Sutton

HERTFORDSHIRE

Weston

NORFOLK

Foulsham

WILTSHIRE

Wexcumb, Kinwardston hundred

WORCESTERSHIRE

Severnstoke

From gifts of the king

HAMPSHIRE

Odiham Castle and manor

WARWICKSHIRE

Kenilworth Castle

Notes*

Introduction: THE TESTIMONY OF THEIR CONTEMPORARIES

page 3, 1. Worcester, *Ann. Mon.*, IV 355.

page 5, 2. Coulton, *From St Francis to Dante*, intro.

    3. Salzman, *Building in England*, 381; quoting from *Gesta Abbatum*, I 314.

page 6, 4. The information on which this section is based is summarized from the new and complete study, Richard Vaughan, *Matthew Paris*.

page 7, 5. Quoted Vaughan, *op. cit.*, 19–20.

    6. *Hist. Angl.*, III 319.

page 9, 7. Denholm-Young, "Thomas Wykes", *EHR*, LXI (1946), 157–79.

page 10, 8. Robt. of Glouc., I, xxxix.

page 11, 9. Walter of Guisborough has usually been referred to as Walter of Hemingburgh, but his new editor feels that his proper name is Walter of Guisborough. Rothwell, *Chronicle of Walter of Guisborough*, intro.

page 12, 10. Bemont, *Simon de Montfort* (unless specifically mentioned otherwise the references to Bemont are always to the French edition), 332–53.

    11. Ms. Clairembault, 1188, f. 2–40, 70–89.

    12. *Manners*, intro.

Chapter 1: MONTFORT-L'AMAURY: THE FAMILY BACKGROUND

page 17, 1. *Pipe Roll, 1206*, 9, 106. *Litt. Claus. 1202–24*, 74. *VCH, Leicester*, II 83.

    2. *Litt. Pat., 1201–16*, 74. *VCH, Leicester*, II 85.

page 20, 3. *Litt. Pat., 1201–16*, 150, 163. *VCH, Leicester*, II 86.

page 21, 4. John of Ox., 144.

    5. Dunstable, *Ann. Mon.*, III 33.

page 23, 6. *Lanercost*, 77.

page 24, 7. Powicke, "Loretta, Countess of Leicester", *Historical Essays in Honour of James Tait*, 247–72. This article gives the facts of Loretta's life and includes the references to the relevant records.

* For key to abbreviations, see Bibliography.

Chapter 2: THE EARLDOM OF LEICESTER

page 27, 1. Rishanger, *De Bellis*, 6–7, trans. by Prothero, *Life of Simon de Montfort*, 380–1.

page 29, 2. *Piers Plowman*, Passus V, ll. 518–9, 67.

page 30, 3. Bemont, *Simon de Montfort*, 333.

4. Vernon-Harcourt, *His Grace the Steward*, 108–14. The relevant entries have all been listed and printed by the author in this section.

5. Bemont suggests that Simon's first trip to England was in 1229. However, since the de Montforts used the Easter dating system, Simon could well have come to England in February 1230, as the Patent Roll would suggest, and still referred to the king's trip to Brittany in the spring and summer of 1230 as the following year.

page 32, 6. Painter, *Studies in the History of the English Feudal Barony*, 174.

7. Vernon-Harcourt, *op. cit.*, 102.

8. *Ibid.*, 99–104.

page 33, 9. Painter, *op. cit.*, 190.

page 34, 10. Bemont, *Simon de Montfort*, 333.

page 35, 11. *Ibid.*, 324–27.

12. Vernon-Harcourt, *op. cit.*, 111.

page 36, 13. Langlois, *La Vie en France au Moyen Age*, 183–209.

page 37, 14. *Ibid.*, 179–82.

15. *CPR 1232–47*, 119.

page 38, 16. Vernon-Harcourt, *op. cit.*, 114.

17. Paris, *Chron. Maj.*, III, 524.

18. Nangis, "Chronicon", *Recueil*, XX 548.

19. *Ibid.*, 549.

Chapter 3: THE KING'S SISTER

page 39, 1. *Royal Letters*, I 114–5.

2. Paris, *Chron. Maj.*, III 320.

page 40, 3. *Royal Letters*, I 244–6.

4. *C. Ch. R. 1226–57*, 102.

5. *CR 1227–31*, 518

page 41, 6. *Select Charters*, 341.

7. Bracton, *De Legibus*, II 49.

8. *CR 1227–31*, 492–3.

page 42, 9. Orpen, G. H., *Ireland under the Normans*, III 78, gives the value of the Irish lands as £1,716 7s. 4½d. The English and Welsh lands are listed, with their value, in the schedule of partition among the Marshal heirs in Chancery Miscellanea, C 49 9/20, 9/21, and the total value, including Eleanor's dower, was £1,854 13s. 5½d. The dower settlement is in *CR 1231–34*, 310.

10. *CPR 1232–47*, 125–6.
11. Gavrilovitch, *Étude sur le Traité de Paris*, app. I 118–9.
page 43, 12. Paris, *Chron. Maj.*, V 235.
    13. *Ibid.*, 235–6.
page 44, 14. *CR 1234–37*, 96.
    15. *CR 1231–34*, 210. *CR 1234–37*, 131.
    16. Paris, *Chron. Maj.*, III 336–9.
page 45, 17. Vernon-Harcourt, *op. cit.*, 82–3.
    18. *CPR 1232–47*, 166.
    19. *CR 1234–37*, 387.
    20. Clark, *Medieval Military Architecture*, II 336–46.
    21. *CR 1234–37*, 386.
page 47, 22. Nangis, "Chronicon", *Recueil*, XX 548.
page 48, 23. Paris, *Chron. Maj.*, III 471.
    24. *Lanercost*, 39–40.
page 49, 25. *CPR 1232–47*, 209.
    26. Tewkesbury, *Ann. Mon.*, I 106.
page 50, 27. Paris, *Chron. Maj.*, III 479–80.
    28. *CPR 1232–47*, 214.
    29. Paris, *Chron. Maj.*, III 480.
    30. *Papal Letters*, I 172.
    31. *Chron. Maj.* III 487.
page 51, 32. *Ibid.*, 498.
    33. *Ibid.*, 518.
    34. *CR 1237–42*, 103.
    35. *CPR 1232–47*, 212.
    36. Paris, *Chron. Maj.*, III 481–4. *Flor. Hist.*, II 224–5.
page 52, 37. Paris, *Chron. Maj.*, III 518.
    38. *Flor. Hist.*, II 229.
    39. *Lib. R.*, I 356.

Chapter 4: CRUSADER AND WARRIOR

page 53, 1. Paris, *Chron. Maj.*, III 539–40.
page 54, 2. *Ibid.*, 566–7.
    3. *CPR 1232–47*, 185.
    4. Bemont, *Simon de Montfort*, 263–4.
page 55, 5. *Ibid.*, 334.
page 56, 6. Paris, *Chron. Maj.*, IV 25.
    7. *Ibid.*, 7.

page 57, 8. *Ibid.*, 44–7.

    9. *Ibid.*, 44.

    10. *Ibid.*, 138–44.

page 58, 11. *Ibid.*, 147.

    12. *Manners*, xix n.

page 59, 13. Bemont, *Simon de Montfort*, 334.

    14. Painter, "The Lords of Lusignan", *Speculum*, XXXII 27–47.

page 61, 15. Lavisse, *Histoire de France*, v. III, pt. II 54–5.

    16. Paris, *Chron. Maj.*, IV 192.

    17. Bemont, *Simon de Montfort*, 334.

page 62, 18. *Ibid.*, 341.

    19. Dante, *Divine Comedy*, *Purgatorio*, canto VII, ll. 130–2.

    20. Salimbene, 305.

page 63, 21. Joinville, *Life*, ch. XXIII, par. 104.

page 64, 22. Paris, *Chron. Maj.*, IV 230.

    23. John of Ox., 171.

    24. Paris, *Chron. Maj.*, IV 224.

page 65, 25. "Chron. de St-Denis", *Recueil*, XXXI 113.

    26. *Flore. Hist.*, II 257.

Chapter 5: THE PEACEFUL YEARS

page 68, 1. *Flore. Hist.*, II 265.

    2. Paris, *Chron. Maj.*, IV 261.

    3. *Ibid.*, 263.

page 69, 4. *Ibid.*, 283.

    5. Bemont, *op. cit.*, 335.

    6. *Exc. e Rot. Fin.*, I 410.

    7. *CPR 1232–47*, 415.

    8. *Ibid.* 416.

    9. *CR 1242–47*, 164.

page 70, 10. *Ibid.*

    11. *C. Ch. R. 1226–57*, 278.

    12. *CR 1242–47*, 195.

    13. *CPR 1232–47*, 419.

    14. *CPR 1247–58*, 5.

page 71, 15. Clark, *Military Architecture*, II 130–53. *VCH, Warwick*, II 379–82; VI 135.

    16. *Lib. R.*, I 220.

page 72, 17. *Lib. R.*, II 33.

    18. *Ibid.*, 71.

    19. *Aucassin and Nicolette*, 4.

page 73, 20. *VCH, Warwick*, II 290.

    21. Denholm-Young, "The 'Paper Constitution' Attributed to

1244", *EHR*, LVIII 401–23. F. M. Powicke, *King Henry III*, pp. vi, 291 n. 2. B. Wilkinson, *Constitutional History*, I 117–26.

page 74, 22. Grosseteste, *Letters*, 141–43.

page 75, 23. *Ibid.*, 243–4

24. Marsh, "Letters", 170.

25. *Ibid.*, 110.

26. W. A. Pantin, "Grosseteste's Relations with the Papacy and the Crown", *Robert Grosseteste*, 205, 212–13.

page 76, 27. Marsh, "Letters", 111.

28. Paris, *Chron. Maj.*, V 284–7.

29. Paris, *Chron. Maj.*, V 415–16.

page 77, 30. Quoted Brewer, *Mon. Franc.*, I, p. ci.

31. Salimbene, 296.

32. *Mon Franciscana*, I, p. c.

page 78, 33. Grosseteste, *Letters*, X 69. trans. Stevenson, *Grosseteste*, 120–1.

34. Marsh, "Letters", *Mon. Franc.*, I 264.

35. *Ibid.*, 298.

36. *Ibid.*, 295.

page 79, 37 *CR 1242–47*, 325–26.

38. Waverley, *Ann. Mon.*, II 336.

39. *Manners*, 5.

page 80, 40. *CR 1242–47*, 214, 264, 268, 288, 424, 441, 458, 518, 521.

41. Paris, *Chron. Maj.*, IV 415.

page 82, 42. *Ibid.*, 420–22.

43. *Ibid.*, 504.

44. *Ibid.*, 527–37.

page 83, 45. *Flor. Hist.*, II 344.

page 84, 46. Paris, *Chron. Maj.*, IV 640–5.

47. *Lib. R.*, II 11–12.

Chapter 6: THE RUNNING OF A NOBLE HOUSEHOLD

page 86, 1. Denholm-Young, N., *Seignorial Administration in England* gives a detailed and clear account of baronial administration of their estates.

2. *Ibid.*, 75–6.

page 87. 3, *Henley's Husbandry*, 125–7.

4. *Cal. of Inq. P.M.*, Vol. II No. 306, p. 176.

page 89, 5. *Henley's Husbandry*, 145, 127–9.

page 91, 6. *Manners*, 4.

7. *Ibid.*, 5.

8. *Henley's Husbandry*, 139.

page 92, 9. *Manners* 5.

10. *CR 1234–37*, 420.
11. *Goodman of Paris*, 272–3.
page 93, 12. *CR 1237–42*, 191. *Lib. R.*, II 100.
page 94, 13. *Manners*, 13.
   14. *Ibid.*, 16.
   15. *Ibid.*, 26.
page 95, 16. *Ibid.* 62.
   17. Tristram, *Wall Painting*, I 62.
   18. *Manners*, 42–3.
page 97, 19. *CR 1234–37*, 563.
   20. *CR 1247–51*, 3–4.
   21. *Ibid.*, 459.
page 98, 22. *Manners*, 14.
   23. Homans, G., *English Villagers of the Thirteenth Century*, 358.
   24. *Goodman of Paris*, 262.
page 99, 25. *Ibid.*, 277.
   26. *Manners*, 39.
   27. *Ibid.*, 34.
   28. *Ibid.*, 18.
page 100, 29. *Ibid.*, 18.
   30. *Ibid.*, 18.
page 101, 31. *Ibid.*, 10.
   32. *Ibid.*, 65.
   33. *Ibid.*, 25.
page 102, 34. *Ibid.*, 72.
   35. *Ibid.*, 10.
   36. *Ibid.*, 31, 41.
   37. *Ibid.*, 57.
   38. *Ibid.*, 8.
   39. *Ibid.*, 9, 24.
page 104, 40. *Henley's Husbandry*, 135, 137, 139, 141.

Chapter 7: THE KING'S LIEUTENANT: GASCONY

page 105, 1. *CR 1242–7*, 293.
   2. *Lib. R.*, II 249.
   3. *Lib. R.*, III 157.
page 106, 4. Paris, *Chron. Maj.*, V 1.
   5. Bemont, *Simon de Montfort*, 264–5.
   6. The general history and background of the Gascon question is covered in E. C. Lodge, *Gascony under English Rule*, and F. B. Marsh, *English Rule in Gascony, 1199–1259*.
page 109, 7. *CR 1247–51*, 43.
   8. *Layettes*, III, no. 3715. Rymer I 269.

page 110, 9. Bemont, *Simon de Montfort*, 265–6.
page 112, 10. Paris, *Chron. Maj.*, V 49.
page 113, 11. Bemont, *Simon de Montfort*, 287.
    12. *CR 1247–51*, 231.
    13. *Ibid.*, 343–4.
page 114, 14. Paris, *Chron. Maj.*, V 104.
    15. Boutaric, *Saint Louis et Alphonse de Poitiers*, 73.
    16. *CR 1247–51*, 302.
    17. Bemont, *Simon de Montfort* (Eng. Ed.), 37, n. 1.
page 115, 18. *Royal Letters*, II 56–7.
    19. Boutaric, *op. cit.*, 75.
    20. *Royal Letters*, II 52–3. Bemont, *Simon de Montfort*, 267.
    21. *CR 1247–51*, 254.
page 116, 22. *CPR 1247–58*, 67.
    23. *CR 1247–51*, 321.
    24. *Ibid.*, 300.
    25. *Royal Letters*, II 63. *CPR 1247–58*, 68.
    26. Bemont, *Simon de Montfort* (Eng. ed.), 90, n. 7.
page 117, 27. Paris, *Chron. Maj.*, V 208–10.
    28. *Ibid.*, 222.
    29. *Papal Letters*, I 266.
    30. Bemont, *Simon de Montfort*, 336.
    31. John of Ox., 185.
page 118, 32. Paris, *Chron. Maj.*, V 263.
    33. *Royal Letters*, II 68–9. *CPR 1247–58*, 124.
    34. *Ibid.*, 69–70.
    35. *Ibid.*, 70–2.
page 119, 36. *Ibid.*, 76–81.
    37. *Royal Letters*, II 81–2.
page, 120 38. Bemont, *Simon de Montfort*, 279–321.
    39. Marsh, "Letters", 122–30. trans. in Green, *Princesses*, App. IV, 448–53.
    40. Paris, *Chron. Maj.*, V 287–96.
page 121, 41. Paris, *Chron. Maj.*, V 290–1.
page 122, 42. *Ibid.*, 313.
    43. *Ibid.*, 313–14.
page 123, 44. Bemont, *Simon de Montfort*, 343.
page 124, 45. *Ibid.*, 321–4.
    46. *Papal Letters*, I 285.
    47. Paris, *Chron. Maj.*, V, 365.
page 125, 48. *Flores Hist.*, II 382–3.
    49. *Rôles Gascons*, I nos. 2641, 2644, 2647.
page 126, 50. Paris, *Chron. Maj.*, V 366, 371–2.
    51. *Ibid.*, 415–16.

52. *CR 1253–54*, 191. *CPR 1247–58*, 251.
53. *CPR 1247–58*, 249–50.
54. *Ibid.*, 250. *Rôles Gascons*, no. 2160.

Chapter 8: SIMON DE MONTFORT, COUNT OF BIGORRE?

page 129, 1. Davezac-Macaya, *Essais Historiques sur le Bigorre*, I 166.
page 130, 2. de Gissey, *Discours Historiques de la Très-Ancienne Devotion de Nostre Dame du Puy*, 478–83.
   3. Davezac-Macaya, *op. cit.*, 249–50, n. 10.
   4. *Ibid.*, 254–56.
page 133, 5. *Layettes*, III, n. 3966.
   6. *Ibid.*
page 134, 7. Bemont, *Simon de Montfort*, 315–6.
   8. *Ibid.*, 370–1.
   9. Rocher, Ch., "Les Rapports de l'Église du Puy", *Tablettes Historiques de Velay*, IV 479–81.
  10. *CPR 1247–58*, 350.
page 135, 11. *CPR 1247–58*, 305–6.
  12. *Ibid.*, 398, 609.
  13. *CR 1254–56*, 426–7.
page 136, 14. Bemont, *Simon de Montfort* (Eng. ed.), 127–8, n. 6.
  15. *Layettes*, III no. 4279.
  16. *Ibid.*, no. 4453.
  17. *Ibid.*, no. 4286.
page 137, 18. *Ibid.*
  19. *Ibid.*, no. 4476.
  20. *Ibid.*, no. 4500.
page 138, 21. Bemont, *Simon de Montfort*, 371–2.
  22. *Recog. Feod.*, 408.
  23. Bemont, *Simon de Montfort*, 346–7.
  24. Vaissete, *Histoire de Languedoc*, VIII, col. 1502–3.
page 139, 25. *Manners*, 75.
  26. *Layettes*, IV, nos. 5101, 5102.
  27. *Ibid.*, no. 5262.

Chapter 9: THE KING'S ENVOY; FRANCE

page 142, 1. Rymer, I 305.
  2. *Rôles Gascons*, II n. 3944.
  3. *Royal Letters*, II 120.
page 143, 4. Paris, *Chron. Maj.*, V 457.
  5. Rymer, I 306.
page 145, 6. Salimbene, 222.

page 146, 7. *Political Songs*, 67.
    8. Paris, *Chron. Maj.*, V 479.
page 147, 9. *Ibid.*, 482–3.
    10. John of Wallingford, 73.
    11. Paris, *Chron. Maj.*, III 324, 334.
    12. John of Ox., 188.
    13. *CR 1254–56*, 153–4.
    14. *Ibid.*, 195–6. *CPR 1247–58*, 411.
page 148, 15. *Layettes*, III n. 4178.
    16. *CPR 1247–58*, 458.
    17. *Ibid.*, 460.
    18. *Ibid.*, 493–4.
page 150, 19. Paris, *Chron. Maj.*, V 706.
    20. *CPR 1247–58*, 542.
page 151, 21. *Ibid.*
    22. *Ibid.*, 594.
page 152, 23. Rymer, I 358. *CPR 1247–58*, 594.
    24. *CPR 1247–58*, 567–8.
    25. Rymer, I 361.
page 153, 26. Paris, *Chron. Maj.*, V 649–50, 659–60. John of Wallingford, 76, 77.
page 154, 27. Paris, *Chron. Maj.*, V 634.
    28. Paris, *Chron. Maj.*, V 677.
    29. *CPR 1247–58*, 628.
page 155, 30. Bemont, *Simon de Montfort*, 344.
    31. Pierre Chaplais, "The Making of the Treaty of Paris (1259) and the Royal Style", *Eng. Hist. Rev.*, LXVII 235–53 gives the sequence of events and an explanation of the formalities of medieval treaties.
page 157, 32. Wykes, *Ann. Mon.*, IV 123.
    33. Rigaud, "Visitations", *Recueil*, XXI 581.
page 158, 34. M. Gavrilovitch, *Étude sur le Traité de Paris*, 118–19. Green *Princesses*, App. I, 453–4.
    35. *C. Ch. R. 1257–1300*, 20. *CPR 1258–66*, 34–5. There is an earlier mention of this gift on May 20 in *CPR 1258–66*, 52–3.
    36. *CR 1256–59*, 433.
    37. *Layettes*, III n. 4454, 4455.
    38. Rigaud, "Visitations", *Recueil*, XXI 581–2.
page 160, 39. *CPR 1258–66*, 106–7. Bemont, *op. cit.*, 330–1.
    40. Rymer, I 392. *Layettes*, III 4565.
    41. Vaissete, *Hist. de Languedoc*, VIII, col. 1451.
    42. Rigaud, "Visitations", *Recueil*, XXI 582. *Layettes*, III n. 4566.
page 161, 43. Gavrilovitch, *op. cit.*, 23–5.
    44. Joinville, *Life*, par. 679.

45. Denholm-Young, "Feudal Society in the 13th Century: The Knights". *Collected Papers*, 58.

Chapter 10: THE COMMON ENTERPRISE

page 163, 1. *Flor. Hist.*, II 418–9. Paris, *Chron. Maj.*, V 674. Tewkesbury, *Ann. Mon.*, I 166.

page 165, 2. H. S. Snellgrove, *The Lusignans in England*, 1247–58, p. 65.
3. Burton, *Ann. Mon.*, I 285.

page 166, 4. John of Ox., 194. Paris, *Chron. Maj.*, V 406.

page 167, 5. F. M. Powicke, *Henry III and the Lord Edward*, I 332.

page 168, 6. The discussion of Bracton has been summarized from F. Schulz, "Bracton on Kingship", V, LX, pp. 136–76; and C. H. McIlwain, *Constitutionalism: Ancient and Modern*, 67–87.
7. C. L. Kingsford, *Song of Lewes*, Intro.

page 169, 8. *Ibid.*, ll. 445–9.

page 170, 9. Robt. of Glouc., II 734.

page 171, 10. Any discussion of the years 1258–63 leans very heavily on R. F. Treharne, *The Baronial Plan of Reform*. His marshalling of the relevant facts is invaluable, though I have differed at times from his interpretation of Simon's character as put forward in this book and the more recent short study, *The Personal Role of Simon de Montfort*.
11. Bemont, *Simon de Montfort*, 327–8.
12. Tewkesbury, *Ann. Mon.*, I 164.

page 172, 13. Rymer, I 370–1.
14. *Select Charters*, 373–8.
15. *Ibid.*, 384.

page 173, 16. Burton, *Ann. Mon.*, I 444–5.
17. Paris, *Chron. Maj.*, V 695–8.
18. Dunstable, *Ann. Mon.*, III 211.
19. *De Ant. Leg.*, 39.

page 174, 20. Bemont, *Simon de Montfort* (Eng. ed.), 162–5 gives a translation of this.
21. *Walter of Guis*, 185.

page 175, 22. *CPR 1258–66*, 3.
23. *Flor. Hist.*, II 421–2.
24. Bemont, *Simon de Montfort*, 328–30.

page 177, 25. Paris, *Chron. Maj.*, V 744.
26. *Flor. Hist.*, II 424–5.
27. Paris, *Chron. Maj.*, V 741, 745.
28. M. A. Hennings, *England under Henry III*, 93–5.
29. *CPR 1258–66*, 18.

page 178, 30. *Ibid.*, 16–17.

31. *Flor. Hist.*, II 428.
32. Bemont, *Simon de Montfort* (Eng. ed.), 173 n. 2.
33. F. M. Powicke, "Some Observations on the Baronial Council", *Essays on Medieval History presented to T. F. Tout*, 119.
34. Burton, *Ann. Mon.*, I 471.
page 179, 35. Bemont, *Simon de Montfort* (Eng. Ed.), 173 n. 3.
36. "Chron. of St Taurin". *Recueil*, XXIII 467.

Chapter 11: ARBITRATIONS AND COMPLAINTS

page 180, 1. Bemont, *Simon de Montfort*, 349.
2. *Ibid.*, 350.
page 181, 3. Nangis, "Chronicon", *Recueil*, XX 552.
4. *Royal Letters*, II 148–50.
5. *Ibid.*, 153–5.
page 182, 6. *Flor. Hist.*, II 443.
7. Bemont, *Simon de Montfort*, 351.
8. *Ibid.*, 350–53.
page 183, 9. *De Ant. Leg.*, 44–5.
page 184, 10. Powicke, "Baronial Council", 133–4.
page 185, 11. Dunstable, *Ann. Mon.*, III 215.
12. *Flor. Hist.*, II 448–9.
13. Treharne, *Baronial Plan of Reform*, 233.
page 186, 14. *Flor. Hist.*, II 449. *De Ant. Leg.*, 45.
15. Tristram, *Wall Painting*, I 575. *CR 1254–56*, 326.
16. F. M. Powicke, "The Archbishop of Rouen, John de Harcourt and Simon de Montfort in 1260", *Eng. Hist. Rev.*, LI 108–13.
page 187, 17. Rigaud, "Visitations", *Recueil*, XXI 583.
18. Powicke, "The Archbishop of Rouen, John de Harcourt, and Simon de Montfort in 1260", LI 108.
19. Bemont, *Simon de Montfort*, 343–53.
20. *Ibid.*, 350.
page 188, 21. Rigaud, "Visitations", *Recueil*, XXI 583. Powicke, "Archbishop of Rouen", 108.
22. *Flor Hist.*, II 454.
page 189, 23. *CPR 1258–66*, 96.
24. *Flor. Hist.*, II 456.
page 190, 25. *CPR 1258–66*, 136.
26. Beaumanoir, *Coutumes de Beauvaisis*, II 155.
page 191, 27. *CPR 1258–66*, 145.
28. Champollion-Figeac, *Lettres*, I 62–3.
29. *Layettes*, II 5049.
page 192, 30. MS. Clairembault, 1188, f. 16v.

page 193, 31. *Ibid.*, f. 18, f. 18v–19, ff. 21, 23, f. 31.

    32. *Flor. Hist.*, II 463–4.

page 194, 33. R. F. Treharne, *Personal Role of Simon de Montfort*, 91–2.

    34. E. F. Jacob, "Complaints of Henry III against the Baronial Council". *EHR*, XLI 559–71. N. Denholm-Young, "Documents of the Barons War", *EHR*, XLVIII 570–5.

page 196, 35. *Flor. Hist.*, II 467–9.

    36. *CPR 1258–66*, 162.

    37. *Ibid.*, 162–4.

    38. Bemont, *Simon de Montfort*, 331–2.

page 197, 39. *CPR 1258–66*, 169.

    40. Rymer, I 408–9.

    41. *Ibid.*, 409.

page 198, 42. *Select Charters*, 394–5.

    43. Dunstable, *Ann. Mon.*, III 217.

    44. Osney, *Ann. Mon.*, IV 128–9.

page 199, 45. *Royal Letters*, II 188–92.

    46. Rymer, I 416.

    47. *CR 1261–64*, 126.

    48. *Royal Letters*, II 174–5.

page 200, 49. Bemont, *Simon de Montfort*, 333–43.

page 201, 50. Rymer, I 422.

    51. Gerv. of Cant., II 217.

page 202, 52. *CPR 1258–66*, 240–1.

    53. Rymer, I 416. trans. M. Hennings, *England under Henry III*, 104–5.

page 203, 54. *CPR 1258–66*, 241.

Chapter 12: THE KING'S OPPONENT

page 205, 1. *CPR 1266–72*, app., pp. 726–7.

    2. *De Ant. Leg.*, 51.

    3. *Flor. Hist.*, II 477.

page 206, 4. *Stat. of the Realm*, 8 n. 3.

    5. *De Ant. Leg.*, 52–3.

page 207, 6. *CPR 1258–66*, 285–6. *De Ant. Leg.*, 53.

    7. John of Ox., 226.

    8. Dunstable, *Ann. Mon.*, III 221.

    9. *De Ant. Leg.*, 53.

page 208, 10. Wykes, *Ann. Mon.*, IV 133.

    11. John of Wallingford, 75.

    12. Rishanger, *De Bellis*, 11. Robt. of Glouc., II 736–9.

page 209, 13. Brieger, *English Art, 1216–1307*, 155–7. *CR 1261–4*, 316.

page 210, 14. Dunstable, *Ann. Mon.*, III 222.

  15. *De Ant. Leg.*, 54.

  16. *Ibid.*, 54–5.

page 211, 17. Dunstable, *Ann. Mon.*, III 222. Gerv. of Cant., II 222 makes it £10,000.

page 212, 18. Dunstable, *Ann. Mon.*, III, 223–4. *Flor. Hist.*, II 481–2.

  19. *CPR 1258–66*, 269–70.

page 213, 20. Gerv. of Cant., II 224.

  21. *Song of Lewes*, II 431–4.

page 214, 22. *Flor. Hist.*, II 482–3.

  23. *CPR 1258–66*, 271–2.

  24. Wykes, *Ann. Mon.*, IV 133–4.

page 215, 25. *CPR 1258–66*, 275.

  26. *Flor. Hist.*, II 484.

  27. *CPR 1258–66*, 276, 280.

  28. *CR 1261–4*, 312.

page 216, 29. *Dover Chron.*, in Gerv. of Cant., II 225.

  30. Dunstable, *Ann. Mon.*, III 225.

  31. Gerv. of Cant., II 225.

  32. Dunstable, *Ann. Mon.*, III 225.

page 217, 33. *De Ant. Leg.*, 58.

  34. Rishanger, *De Bellis*, 17.

page 218, 35. *Ibid.*

  36. *Ibid.*, 18.

  37. Trevet, 253.

  38. *CPR 1258–66*, 292, 294.

page 219, 39. Tewkesbury, *Ann. Mon.*, I 179–80.

  40. *CPR 1258–66*, 273.

page 220, 41. Gerv. of Cant., II 230–1.

  42. Dunstable, *Ann. Mon.*, III 226. *Flor. Hist.*, II 485.

  43. Rishanger, *De Bellis*, app., 121–2. Rymer, I 433.

  44. Rishanger, *De Bellis*, app., 120–1. Rymer, I 433.

page 221, 45. Dunstable, *Ann. Mon.*, III 226.

  46. Rishanger, *De Bellis*, app. 122–3. Dunstable, *Ann. Mon.*, III 227.

page 222, 47. Treharne, "Mise of Amiens", *Studies in Medieval History presented to F. M. Powicke*, 223–9. Walne, "The Barons' Argument at Amiens", *Eng. Hist. Rev.*, LXIX 418–25; LXXIV 453–9.

  48. Treharne, *op. cit.*, 238.

  49. Walne, *op. cit. EHR*, LXXXIV 455–9, also *EHR*, LXIX 421–2.

page 223, 50. *Ibid.*, *EHR*, LXIX 421–5.

  51. *Papal Letters*, I 396–400.

page 224, 52. Tewkesbury, *Ann. Mon.*, I 177.

53. *Select Charters*, 395–7. Wilkinson, *Constitutional History of Medieval England*, I 175–7.

Chapter 13: THE RISE TO ROYAL STATE

page 226, 1. Dunstable, *Ann. Mon.*, III 227. *Flor. Hist.*, II 486–7.
  2. *Robt. of Glouc.*, II 740–1.
page 227, 3. Dunstable, *Ann. Mon.*, III 227–8. *Flor. Hist.*, II 487.
  4. Gerv. of Cant., II 232–3.
  5. *CPR 1258–66*, 307.
  6. Osney, *Ann. Mon.*, IV 139–41. *Robt. of Glouc.*, II 741–3.
page 228, 7. *CPR 1258–66*, 358.
  8. *Ibid.*, 307.
  9. *Ibid.*, 308.
  10. Dunstable, *Ann. Mon.*, III 228.
  11. Wykes, *Ann. Mon.*, IV 140–1. *De Ant. Leg.*, 61.
page 229, 12. *CR 1242–47*, 201.
  13. Dunstable, *Ann. Mon.*, III 229–30. Trevet, 256.
  14. Dunstable, *Ann. Mon.*, III 230.
page 230, 15. Wykes, *Ann. Mon.*, IV 141–3.
  16. *Flor. Hist.*, II 489.
page 231, 17. *Ibid.*, 490.
  18. Rishanger, *De Bellis*, 26–7. *Flor. Hist.*, II 489–92. Gerv. of Cant., II 235–6.
page 232, 19. Dunstable, *Ann. Mon.*, III 231. Trevet, 256.
  20. The best summary of all the details about the battle of Lewes is to be found in the notes and chronology provided by C. L. Kingsford, *The Song of Lewes*.
page 236, 21. Gerv. of Cant., II 237–8.
  22. Walter of Guis., 196.
  23. *CPR 1258–66*, 318.
page 237, 24. The best discussion of these negotiations is in the paper by N. Denholm-Young, "Documents of the Barons' War", *Collected Papers on Medieval History*, 111–29.
  25. *Ibid.*, 122.
  26. *CPR 1258–66*, 319, 335.
page 238, 27. *Ibid.*, 321, 324, 325, 329.
  28. Wykes, *Ann. Mon.*, IV 152.
  29. Boutaric, *St Louis et Alphonse de Poitiers*, 108–10.
page 239, 30. Gavrilovitch, *op. cit.*, 121–3; 120–1.
  31. *De Ant. Leg.*, 67–9.
page 240, 32. Wykes, *Ann. Mon.*, IV 156–7.
page 241, 33. *CPR 1258–66*, 370–1.
  34. *Ibid.*, 344.

35. *Ibid.*, 366–7.
36. *Flor. Hist.*, II 503. Robt. of Glouc., II 751–2.
page 242, 37. *Manners*, 55, 57, 67.
38. *Ibid.*, 14, 25.
39. Rishanger, *Chron.*, 29.
40. *Ibid.*, 29. Wykes, *Ann. Mon.*, IV 157–8.
page 243, 41. *CPR 1258–66*, 394, 395, 397.
42. *Ibid.*, 398, 399.
43. *Flor. Hist.*, II 504–5.

Chapter 14: THE SPIN OF FORTUNE'S WHEEL

page 245, 1. *De Ant. Leg.*, 71–2.
2. *C. Ch.R.*, 1257–1300, 540.
3. Rishanger, *Chron.*, 32.
page 246, 4. Walter of Guis., 197.
5. Rishanger, *Chron.*, 32.
page 247, 6. *Battle Chronicle*, printed in Bemont, *Simon de Montfort*, 378.
7. Wykes, *Ann. Mon.*, IV 158–9.
page 248, 8. *VCH Hampshire*, IV 645.
9. *CR 1264–68*, 53.
10. *CPR 1258–66*, 404.
11. *CR 1264–68*, 4, 26.
12. *Manners*, 13.
13. *Ibid.*, 14.
14. *Ibid.*, 15.
page 249, 15. Dunstable, *Ann. Mon.*, III 238–9.
16. Wykes, *Ann. Mon.*, IV 161.
page 250, 17. Waverley, *Ann. Mon.*, II 361–2. *De Ant. Leg.*, 73.
page 251, 18. *CPR 1258–66*, 423–4.
19. Osney, *Ann. Mon.*, IV 164.
20. Robt. of Glouc., II 756–8. Wykes, *Ann. Mon.*, IV 163–4. Waverley, *Ann. Mon.*, II 362. Walter of Guis, 198. Rishanger, *Chron.*, 33–4.
page 252, 21. Wykes, *Ann. Mon.*, IV 164–8.
22. *CPR 1258–66*, 428, 429, 434.
page 253, 23. Wykes, *Ann. Mon.*, IV 165–8. Rishanger, *Chron.*, 34.
page 254, 24. Osney, *Ann. Mon.*, IV 164–8. Wykes, *Ann. Mon.*, IV 169–71. Waverley, *Ann. Mon.*, II 363–4. Walter of Guis, 199–200.
page 255, 25. Walter of Guis., 200.
26. Rishanger, *De Bellis*, 45. Walter of Guis., 200–1.
27. Rishanger, *De Bellis*, 45.

page 256, 28. Walter of Guis., 201.

29. Robert of Gloucester, II 765.

30. All the chroniclers have accounts of the momentous battle, which are more or less full and vary slightly. This is a composite account made up from the information furnished by: Rishanger, *De Bellis*, 45–7; Walter of Guis., 200–2; Robt. of Glouc., II 762–6; John of Ox., 228–30; *De Ant. Leg.*, 75–6; Waverley, *Ann. Mon.*, II 364–5; Wykes, *Ann. Mon.*, IV 171–5; Osney, *Ann. Mon.*, IV 168–73.

31. Robt. of Glouc., II 766.

page 257, 32. Rishanger, *Chron.*, 37.

33. Osney, *Ann. Mon.*, IV 176–7.

34. *Papal Letters*, I 419.

35. *Ibid.*, 434.

36. Gerv. of Cant., II 247.

page 258, 37. Waverley, *Ann. Mon.*, II 365.

Chapter 15: FULL CIRCLE

page 260, 1. *CR 1264–68*, 74.

2. Wykes, *Ann. Mon.*, IV 175–6.

3. *Manners*, 66.

page 261, 4. Rishanger, *De Bellis*, 49. *De Ant. Leg.*, 76–7. Trevet, 267.

5. *Manners*, 73.

6. *Ibid.*, 67.

7. Blauuw, *The Barons' War*, 361–2.

8. Rishanger, *De Bellis*, 50–1.

9. *Manners*, 74.

10. *Royal Letters*, II 292.

page 262, 11. *CR 1264–68*, 136.

12. This has been very carefully gone into by E. F. Jacob in his *Studies in the Period of Baronial Reform and Rebellion*.

13. Waverley, *Ann. Mon.*, II 367. Trevet, 267.

14. Gerv. of Cant., II 243.

page 263, 15. *CR 1264–68*, 217–8, 306. *Royal Letters*, II 294–6.

16. *Royal Letters*, II 294.

17. Waverley, *Ann. Mon.*, II 367.

18. Rishanger, *De Bellis*, 50–1.

page 264, 19. *Olim*, I 263.

20. MS. Clairem., 1188, f. 29.

page 265, 21. *Papal Letters*, I 434.

22. *CPR 1258–66*, 641.

23. *Ibid.*, 678.

24. *CPR 1266–72*, 140–1.

U*

page 266, 25. *Select Charters*, 407–11.

    26. Rishanger, *De Bellis*, 67–110. Prothero, *Life of Simon de Montfort*, App. IV, 388–91.

page 267, 27. *Papal Letters*, I 422.

    28. F. M. Powicke, "Guy de Montfort", *Ways of Medieval Life and Thought*, 69–89, gathers together the references and details of the adventures of the brothers.

page 269, 29. Bemont, *Simon de Montfort* (Eng. ed.), 260 n. 6.

    30. Bemont, *Simon de Montfort*, 367.

page 270, 31. Green, *Princesses*, II, App. VIII 456.

    32. *CPR 1272–81*, 159.

    33. Green, *op. cit.*, App. X 456–7.

    34. *CR 1272–79*, 35.

    35. *CPR 1266–72*, 549.

page 271, 36. Dunstable, *Ann. Mon.*, III 258–9.

    37. *CR 1272–79*, 181.

    38. *Cal. of Fine Rolls, 1272–1307*, 44.

    39. Green, *op. cit.*, App. XI 457–8.

    40. Bemont, *Simon de Montfort*, 369–70.

    41. *Issues of the Exchequer*, 98.

page 272, 42. Rishanger, *Chron.*, 87.

    43. Rymer, I 576, 577–8, 587.

    44. Powicke, *Henry III and the Lord Edward*, II 610 n. 1.

page 273, 45. *Flor. Hist.*, III 67.

Chapter 16: CONCLUSION

page 274, 1. Rishanger, *De Bellis*, 109–10: trans. by G. G. A. Murray in Hutton, *Simon de Montfort and His Cause*, 169.

page 275, 2. Rishanger, *De Bellis*, 6–7. *Mailros*, 207–8.

page 276, 3. *Political Songs*, 126.

    4. Prothero, *op. cit.*, 389.

    5. Knowles, *Archbishop Thomas Becket*, 1–8.

Bibliography

PRIMARY WORKS

A. *Manuscript*
Bibliothèque Nationale
  Clairembault 1188, ff. 2–40, 70–89.
Public Record Office
  Chancery Miscellanea, bundle 9, nos. 20 and 21. C 49 9/20, 9/21.

B. *Printed*
Ann. Mon. = *Annales Monastici.* ed. by H. E. Luard. Rolls Series,
    1864–9.

> vol. I. Tewkesbury, Burton.
> vol. II. Winchester, Waverley.
> vol. III. Dunstable.
> vol. IV. Osney, Thomas Wykes, Worcester.

Aucassin and Nicolette = *Aucassin and Nicolette and other Medieval Romances and Legends.* trans. by E. Mason. Everymans, 1928.
Beaumanoir, Philippe de. *Coutumes de Beauvaisis.* ed. by A. Salmon. 2 vols. Paris, 1899–1900.
Bracton, Henry de. *De Legibus et Consuetudinibus Anglie.* 6 vols. ed. by T. Twiss. Rolls Series, 1878–83.
CPR. = *Calendar of Patent Rolls.* Henry III, 7 vols. Edward I, 1272–81. Public Record Office.
CR. = *Close Rolls.* Henry III, 14 vols. Edward I, 1272–9. Public Record Office.
C.Ch.R. = *Calendar of Charter Rolls.* vol. I, 1226–57; vol. II, 1257–1300. Public Record Office.
Champollion-Figeac, M., ed. *Lettres des Rois Reines, et Autres Personages des Cours* de France et d'Angleterre. vol. I. Paris, 1839.
"Chron. de St-Denis". *Recueil.* = "Extraits des Chroniques de St-Denis", *Recueil des Historiens des Gaules et de la France,* vol. XXI.
"Chron. of St-Taurin", *Recueil.* = "Extracts from the Chronicle of the Monastery of St-Taurin", *Recueil des Historiens des Gaules et de la France,* vol. XXIII, pp. 465–7.
De Ant. Leg. = *De Antiquis Legibus Liber: Cronica Maiorum et Vicecomitum Londoniarum.* ed. by T. Stapleton. Camden Series, 1846.
Exc. e Rot. Fin. = *Excerpta e Rotulis Finium in Turri Londinensi Asservatis*

Henry III, 1216–72. 2 vols. ed. by C. Roberts, 1835–6. Public Record Office.

Flor. Hist. = *Flores Historiarum, per Matthaeum Westmonasteriensem Collecti.* vols. II–III. Rolls Series, 1890.

Gerv. of Cant = *Historical Works of Gervase of Canterbury.* ed. by W. Stubbs. 2 vol. Rolls Series, 1880.

Goodman of Paris = *The Goodman of Paris (Le Ménagier de Paris).* trans. with intro. and notes by E. Power. London, 1928.

Grosseteste *Letters* = *Roberti Grosseteste Episcopi quondam Lincolniensis Epistolae.* ed. by H. R. Luard. Rolls Series, 1861.

Henley's Husbandary = *Walter of Henley's Husbandry.* transcription and translation by E. Lamond. Intro. by W. Cunningham. Royal Historical Society, 1890.

Hennings, M. A. *England under Henry III.* London, 1924.

Hist. Angl. = *Matthaei Parisiensis Historia Minor 1067-1253.* vol. III, ed. by Sir F. Madden. Rolls Series. 1869.

Hutton, W. H. *The Misrule of Henry III.* London, 1887.

Simon de Montfort and His Cause. 1251–66. London, 1888.

Issues of the Exchequer = *Issues of the Exchequer Henry III–Henry VI* from the Pell Records. ed. by F. Devon. Public Record Office.

John of Ox. = *Chronica Johannis de Oxenedes.* ed. by H. Ellis. Rolls Series, 1859.

John of Wallingford. = Vaughan, R. "The Chronicle of John Wallingford", *English Historical Review*, vol. LXXIII (1958), pp. 66–77.

Joinville, *Life* = Joinville, Jean de. *Histoire de Saint Louis, Credo, et Lettre a Louis X.* ed. and trans. by N. de Wailly. 2nd ed. Paris, 1874.

Lanercost = Chronicon de Lanercost. ed. by J. Stevenson. Edinburgh, 1839.

Layettes = *Layettes du Tresor des Chartres.* vol. III, ed. by J. Delaborde; vol. IV, ed. by E. Berger. Paris, 1876, 1902.

Lib. R. = *Calendar of Liberate Rolls,* vol. I, 1226–40; vol. II, 1240–45; vol. III, 1245–51. Public Record Office.

Litt. Claus. = *Rotuli Litterarum Clausarum in Turri Londinensi Asservati,* vol. I, 1202–24. ed. by T. D. Hardy, 1833. Public Record Office.

Litt. Pat. = *Rotuli Litterarum Patentium in Turri Londinensi Asservati, 1201–1216.* ed. by T. D. Hardy, 1835. Public Record Office.

Mailros. = *Chronica de Mailros.* ed. by J. Stevenson. Edinburgh, 1839.

Manners = *Manners and Household Expenses of England in the Thirteenth and Fifteenth Centuries.* ed. by H. T. Turner, intro. by Beriah Botfield. Roxburghe Club, London, 1841.

Marsh "Letters" = "Adae de Marisco Epistolae", *Monumenta Franciscana,* vol. I, ed. by J. S. Brewer. Rolls Series, 1858.

Nangis, "Chronicon". = Nangis, Guillaume de. "Chronicon", *Recueil des Historiens des Gaules et de la France,* vol. XX, pp. 543–82.

Nangis, "Vie". = Nangis, Guillaume de. "Vie de Daint Louis", *Recueil des Historiens des Gaules et de la France*, vol. XX, pp. 312–465.

Olim = *Les Olim ou Registre des Arrets*. vols. I–II. ed. by A. Beugnot, Paris, 1839–42.

Papal Letters = *Entries in the Papal Registers Relating to Great Britain and Ireland: Papal Letters*. vol. I. ed. by W. H. Bliss, 1894.

Paris, *Chron. Maj.* = *Matthaei Parisiensis Chronica Majora*. vols. III–VI. ed. by H. R. Luard. Rolls Series, 1876–82.

Piers Plowman. = Langland, W. *The Vision of Piers Plowman*. trans. by H. W. Wells, intr. by N. Coghill. New York, 1935.

Pol. Songs. = *The Political Songs of England from the Reign of John to that of Edward II*. ed. and trans. by T. Wright. Camden Series, 1839.

Recog. Feod. = *Recueil d'Actes relatifs a l'Administration des Rois d'Angleterre en Guyenne, au XIII Siecle*. (Recogniciones Feodorum). ed. by C. Bemont. Paris, 1914.

Rigaud, "Visitations". = E Visitationibus Odonis Rigaudi, archiepiscopi Rothomagensis", *Recueil des Historiens de Gaules et de la France*, vol. XXI, pp. 571–93.

Rishanger, *Chron.* = *Willelmi Rishanger Chronica et Annales 1259–1307*. ed by H. T. Riley. Rolls Series, 1865.

Rishanger, *De Bellis.* = *The Chronicle of William de Rishanger of the Barons' War: The Miracles of Simon de Montfort*. ed. by J. O. Halliwell. Camden Series, 1840.

Robt. of Glouc. = *Metrical Chronicle of Robert of Gloucester*. vols. I–II. ed. by W. A. Wright. Rolls Series, 1887.

R^les Gascons = *Rôles Gascons*, vol. I. 1242–54, ed. by F. Michel. Supplement, 1254–5, ed. by C. Bemont. Paris. 1885, 1896.

Royal Letters. = *Royal Letters, Henry III*. ed. by W. W. Shirley. vols. I–II. Rolls Series, 1862–6.

Rymer. = Rymer, T. *Foedera, Conventiones, Litterae, et cujuscunque generis Acta Publica*. ed. by T. D. Hardy and D. Sandeman. vol. I, pts. I and II (1066–1307). London, 1816.

Salimbene = "Cronica Fratris Salimbene de Adam", *Monumenta Germaniae Historica*, scriptores, vol. XXXII, 1905.

Select Charters. = Stubbs, W. *Select Charters*. 9th ed. ed. and rev. by H. W. C. Davis. Oxford, 1929.

Trevet = Trevet, Nicholas. *Annales Sex Regum Angliae. 1135–1307*. ed. T. Ogg. English Historical Society, 1845.

Walter of Guis. = *Chronicle of Walter of Guisborough*, ed. for the Royal Historical Society by H. Rothwell. Camden Series, vol. LXXXIX, 1957.

Secondary Works

Bemont, Charles. *Simon de Montfort, comte de Leicester*. Paris, 1884.

Simon de Montfort, earl of Leicester. trans. by E. F. Jacob. Oxford, 1930.

Blauuw, W. H. *The Barons' War.* 2nd ed. London, 1871.

Boutaric, Edgard. *St Louis et Alphonse de Poitiers.* Paris, 1870.

Braun, Hugh. *An Introduction to English Medieval Architecture.* London, 1951.

Brieger, Peter. *English Art, 1216–1307.* vol. IV of Oxford History of English Art. Oxford, 1957.

Cam, Helen. *Liberties and Communities in Medieval England.* Cambridge, 1944.
"The Medieval English Franchise". *Speculum,* vol. XXXII, no. 3. July, 1957.
Studies in the Hundred Rolls. Oxford, 1921.

Carlyle, R. W. and A. J. *History of Medieval Political Thought in the West.* vol. III. London, 1950.

Carus-Wilson, E. M. "The English Cloth Industry in the Twelfth and Thirteenth Centuries", *Medieval Merchant Venturers,* pp. 211–38. London, 1954.

Chaplais, Pierre. "The Making of the Treaty of Paris (1259) and the Royal Style". *English Historical Review,* vol. LXVII (1952), pp. 235–53.

Clark, G. T. *Medieval Military Architecture in England.* 2 vols. London, 1884.

Coulton, G. G. *From St Francis to Dante.* London, 1906.

Darlington, O. G. *Travels of Odo Rigaud, Archbishop of Rouen (1248–75).* Philadelphia, 1940.

Davezac-Macaya, M.A. *Essais Historiques sur le Bigorre.* 2 vols. Bagneres, 1823.

Denholm-Young, N. *Collected Papers on Medieval Subjects.* Oxford, 1946.
"Documents of the Barons' War", *English Historical Review,* vol. XLVIII (1933), pp. 570–5.
Richard of Cornwall. Oxford, 1947.
Seignorial Administration in England. Oxford, 1937.
"Thomas de Wykes and his Chronicle." *English Historical Review.* LXI (1946), pp. 157–79.
"The Tournament in the Thirteen Century", *Studies in Medieval History presented to F. M. Powicke,* pp. 240–68. ed. by R. W. Hunt, W. A. Pantin, R. W. Southern. Oxford, 1948.

EHR = English Historical Review.

Faral, E. *La Vie Quotidienne au temps de St Louis.* Paris, 1938.

Gasquet, F. A. *Henry III and the Church.* London, 1905.

Gavrilovitch, M. *Étude sur le Traité de Paris, 1259.* Paris, 1899.

Gibbs, M. and Lang, J. *Bishops and Reform, 1215–72.* Oxford Historical Series. London, 1934.

Gissey, Odo de. *Discours Historique du tres ancien Devotion de Notre Dame du Puy.* 2nd ed. Toulouse, 1627.

Green, Mary Anne Everett. *Lives of the Princesses of England.* vol. II. London, 1849.

Hill, J. W. F. *Medieval Lincoln.* Cambridge, 1948.

Hill, Mary. "King's Messengers and Administrative Developments in the Thirteenth and Fourteenth Centuries." *English Historical Review.* LXI (1946), pp. 315–28.

Hinnebusch, W. A., O.P. *The Early English Friars Preachers.* Rome, 1951.

Histoire Generale de Languedoc. ed. by Devic and Vaissete. vol. IV and VIII. new ed. Toulouse, 1897.

Homans, G. *English Villagers in the Thirteenth Century.* Cambridge, 1941.

Houston, M. G. *Medieval Costume in England and France.* London, 1950.

Jacob, E. F. "Complaints of Henry III against the Baronial Council in 1261." *English Historical Review,* vol. XLI (1926), pp. 559–71.

"The Political Assumptions of Some Medieval Men of Action." *History,* vol. XI. no. 42 (July, 1926), pp. 116–29.

"The Reign of Henry III. Some Suggestions." *Transactions of the Royal Historical Society,* 4th ser., vol. X., pp. 21–53. London, 1927.

Studies in the Period of Baronial Reform and Rebellion, 1258–1267. Oxford Studies in Social and Legal History, VIII. Oxford, 1925.

Kingsford, C. L. *The Song of Lewes.* Oxford, 1890.

Knowles, David. *Archbishop Thomas Becket: A Character Study.* Raleigh Lecture on History, 1949. Proceedings of the British Academy, vol. XXXV.

The Religious Orders in England. Cambridge, 1948.

Langlois, Ch. V. *La Vie en France au Moyen Age d'apres les romans mondains du temps.* Paris, 1926.

Lavisse, E. *Histoire de France depuis les Origines jusqu'a la Revolution.* t. III, pt. II, by C. V. Langlois. Paris, 1901.

Lethaby, W. R. "The Painted Chamber and the Early Masters of the Westminster School", *Burlington Magazine,* vol. VII (1905).

Lewis, Ewart. *Medieval Political Ideas.* 2 vols. London, 1954.

Little, A. G. *The Grey Friars in Oxford.* Oxford, 1892.

Medieval Wales. London, 1902.

Lodge, E. C. *Gascony under English Rule.* London, 1926.

Marca, Pierre de. *Histoire de Bearn.* Paris, 1640.

Marsh, F. B. *English Rule in Gascony, 1199–1259.* 1912.

McIlwain, C. H. *Constitutionalism Ancient and Modern.* Ithaca, 1947.

Oman, Charles. *Castles.* London, 1926.

Owst, G. R. *Preaching in Medieval England.* Cambridge, 1926.

Painter, S. "The Lords of Lusignan in the Eleventh and Twelfth Centuries", *Speculum,* vol. XXXII (1957), pp. 27–47.

Studies in the History of the English Feudal Barony. Baltimore, 1943.

Poole, A. L. *Obligations of Society in the XII and XIII Centuries*. Oxford, 1949.

Postan, M. M. The Famulus. *Economic History Review supplements*, n. 2.

Powicke, F. M. "The Archbishop of Rouen, John de Harcourt, and Simon de Montfort in 1260", *English Historical Review*, vol. LI (1936), pp. 108–13.

King Henry III and the Lord Edward. 2 vols. Oxford, 1947.

"Loretta, Countess of Leicester", *Historical Essays in Honour of James Tait*. Manchester, 1933.

Modern Historians and the Study of History. London, 1955.

"Some Observations on the Baronial Council (1258–60) and the Provisions of Westminster", *Essays in Medieval History presented to T. F. Tout*, ed. by A. G. Little and F. M. Powicke. Manchester, 1925.

The Thirteenth Century. Oxford, 1953.

Ways of Medieval Life and Thought. London, 1949.

Prothero, G. S. *Life of Simon de Montfort, earl of Leicester*. London, 1877.

Richardson, H. G. "The Marriage and Coronation of Isabelle of Angoulême", *English Historical Review*, vol. LXI (1946), pp. 289–314.

Richardson, H. G. and Sayles, G. O. "The Provisions of Oxford: a Forgotten Document and Some Comments", *Bulletin of the John Rylands Library*, vol. XVII, pp. 291–321.

Riesenberg, Peter. *Inalienability of Sovereignty in Medieval Political Thought*. New York, 1956.

Robert Grosseteste, Scholar and Bishop. ed. by D. A. Callus. Intro. by F. M. Powicke. Oxford, 1955.

Rocher, Ch. "Les Rapports, de l'Eglise du Puy avec la ville, de Gerone en Espagne et le Comté de Bigorre." *Tablettes Historiques de Velay*, III, pp. 337–404; IV, pp. 463–501. Le Puy, 1873–74.

Salzman, L. F. *Building in England down to 1540*. Oxford, 1952.

Sanders, I. J. "The Texts of the Peace of Paris, 1259." *English Historical Review*. vol. LXV (1951), pp. 81–97.

Schulz, F. "Bracton on Kingship." *English Historical Review*, vol. LX (1945), pp. 136–76.

Snellgrove, H. S. *The Lusignans in England, 1247–58*. Univ. of New Mexico, 1950.

Stenton, F. M. "The Road System of Medieval England." *Economic History Review*, vol. VII, no. 1 (November, 1936), pp. 1–21.

Stevenson, F. S. *Robert Grosseteste, Bishop of Lincoln*. London, 1899.

Tout, T. F. *Chapters in the Administrative History of Medieval England*. Manchester, 1937.

Edward the First. London, 1920.

Toy, Sidney. *Castles*. London, 1939.

Treharne, R. F. *The Baronial Plan of Reform, 1258–63.* Manchester, 1932.

"The Mise of Amiens", *Studies in Medieval History presented to F. M. Powicke*, ed. by R. W. Hunt, W. A. Pantin, R. W. Southern. Oxford, 1948, pp. 223–39.

The Personal Role of Simon de Montfort in the Period of Baronial Reform and Rebellion 1258–65. Proceedings of the British Academy, vol. XL. Raleigh Lecture on History, 1954.

Tristram, E. W. *English Medieval Wall Painting. The Thirteenth Century.* vol. I, text; vol. II, plates. London, 1950.

Vaughan, R. *Matthew Paris.* Cambridge, 1958.

Vernon-Harcourt, L. W. *His Grace the Steward and Trial of Peers.* London, 1907.

VCH = Victoria County History.

Walne, P. "The Barons' Argument at Amiens, 1264." *English Historical Review*, vol. LXIX (1954), pp. 418–25.

vol. LXXIV, "The Barons' Argument at Amiens, 1264." *EHR*, 1958.

Wilkinson, B. *The Constitutional History of England, 1216–1399.* vol. I, Toronto, 1948. vol. III, Toronto, 1958.

"English Politics and Politicians of the Thirteenth and Fourteenth Centuries", *Speculum*, vol. XXX (1955), pp. 37–48.

Index

Acre, John of, 265
Agenais, 160
Aigueblanche, Peter, bishop of Hereford, 143, 208, 215, 216
Albigenian Crusade, 16, 17, 19, 21, 28, 64, 130
Aldobrandesca, Margherita, wife of Guy de Montfort, 268
Alexander II, king of Scotland, 39, 47
Alexander III, king of Scotland, 118, 142
Alexander IV, pope, 155, 174, 195, 199
Alice, daughter of Perronelle, countess of Bigorre, 131, 133
Alfonso, king of Castile, 124, 141, 142, 151
Alphonse of Poitiers, count of Poitou, brother of Louis IX, 59, 60, 114, 193, 216, 238, 239
Alton, 194
Amiens, 220, 223
    Mise of, see Mise of Amiens
Angoulême, 60, 191, 192, 201, 264
Anjou, 108, 145, 155, 156, 160
    count of, see Charles of Anjou
Annals, 3
    of Burton, 172
    of Dunstable, 48, 270
    of Osney, 9
    of Tewkesbury, 3, 218
    of Waverley, 3, 257
    of Winchester, 34
    of Worcester, 3
Aquitaine, 106, 108, 161
Aragon, kingdom of, 21, 64, 108, 110, 130
Armagnac, 161

Ascalon, 55
Audley, James of, 241
Axholm, Isle of, 263

Bacon, Roger, 23, 77
Balliol, John de, 125, 177, 243
Barentin, Drogo de, 236, 238
Basingstoke, John of, 76
Basset, Fulk, bishop of London, 160, 172
    Philip, 182, 183, 185, 196, 201, 206, 212, 260, 262
Bassingbourn, Warin of, 241
Bayonne, 108, 248
Bazas, 110, 116
Bearn, Constance de, 139
    Gaston, viscount de, 64, 109, 111, 112, 114, 115, 116, 124, 131, 133, 134, 135, 136, 137, 138, 139, 141
Beatrice, daughter of Henry III, 63, 180, 181
Beatrice of Savoy, countess of Provence, 67, 68, 69, 70, 80, 146
Beatrice of Provence, wife of Charles of Anjou, 68
Beaumanoir, Philippe de, 37, 190
Becket, St Thomas, archbishop of Canterbury, 236, 276-7
Bere Regis, 158
Beziers, 148, 160
Bezil, Matthew de, 208, 215
Bigod, Hugh, 151, 154, 155, 171, 172, 174, 175, 181, 184, 189, 195, 206, 221, 227
    Roger, earl of Norfolk, 44, 125, 152, 156, 171, 172, 174, 175, 182, 206, 262

Bigorre, county of, 21, 64, 100, 101, 104, 111, 128, 129, 130, 131, 133, 134, 135, 136, 137, 138, 139, 140, 148, 149, 161, 187, 200, 206, 261
countess of, *see* Perronelle
Blanche of Castile, mother of Louis IX, 47, 60, 109, 118, 119, 125
Blaye, 62, 63
Bodin, Raymond, 138, 200
Bohun, Humphrey de, earl of Hereford, 120, 125, 172, 177, 184, 205
Humphrey de, the younger, 221, 225, 237
Bordeaux, 31, 61, 63, 104, 108, 110, 111, 112, 113, 114, 116, 124, 142
Boulogne, 122, 158, 173, 211, 215, 240
Brabourne, Brayburn, 95, 96, 279
Brackley, 228
Bracton, Henry de, 41, 166–8, 169, 194
Bramber, 89, 253
Bridgnorth, 208
Brimpsfield, 226
Bristol, 86, 92, 163, 185, 213, 243, 252, 253, 272
Brittany, count of, *see* Mauclerc
John of, see John of Brittany
Builth castle, 188
Burchard, count of Vendome, 192

Cahors, 157, 160, 239
Cambrai, 155, 175
Canterbury, 24, 37, 158, 187, 211, 227, 230, 240
archbishop of, *see* Edmund, St, of Abingdon, and Savoy, Boniface of
Cantilupe, Thomas de, 215, 221
Walter de, bishop of Worcester, 118, 151, 152, 156, 175, 196, 197, 213, 215, 226, 233, 234, 250
William de, 125
Cardiff, 99
Caseneuve, 116

Castelnau, Peter de, papal legate, 19
Castelnaudary, 22, 131
Castile, kingdom of, 108, 110, 141, 143
see also Alfonso, Blanche, and Eleanor
Catesby, 221
Catherington, 94, 95
Caupenne, Vital de, 115
Chabanais, Esquivat de, 133, 134, 135, 136, 137, 138, 139, 149
Jourdain de, 133, 136
Lore de, 133, 139
Chaceporc, Peter, 143
Charles of Anjou, count of Anjou, brother of Louis IX, 68, 146, 268, 269
Chawton, Chalton, 95, 278
Chester, 188, 212, 243, 245, 247, 250
earl of, *see* Ranulf, Edward
Cheyham, John de, bishop of Glasgow, 215
Chichester, 100
bishop of, (Stephen Berksted), 232, 237
Chishull, John of, 201
Cinque Ports, 49, 96, 147, 195, 211, 231, 237, 240, 242, 247
Clare, Gilbert de, earl of Gloucester, 204, 205, 207, 218, 219, 229, 230, 231, 232, 233, 234, 237, 240, 241, 245, 246, 247, 248, 249, 250, 251, 253, 255, 276
Richard de, earl of Gloucester, 32, 63, 120, 154, 157, 158, 171, 172, 173, 175, 176, 177, 178, 179, 181, 182, 183, 184, 185, 186, 188, 196, 197, 198, 204, 276
Thomas de, 251
Clarendon, 105
Clement IV, pope, 223, 239, 257, 264, 267, 268
Clifford, Roger, 207, 217, 226
Colom family, 110, 112, 113
Committee of Fifteen, 150, 172, 237
Corfe castle, 237, 247, 272
Crakhall, John of, 189

Crendon, 271
Crioll, Bertram de, 148

Dante, 62
David, Jew of Oxford, 70
Dax, 110, 112
Delsoler family, 110, 112, 113
Derby, earl of, *see* Ferrers
Devon, countess of, *see* Fortibus
Dictum de Kenilworth, 86, 266, 267
Dispenser, Hugh, 172, 189, 212, 214,
 228, 256, 257, 260
Dominic, St, 19
Dover, 68, 89, 90, 95, 96, 97, 99,
 118, 147, 158, 195, 206, 209,
 211, 219, 220, 227, 230, 232,
 237, 240, 260, 261, 262, 263
 castle, 86, 95, 96, 97, 195, 212,
 219, 231, 247, 249, 253, 259,
 260, 262
 priory, 227, 260
Dunstable, 81, 220, 245
Dylwin, 223

Eardisley castle, 208
Edmund, St, of Abingdon, archbishop of Canterbury, 43, 48, 54,
 146
Edmund, son of Henry III, 142, 143,
 152, 156, 211, 212, 265
Edmund, son of Richard of Cornwall,
 101, 242
Edward, oldest son of Henry III, in
 1272 Edward I, king of England,
 53, 80, 100, 117, 122, 123, 141,
 142, 145, 156, 169, 171, 177, 178,
 179, 182, 183, 184, 185, 186, 189,
 202, 205, 206, 207, 208, 210, 212,
 213, 216, 217, 218, 220, 221, 225,
 226, 228, 230, 232, 233, 234, 235,
 236, 241, 242, 243, 244, 245, 248,
 250, 251, 252, 253, 254, 255, 256,
 257, 262, 263, 265, 266, 267, 268,
 269, 270, 271, 272, 275
Eleanor de Montfort, countess of
 Leicester, sister of Henry III,
 40, 43, 44, 45, 51, 52, 53, 54,
 57, 67, 69, 70, 73, 75, 78, 79,
 89, 105, 106, 114, 117, 122,
 128, 139, 248, 249, 253, 275
 first marriage to William Marshal
 the younger, earl of Pembroke,
 40, 47
 dower lands, 40–42, 52, 69, 87,
 148, 149, 157–8, 265, 270–1
 279
 marriage to Simon de Montfort,
 47–8
 household accounts, 12, 90–1,
 92, 94–5, 97–8, 99–100, 101–3,
 242
 share in treaty of Paris, 149, 154,
 155, 156–7, 158, 160, 221
 legal quarrels over Angoulême,
 191, 192–3, 201, 264
 life after Evesham, and death,
 259, 260, 261, 262, 263, 264,
 265, 267, 270, 271
Eleanor of Aquitaine, wife of Henry II
 of England, 106, 146
Eleanor of Castile, wife of Edward I,
 141, 142, 238
Eleanor of Provence, wife of Henry
 III, 44, 53, 55, 212, 216, 238, 239
Evesham, 2, 23, 86, 139, 242, 248,
 254, 255, 256, 257, 258, 259, 260,
 261, 262, 268, 269, 275
Evreux, 149, 160, 179
Exeter, Master John of, bishop of
 Winchester, 240
Eye, Philip of, 10

Ferrers, Robert de, earl of Derby,
 218, 225, 226, 230, 246, 260
Fezansac, 161
Fitz Geoffrey, John, 171
Flanders, count of, *see* Savoy (Thomas)
 countess of, see Joan
Flores Historiarum, 10
Foix, Roger, count of, 136, 137
Fontevrault, 65, 145
Forme of Cury, 88
Fortibus, Isabella de, countess of
 Devon and Aumale, 86, 100, 248
Fos, Roscelin de, Master of the
 Temple, 118, 119, 123

Foucod, Guy, cardinal bishop of Sabina, *see* Clement IV
Frederick II, emperor, 39, 50, 53, 57, 58, 81, 82, 143, 147
Fronsac, 116

Garland, John of, 88
Gascony, 22, 58, 64, 76, 96, 97, 104, 105, 106, 108, 109, 110, 111, 112, 113, 114, 115, 116, 117, 118, 119, 120, 121, 122, 123, 124, 125, 126, 127, 131, 134, 135, 138, 140, 141, 142, 145, 161, 200
Gaza, 38, 57
Geddington, 105
Giffard, John, 226, 230, 247
Gisors, 157
Gloucester, 208, 226, 228, 243, 250, 253
    earl of, *see* Clare
    Robert of, 10, 11, 256
Gravelines, 261
Gravesend, Richard, bishop of Lincoln, 156, 160, 175
Gregory IX, pope, 6n., 50, 53
Grey, Richard de, 219, 231
Grosseteste, Robert, bishop of Lincoln, 23, 73, 74, 75, 76, 77, 78, 80, 81, 88, 89, 91, 103, 114, 120, 122, 126, 151, 277
Guisborough, Walter, of, 11, 174

Haakon, king of Norway, 6
Hackington, 24, 37, 249
Harcourt, John, 186, 187
Hastings, Henry of, 234
Havering, Richard de, 100, 115
Haye, John de la, 101, 219, 262
Hayles, abbey of, 63n
Henry of Almain, oldest son of Richard of Cornwall, 156, 189, 207, 211, 213, 217, 226, 235, 236, 240, 245, 248, 268, 269, 270
Henry III, king of England, 12, 28, 30, 31, 35, 47, 48, 52, 53, 61, 62, 63, 64, 67, 72, 73, 83, 92, 105, 106, 109, 112, 113, 114, 115, 117, 118, 121, 122, 124, 126, 134, 135, 137,
138, 141, 142, 143, 144, 145, 147, 149, 150, 151, 153, 155, 156, 157, 158, 160, 161, 164, 171, 180, 181, 182, 184, 185, 187, 190, 193, 194, 195, 196, 197, 199, 200, 205, 206, 209, 211, 212, 214, 216, 127, 219, 220, 221, 222, 227, 228, 231, 233, 235, 254, 255, 256, 258, 259, 262, 265, 267, 276
Hereford, 99, 250, 251, 252, 253, 254
    bishop of, *see* Aigueblanche
    earl of, *see* Bohun
Hertford, John of, abbot of St Albans, 5
Hugh X Le Brun, count of La Marche, 39, 59, 60, 61, 63, 154, 165, 191

Ile-de-France, 15, 122, 137, 151
Ilmington, 187, 278
Inkberrow, 41
Innocent III, pope, 17, 19, 20
Innocent IV, pope, 75, 80, 81, 82, 106, 117, 124, 143, 152
Isabella, sister of Henry III, wife of Frederick II, 39, 57, 58, 155
Isabella of Angoulême, wife of (1) King John, (2) Hugh X Le Brun, 39, 59, 60, 61, 64–5, 84, 165, 191
Isleworth, 228

Jeanne of Navarre, wife of Philip IV, 140
Jehan et Blonde, 36
Jerusalem, 50, 106
Joan, countess of Flanders, 45, 47, 54
Joanna, sister of Henry III, wife of Alexander II, 39, 191
John, king of England, 17, 21, 24, 28, 32, 35, 39, 60, 70, 108, 144, 191
John of Brittany, 180, 189
Joinville, Jean, sire de, 4, 5, 9, 56, 63, 161

Kempsey, 254
Kemsing, 44, 94, 95, 279

Kenilworth castle, 51, 52, 70–3, 87, 97, 99, 101, 103, 126, 174, 182, 218, 220, 221, 227, 228, 230, 242, 243, 247, 253, 254, 255, 256, 259, 261, 263, 266, 279
Dictum de, *see* Dictum de Kenilworth
Kingston, 198

La Marche, 59, 60, 191, 193, 264
count of, *see* Hugh X Le Brun
countess of, *see* Isabella of Angoulême
Lands of the Normans, 35–6, 278
Lanercost chronicle, 11, 48
Languedoc, 17, 18, 19, 20
La Réole, 114, 119, 123, 125
La Warre, John, 86
Le Chambellan, Peter, 190, 196, 197
Leicester, borough of, 17, 31, 32, 56, 230, 278
countess of, *see* Loretta, Eleanor
earl of, *see* Montfort (Simon)
earldom of, 16–17, 28, 32–3, 34, 69, 85, 117, 200, 272
Le Puy, 100, 129, 130, 134, 137, 138, 139, 140, 200
Lewes, 2, 232, 233, 234, 235, 238, 240, 245, 236, 248, 250, 255, 260, 275
castle, 232, 234, 235
mise of, *see* Mise of Lewes
priory, 232, 233, 234, 235
Leyburne, Roger, 184, 206, 213, 217, 227, 230
Limoges, 160, 239
Lincoln, bishop of, *see* Grosseteste, Gravesend
Llywelyn, prince of Wales, 164, 205, 215, 225, 243, 250, 252, 272
London, 99, 116, 118, 173, 182, 183, 184, 198, 205, 207, 209, 210, 211, 212, 214, 215, 218, 220, 221, 225, 227, 228, 229, 230, 231, 232, 244, 245, 248, 253, 254, 259, 262, 263
bishop of, *see* Basset (Fulk), Wingham, Sandwich (Henry)

Tower of, 54, 147, 193, 195, 196, 209, 210, 211, 212, 228, 246, 260
Loretta, countess of Leicester, 24, 25, 37, 249
Lorris, 109
Louis IX, king of France, 4, 6, 55, 56, 59, 60, 62, 63, 82, 83, 106, 109, 114, 125, 144–5, 146, 147, 150, 151, 153, 155, 156, 158, 160, 161, 169, 173, 176, 180, 181, 184, 187, 188, 190, 192, 196, 197, 198, 199, 201, 206, 207, 214, 218, 220, 221, 223, 224, 225, 236, 238, 239, 262, 264, 265, 266, 267
Lourdes, 100, 104, 130, 135, 138, 139
Ludlow, 251
Lugwardin, 223
Lungespee, William, earl of Salisbury, 63
Stephen, 125
Lusignan, Geoffrey de, 119, 154, 165, 192, 193
Geoffrey de, count of Eu, 60, 154
Guy de, 118, 125, 154, 165, 192
Luton, 81, 87, 271, 279
Lyons, council of, 75, 82, 106, 221

Magna Carta, 21, 40, 41, 170
Mahaut, countess of Boulogne, 45, 47
Maine, 145, 155, 156, 160
Mansel, John, 143, 148, 152, 157, 158, 177, 178, 181, 196, 198, 211, 216, 219, 248
Master John, 193–4, 195
Marden, 223
Margaret, countess of Winchester, 17, 35
Marguerite of Provence, wife of Louis IX, 68, 125, 180, 190, 197, 202, 215, 223, 238, 271
Marsh, Adam, 74, 75, 76, 77, 78, 102, 114, 120, 121, 122, 123, 151, 157, 175
Marshal, Gilbert, earl of Pembroke, 42, 49, 69
Richard, earl of Pembroke, 41, 42

Walter, earl of Pembroke, 69
William, earl of Pembroke and Regent, 25
William the younger, earl of Pembroke, first husband of Eleanor, 40, 41, 43, 47, 149
Martin, Master, papal collector, 81–2
Mathe, daughter of Perronelle of Bigorre, 131, 133
Mauclerc, Peter, count of Brittany, 54
Melrose chronicle, 11
Melun, 119, 270
Menagier de Paris, 88, 92, 98
Mepham, Richard de, archdeacon of Oxford, 215
Merton, Walter de, 201
Meulles, Nicholas de, 123
Mise of Amiens, 220, 223–4, 225, 227, 237
  of Lewes, 237, 247
Monmouth, 252
Montargis, 90, 264, 271, 272
Montferrand, Imbert de, 201
Montfort, Amaury, brother of Simon, 21, 22, 25, 30, 37, 38, 55, 56, 100, 148
  Amaury, son of Simon, 22, 23, 97, 101, 188, 248, 257, 262, 263, 269, 271, 272
  Eleanor, countess of Leicester, wife of Simon, *see* Eleanor
  Eleanor, daughter of Simon, 99, 100, 101, 263, 271, 272, 273
  Guy, brother of Simon, 21, 22, 24, 25, 131, 133
  Guy, son of Simon, 234, 248, 259, 263, 267, 268, 269, 271, 272, 273
  Henry, oldest son of Simon, 22, 96, 122, 173, 175, 189, 207, 221, 225, 226, 234, 237, 247, 248, 256, 257
  John, lord of Tyre, 24
  Loretta, daughter of Amaury and niece of Simon, 100
  Philip, lord of La-Ferte-Alais and Castres, 24, 137, 268

Richard, son of Simon, 101, 139, 231, 248, 261, 262, 263, 269
Simon the Crusader, father of Simon, 16–17, 20–1, 25, 28, 55, 88, 113, 131
Simon, earl of Leicester, 10, 11, 12, 45, 67, 69, 70, 73–4, 80, 83, 84, 85, 95, 142, 147, 150, 153–4, 163, 175, 180, 181–2, 188, 198, 221, 223, 228
  character, 27, 76–7, 200, 219, 275–7
  birth and childhood, 15, 22, 23, 24, 25
  becomes earl of Leicester, 28, 29–31, 35, 37, 38, 52
  marriage to Eleanor, 47–8, 49, 50, 51, 53–4
  on crusade, 53, 56–7, 58–9
  first expedition to Gascony, 1242, 61, 62, 63, 64
  friendship with Grosseteste and Adam Marsh, 74–9
  king's lieutenant in Gascony, 97, 106, 109–14, 115, 116, 117, 118, 119–22, 123–4, 125–6, 141
  claim to Bigorre, 131, 136, 137, 138, 139, 140, 187, 200
  share in the treaty of Paris, 148–9, 150, 151, 152, 154, 155, 156, 157, 158, 160, 162, 170, 175, 176, 177, 178, 179, 180, 187, 190, 204, 221
  share in Provisions of Oxford, 169–70, 171, 174, 182, 187
  trial of 1260, 186, 187, 188
  trial of 1262, 199, 200
  French arbitration over personal matters, 190, 191, 196, 197, 201, 202, 203, 265
  leader of the barons, 1263–4, 204, 207, 208, 210, 211,

Montfort, Simon (*cont.*)
212, 213, 214, 216, 217, 218, 219, 224, 228, 229, 230, 231
Lewes and baronial government, 232–5, 236, 237, 239, 240, 241, 243, 244, 245, 246, 247, 250, 253
Evesham and death, 254–7, 259
Simon the younger, son of Simon, 139, 189, 219, 225, 229, 236, 241, 243, 247, 248, 253, 254, 256, 261, 262, 263, 265, 267, 268, 269
Montfort, Peter de, 148, 171, 184, 196, 214, 221, 229, 236, 237, 256
Montfort-l'Amaury, 15, 23, 24, 55, 273
Montgomery, 241
Morlaas, 111n
Mortimer, Edmund, 269
Roger, 172, 188, 221, 223, 225, 241, 251, 255, 256
Munchesney, Joan of, wife of William de Valence, 165, 238

Nangis, Guillaume de, 4, 11, 47
Narbonne, 20, 21
Navarre, kingdom of, 108, 109–10, 140. *See* Jeanne, Thibault
Néaufle-le-Chateau, 157
Newcastle-under-Lyme, 245
Norfolk, earl of, see Bigod
Normandy, duchy of, 15, 16, 17, 29, 40, 83, 108, 145, 149, 155, 156, 160, 180, 181, 187
Northampton, 220, 229, 236, 241, 249, 263
Norway, 6
Nottingham, 21, 230, 231

Odiham castle, 3, 45, 73, 79, 87, 89, 92, 94, 95, 99, 100, 104, 126, 174, 248, 249, 253, 279
Ordinances, 176, 177, 204
Orleans, 117, 221
Osney abbey, 9, 51

Otto, papal legate, 50, 51
Ottobuono, papal legate, 257, 263, 266
Oxford, 9, 51, 77, 102, 172, 173, 207, 221, 227, 228, 232, 243, 253
Provisions of, *see* Provisions of Oxford
Padua, 269
Paper Constitution, 73
Paris, 15, 146, 152, 153, 154, 158, 163, 180, 187, 192, 193, 200, 201, 202, 221, 270
treaty of, *see* Treaty of Paris
Paris, Matthew, 5–9, 39, 43, 50, 54, 58, 63, 68, 80, 81, 83, 84, 112, 113–4, 118, 120, 121, 125, 146, 147, 150, 152
Parthenai, 60
Pastoureaux, 117
Peak, castle of the, 245
Pembroke, earl of, *see* Marshal
lands, 25, 40, 165, 251
Perigord, 157, 160, 239
Perronelle, countess of Bigorre, 21, 22, 64, 111, 128, 130, 131, 133, 139
daughter of Perronelle, countess of Bigorre, 131, 133
Pevensey, 235, 238, 241, 248, 253
Philip Augustus, king of France, 17, 35, 108, 144
Philip III, king of France, 268, 270
Philip IV, the Fair, king of France, 140
Pigorel, William, 119
Poitiers, 192
Poitou, county of, 39, 59, 60, 64, 105, 108, 134, 144, 145, 155, 156, 160, 173, 191, 238, 264
count of, *see* Alphonse of Poitiers
Pontigny, 146
Porchester, 89, 243, 247, 248, 253
Portsmouth, 67, 243
Provence, count of, *see* Raymond
countess of, *see* Beatrice of Savoy
see also Beatrice, Eleanor, Marguerite, and Sanchia

Provisions of Oxford, 11, 73, 162, 163, 164, 169, 170, 172, 173, 176, 181, 182, 183, 187, 194, 195, 196, 197, 199, 201, 204, 206, 207, 208, 209, 212, 214, 215, 216, 219, 221, 222, 223, 224, 236, 246, 252, 275
Provisions of Westminster, 178, 206, 267

Quercy, 159, 160

Radnor, 225
Rancon, Geoffrey de, 63
Ranulf, earl of Chester, 20, 28–30, 31, 37, 54
Raymond, count of Provence, 56, 69
Reading, 219
Remi, Philippe de, 36, 37. *See* also Beaumanoir
Richard of Cornwall, king of the Germans, brother of Henry III, 10, 32, 38, 49, 53, 54, 56, 57, 58, 61, 62, 63, 67, 68, 80, 97, 98, 101, 103, 118, 120, 121, 143, 146, 147, 149, 151, 152, 154, 155, 156, 157, 164, 176, 182, 183, 184, 185, 191, 198, 199, 206, 207, 210, 211, 227, 228, 231, 232, 233, 235, 241, 242, 261, 262, 263, 267
his sons, *see* Henry of Almain, Edmund
Rigaud, Odo, archbishop of Rouen, 155, 157, 158, 160, 186, 187, 188, 240, 269
Rishanger, 232
Rochester, 195, 227, 230, 231
Romney, 211
Rouen, archbishop of, *see* Rigaud
Royaumont, 180
Rules of Seynt Robert, 88

Saint Albans, 5, 6, 23, 43, 147, 182, 197, 198, 229
Saint-Denis, 158, 180, 268
St James-de-Beuvron, 30, 31
St Martin, Walter of, 43
Saint-Omer, 182, 183

Saint-Sever, 110, 111
Saintes, 62
Saintonge, 160
Salimbene, 5, 9, 62, 77
Salisbury, earl of, *see* Lungespee
Sanchia of Provence, wife of Richard of Cornwall, 56, 67, 68
Sandwich, 95
Henry de, bishop of London, 233, 237, 240
Sanford, Cecily de, 43
Savoy, Beatrice of, *see* Beatrice, countess of Provence
Boniface of, archbishop of Canterbury, 75, 142, 216, 219, 239
Peter of, 120, 143, 147, 148, 151, 152, 154, 155, 157, 158, 171, 174, 177, 178, 181, 182, 204, 216, 219
Thomas of, count of Flanders, 54, 55, 61, 143
William of, bishop-elect of Valence, 153n., 208
Scotland, king of, *see* Alexander
Segin, Arnold, 115
Segrave, Nicholas, 234
Sempringham nunnery, 273
Shrewsbury, 163, 188
Sicilian affair, 143–4, 145, 152, 153, 164, 174, 208, 222, 223
Song of Lewes, 11, 168–9, 213
Statute of Marlborough, 266, 267
Stavensby, Alexander, bishop of Lichfield, 51
Steward of England, the office of, 17, 24, 31, 34–5, 44–5, 188–6, 212–3, 249, 272
Surrey, earl of, *see* Warenne
Sutton, 122, 279

Taillebourg, 62, 65
Tarbes, 136, 138
Tarentaise, archbishop of, 152, 155
Templar of Tyre, 23
Tewkesbury, 44
Thibault, count of Champagne, king of Navarre, 110, 139
Tonbridge castle, 230, 231

Tours, 119
Toulouse, 20, 21, 29, 88, 148, 160
  count of, 19, 20, 64, 114, 130
Touraine, 145, 155, 156, 160
Treaty of Paris, 1259, 42, 137, 140,
  147, 148, 150, 151, 154–5, 156,
  157, 158, 160–1, 162, 180, 203,
  221, 239
Trevet, Nicholas, 11
Tyre, 55, 59

Umfravill, Gilbert de, 80, 117
Urban IV, pope, 199, 201

Valence, Aymer de, 153, 165, 173, 174
  William de, 84, 153, 154, 164,
  165, 173, 192, 228, 234, 238,
  251
Valenciennes, John de, 228
Viterbo, 257, 264, 268

Walerand, Robert, 150, 152, 157,
  177, 195, 210
Wallingford castle, 68, 92, 211, 241
Warenne, John de, earl of Surrey,
  86, 165, 196, 207, 217, 230, 232,
  234, 251
Warwick castle, 230
Waverley abbey, 3, 79, 91, 92
Westminster, 30, 47, 68, 84, 150, 158,
  183, 184, 228, 238, 244
  abbey, 44, 53, 67, 83, 84, 112, 120
  hall, 38, 84
  palace, 30, 47, 64, 69, 72, 105,
  186, 205, 209
  Edward of, 105
Weston, 271, 279
Wexcumb, 44, 271, 279
Wigmore castle, 251, 256
William the Engineer, Master, 103,
  242
Winchelsea, 89, 95, 231, 253, 263
Winchester, 38, 44, 45, 52, 173, 174,
  195, 238, 253, 260
  bishop of, see Valence (Aymer)
  countess of, see Margaret
Windsor, 45, 106, 198, 211, 212, 213,
  217, 218, 221, 227, 229, 236, 238
Wingham, Henry of, bishop of
  London, 118, 119, 189
Wissant, 118, 158, 227
Woodstock, 243
Worcester, 41, 226, 243, 252, 253,
  254, 272
  bishop of, see Cantilupe (Walter)
Wortham, William de, 97, 100
Wykes, Thomas, 9–10, 157, 207, 214,
  229, 230, 240, 249

York, 99, 118